What People Are Saying About
Monopolize Your Marketplace

"*Monopolize Your Marketplace* is a book that takes no prisoners and fights until victory has been achieved. Richard Harshaw shows readers how to triumph in the marketing wars, using tactics that are realistic and simple. If you own a business, this book is mandatory reading."

—Jay Conrad Levinson,
Author of the best-selling
Guerrilla Marketing series of books.

Many people have great ideas, but few of us turn these ideas into great businesses. In *Monopolize Your Marketplace,* Rich Harshaw provides a great road map for making this transition!

Real leaders have to get beyond theoretical concepts and focus on practical application. *Monopolize Your Marketplace* is filled with ideas that you can actually use!

—Marshall Goldsmith,
named one of 50 great thinkers in management, top 10
executive educators, five most-respected executive coaches
and most credible consultants in the new era of business

"*Monopolize Your Marketplace* provides an insightful and practical look at how to differentiate your business and capture greater market share. Richard Harshaw's book will definitely help you re-ignite and leverage the passion you have for your business and to help achieve improved business results!"

—Richard Chang
CEO, Richard Chang Associates, Inc., and author of
The Passion Plan and *The Passion Plan at Work*

"Richard Harshaw highlights the difference between strategic and tactical marketing, which is indeed a trap for many of us, and does so with his great deal of experience. "

—Beverly Kaye
Founder/CEO of Career Systems International

The Authoritative, Hands-on, Real-Life
"Here's How You Do It," Make-More-Money-Right-Now
Guide to Success in Marketing, Advertising and Business.

MONOPOLIZE YOUR MARKETPLACE

SEPARATE YOUR BUSINESS FROM THE COMPETITION.

THEN ELIMINATE THEM.

Richard Harshaw

CEO of Y2Marketing

One of *Inc.'s* Top 50 Fastest-Growing Companies

For permission requests, contact the publisher at:

Executive Excellence Publishing
1366 East 1120 South
Provo, UT 84606
Phone: 1-801-375-4060
Toll Free: 1-800-304-9782
Fax: 1-801-377-5960
www.eep.com

Monopolize Your Marketplace
2321 Ira E. Woods Ave.
Suite 200
Grapevine, TX 76051
Phone: (817) 310-0013
Fax: (817) 796-2967
www.MYMBook.com

For additional Monopolize Your Marketplace products, please visit www.MYMbook.com.

For Executive Excellence books, magazines and other products, contact Executive Excellence directly. Call 1-800-304-9782, fax 1-801-377-5960, or visit our website at www.eep.com.

First edition.
Printed in the United States of America
10 9 8 7 6 5 4 3 2 1

$24.95USA
Business/Marketing
ISBN 1-930771-04-5

Harshaw, Richard.
  Monopolize your marketplace : separate your business from the competition, then eliminate them / Richard Harshaw.—1st ed.
      p. cm.
  "The authoritative, hands-on, real-life 'here's how you do it,' make-more-money-right-now, guide to success in marketing, advertising, and business."
  ISBN 1-930771-04-5 (alk. paper)
  1. Marketing. 2. Competition. I. Title.
  HF5415.H237 2004
  658.8—dc22
                          2004021851

Acknowledgements

This book was started on January 15th, 1995, as a collection of marketing tips written in my Franklin planner. Over the next several years, we worked on perfecting what would become the Monopolize Your Marketplace system as we worked with hundreds of clients. As we worked, the system developed into what you are holding in your hands—as true step-by-step guide to innovating and marketing any business.

During the nearly 10 years between the beginning of the book and the initial publication, there have been many along the way who have helped our cause, cheered us along, and invested their time, sweat, and money with us. We wish to extend formal appreciation to each of the following people:

- **Clients from the early days.** They didn't know it at the time, but they were the guinea pigs of the MYM system. From 1995 to 1998, these brave clients had the courage to invest in our program even though we were young and unpolished. The principles worked back then, but we had no track record to back it up. A few names of many that could be mentioned: Tommy Aiken, V.K. Gupta, David Atwell, Ken Andrews, Curtis Miller, Jacob Garza, Bill Rickett, Chris Brady, Lon Smith, Scott Hamilton, Rick Sapio and others.

- **Clients from the later days:** They allowed us to have a symbiotic relationship with them in which we both made good money using our system. This shorter list includes Al Boenker, David Boenker, David Whitt, and Andy Johnson. Special thanks go to Patrick Phillips and Dennis Brown who gave us the opportunity of a lifetime while helping them take their new business to great heights.

- **Consultants all over North America.** Since there are over 1,000 of them, we won't thank them by name. But their faith in us personally as well as the MYM system has taken our company from a two-man operation in Dallas, Texas, to an international company with a presence in every major and most minor markets. They are the backbone of Monopolize Your Marketplace; a fulfillment of a dream we had a decade ago. They are the ones who shoulder the workload of implementing our system into businesses everywhere. Thank you!

- **Employees:** Thanks go out to the 100+ employees who have worked for us over the last decade. Your efforts have been valuable to our cause. Special thanks go out to Glen Nelson, Sam Scarlett, Jim Owsley, Dan Billings, and Bryan Bauman.

- **My Publisher:** Thanks to Ken Shelton and his staff at Executive Excellence Publishing. They have taken a long project that seemed impossible at times and led us through all the many steps to bring this book to the market. You are an amazing man, Ken!

- **Finally, to my family:** As I have juggled work, church, and family duties for the last decade, the heaviest lifting has been done by my family. My wife has spent many days and nights at home alone with a house full of children while dad was out building the business and developing the system. My kids have picked up the load and helped out in every imaginable way. This book would not have been possible without all of their collective efforts. So thank you Tonia, Sam, Kelsie, Ben, Jonah, Grace, and the new baby. I love you all!

A special thank you: I am who I am because of my parents, Curtis and Janice Harshaw. Every good idea I ever had originated from my dad. He taught me how to work hard and think smart. Thank you for those $1 per hour opportunities to pick up trash at Spring Creek mobile home park on Saturday mornings in the late 1970's! My mother taught me by example to be a good, honest, decent person. She is an angel on earth. Thank you both for everything.

Rich Harshaw
October 8, 2004

Contents

Introduction:

What You Will Find in This Book

When I started my career as a marketing consultant in 1994, I was full of big ideas and impossible dreams. My original goal was to take all of what I had learned about marketing, advertising and business development and create a step-by-step system for innovating and marketing any product, service or company.

Of course, there were dozens of other marketing programs, books, seminars and gurus offering advice at that time, but nothing out there said: "Ask why before how or what. Do this first. Do this second. After that, do this, this and this. And use these templates and evaluations to make sure you're doing it right. And if you need to make corrections, take these steps. And, you will be assured of this result."

That kind of *systematic and strategic approach* just didn't exist. My partner and I knew that we could create it; but since it had never been done before, it was a big project.

With a system in place, we could show companies exactly what we were going to do, exactly how we were going to do it, and predict the results they could expect. We knew if we had a system, we could show them our strategy and methodology for getting results—something no other marketing consultant, advertising agency, or growth guru in the world could do—then or now.

We also knew that if we could create a marketing system, we could scale our business. If we had a system, we could train other qualified people to run that system, leverage the system, and grow our company into a national powerhouse. We could add more value to more companies worldwide.

During our first three years, we worked non-stop to develop and perfect the system. During that time, we held seminars every month while we tweaked and fine-tuned the system. We also worked with hundreds of clients and proved that the system got results. The end product of those long days, weeks, and months is the *Monopolize Your Marketplace* (MYM) system.

We successfully introduced the MYM program in 1997. During 1998 and 1999, we focused on getting bigger and better clients, and adding more value to the marketplace. With the MYM system in place, we found the caliber of our clients went up dramatically. Now, we could participate in the profitability of the projects, too. This proved to be extraordinarily profitable for both us and our clients.

By June 1999, as I turned 30 years old, we were providing enough value to the marketplace and making our clients enough money to allow me to take home an income in excess of $50,000 a month and invest *at least that much* back into the business for expansion.

In 1999, when we were making that money, we were working with only three clients who occupied only 30 hours a week. Think about it—we were only serving three companies out of 13 million businesses nationwide with the *Monopolize Your Marketplace* system.

At that time, we had to decide: Either we could add more clients and double our client load, triple our income, and within a few years, amass personal fortunes of $10 million each and retire by age 35. Or, we could expand our reach and make this incredible marketing system available to millions of companies.

The Principle of Stewardship

Our dilemma wasn't financial—it was philosophical. We felt then, as now, that we have a stewardship over this information, and we take that responsibility seriously.

Perhaps you remember the *Parable of the Talents* from the New Testament of the Bible. The master of the servants gave one servant five talents, or units of value, the second servant two talents, and the third servant just one. The master then left, but returned after a season to see what they had done. The servant who had been given five talents turned them into 10, doubling his value. The second servant turned his two talents into four. The third servant, however, buried his talent and didn't turn it into anything. The master cast the servant out and gave the one talent to the servant who now had 10—the one the master knew he could trust with things of value.

So, when we assess our situation and the MYM system we have developed, we feel like the servant who has five talents. But with talent comes responsibility. It would have been easy to limit our clients, make a few extra million dollars apiece, and then retire. But we knew that route would be like burying the talent we had been given. Instead of burying that talent, we decided to expand our horizons and make the MYM system available to a wider audience.

Why We're Talking to You

We want you to grow your business using the *Monopolize Your Marketplace* system.

People ask us constantly, "Why do you do this?" Answer: We want to rule the world of marketing and advertising. We loathe the current state of our industry—the ad agencies, consultants, and gurus who are ripping off their clients with no accountability for results. Their clients just open up the checkbooks and turn over the marketing decisions to incompetent creative types who know next to nothing about selling something or growing a company.

Wanting to expand the value we bring to the marketplace, we decided to seek out qualified individuals with the right skill-sets and mindsets and allow them to license the MYM system under our training and supervision. We knew this would be *the* most effective way to expand. The people we recruit as consultants—professionals, entrepreneurs, and executives—are people who make things happen.

We have two passions. Number *two*, ironically, is marketing. Number *one* is people. Specifically, **our passion is to help people like you become financially free**. We offer this program to you as a way to achieve financial freedom—the ability to do whatever you want with your time and money long before you reach age 65, when most people's lives and energy have been sapped by running a rat race for 40 years.

We all have a bigger purpose in life than just making money. It's what money can buy us that makes it so valuable—the freedom to pursue worthy causes in life.

What's Your Passion and Life Calling?

Financial freedom buys you the time to dedicate your life to your true passion. What is your passion and your life calling? Perhaps you have a business already. Or you're in a position to influence the business that you work for. I invite you to take this powerful information and use it. It can take you where you want to go, financially and personally.

I remember talking with one of our consultants in Chicago, Illinois. He had just signed a consulting agreement with a new client; the company had a great product that was worthy of the lion's share of the dollars in its industry. When I joined a conference call with the owner of the company and our consultant, I could sense the genuine nature of this man. Like many of our clients, he was bright, energetic, and confident. His business was doing well, but he knew it could do better.

He came to Dallas a short time later, and I met him for dinner to discuss his business. As we talked, I realized he was making about $300,000 a year in personal income. But as I explored his situation from a marketing perspective, I could also see that he had a ton of upside. So, after dinner, I called our consultant and said, "You are going to turn up his *profit faucet* so he can make $1.5 million a year in personal income. You are going to make a difference in this person's life. He'll be financially free in five years—free to sell the business and retire to other projects or free to grow the company even more."

I'm offering you the same opportunity with this program. I strongly encourage you to act on what you learn. In marketing, there's a lot of difference between knowing what the business is supposed to look like and knowing how to make it happen—and then doing it.

When we work with clients individually, we do it in one of two ways. The first way is a straight project fee basis. We evaluate your situation and quote you a price to create the strategy and write the marketing. Sometimes, we will work on a reduced fee plus what we call a *participation fee*, meaning we will work for less money up front in exchange for a percentage of the increased profitability our program brings your company. This option works well for aggressive companies looking for a long-term marketing partnership.

And yet some people think that the main goal of *Monopolize Your Marketplace* is to eliminate competitors for the fun of it. That's not the case. We're just trying to be the best we can be. Soon after he won his fifth MVP of the NBA award, Michael Jordan said, "I'm not sitting around trying to figure out how to be the best player in the league. I'm continually trying to figure out how I can be *the best I can be*. Then the rest—the MVP awards and championships—will all fall into place."

We're looking for people who sincerely want to be the best *they* can be—people who strive for excellence, people who want to take their business to the next level, people who have such passion for their customers and for doing things right that they can't stomach the thought of their customers doing business with their competitors.

e MYM Model

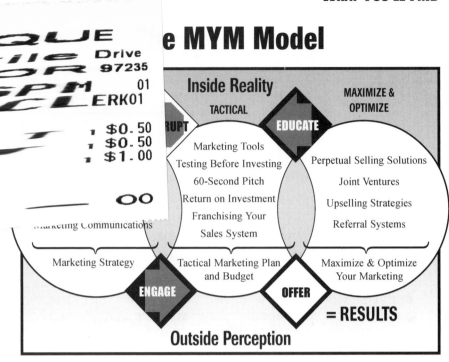

Our marketing system is a series of steps implemented over the course of a few months. Each step is multi-tiered and takes some understanding and know-how to properly execute. The following model shows how these steps are integrated into a business growth system.

We have spent thousands of hours perfecting this system to allow us to put your marketing together *relatively* quickly and easily. Our principal consultants are seasoned business professionals who are extensively trained how to implement this system for our clients.

We want to give your business an extreme makeover. Obviously, going from the "before" picture to the "after" picture takes know-how and hard work. It's easy to understand *how* to overhaul your marketing program, but it's not so easy to *do*. The purpose of this book is NOT to train you on every detail of marketing; instead, I want to educate you so you have a clear vision of what your marketing is supposed to achieve, along with the steps, processes and strategies for making it work. I also want you to apply these principles and thereby gain a significant advantage over your competitors.

Here is a brief overview of what we'll share with you.

- First, we'll discuss what marketing is supposed to do and why most marketing doesn't do it. We'll explain exactly *why* everything you now know about marketing and advertising is wrong.

- After that, we'll talk about creating strategic marketing messages. Strategic marketing is the content of your message and the positioning of your brand, company or product. It's what you say and how you say it. It makes your marketing program easy to implement and ensures your brand message is always consistent.

- Then we'll talk about executing a tactical marketing program. Tactical marketing is the execution of the strategic marketing plan.

- We'll next describe the *marketing equation*, the backbone of the MYM system. It's a road map to ensure you're always saying the right thing to the right people every single time.

- We'll show you how to systematize your tactical marketing program to generate leads, place media, and implement a follow-up system. We'll cover the principles of lead generation, marketing tools, hopper systems, knock-down lists, and master strategies.

- We'll also discuss how to maximize and optimize your marketing program—two of the more advanced tactical execution strategies.

Many business people assume that when you talk about marketing, you're automatically talking about tactical marketing—placing ads, generating leads, sending out mailers, attending trade shows, and implementing a follow-up system. They fail to realize that the strategic side—WHY you do what you do in your marketing and WHAT you say—is almost always more important than WHEN and WHERE and even HOW you say it.

If you fail to make the distinction between strategic and tactical marketing, you risk eliminating some forms of marketing and advertising that should be part of your tactical plan, simply because these methods haven't worked for you in the past. When results are less than optimal, most people blame the marketing medium—the tactical part of the plan—without regard

for the strategy behind that marketing piece! People often say, "We t̸
radio and it doesn't work for our business." Or, "We sent 50,000 r̸
direct mail and only got back 16 orders. It doesn't work!" Well, n̸
true. But just because it *didn't* work, don't assume that it *won't*

We'll give you the evaluation tools and know-how to ju̸
poor marketing result stems from poor strategy or poor tac̸
Bottom line: We'll teach you how to grow your business̸
communicate your unique advantages to your target marke̸

Inside Reality vs. Outside Perception

Everything you've ever learned about marketing is wrong.

The *Monopolize Your Marketplace* system is a step-by-step program for innovating and marketing your company. The system first teaches you how to **be better** than the competition. Then, you learn how to **out-market** the competition. You become the obvious choice to do business with.

Chapter 1:

The Two Sides of Your Business

When the outside perception of your organization
is an accurate reflection of an amazing inside realty,
you can monopolize your marketplace.

Monopolize Your Marketplace focuses on both sides of your business: the inside reality and the outside perception. We find that these two sides of a business are rarely aligned.

In fact, we venture to say that the crux of all marketing problems—including yours—can be wrapped up into one simple statement:

> **Most companies' outside perception is not**
> **an accurate reflection of their inside reality.**

What the MYM system does, first and foremost, is fix that problem.

The inside reality has to do with all the things your business does that makes you valuable to your customers from a product, operations, and management standpoint. The *inside reality* is about what you do and what you are that allows your business to perform better. It's what gives you a competitive advantage in the marketplace. The reason we call it the *inside reality* is because the reality of what you do, and the customers' perceptions of what you do, aren't necessarily the same. These two words—reality and perception—are vital to winning in business.

The inside reality encompasses everything you do and everything you are that makes you good. It's all your skills, your people, your expertise, your service to the customer—before, during *and* after the sale—your systems, your operational procedures, your commitment to excellence, your passion, and the way you conduct your business. You might think you're actually better than you are, or, you might not be giving yourself enough credit for the things you do well. Regardless, *there is a reality of how valuable you are to the marketplace* based on these things. That's what we call the inside *reality*.

What is the inside reality in your business? You probably already know, even though you may not have really thought of it before. If you asked your customers why they bought from you, they could tell you something quantifiable, specific, and instantly obvious. They could point to certain advantages of doing business with you and say, "That's why I do business here; that's why I refer my friends to come here; that's why I'm a loyal customer of this place; that's why I don't mind paying more here; that's why I keep coming back." That's your inside reality.

This is what business gurus like Tom Peters, Ken Blanchard, and Michael Gerber are all about—innovating your business so it's valuable to the marketplace. Tom Peters calls it the "Pursuit of Wow!"—making your business so good that your customers say "WOW!" Ken Blanchard calls it developing "Raving Fans."

You need to innovate your company so that there's a reason for people to buy from you. These popular gurus do a great job of teaching you how to do those things. But here's the problem: Just because you've achieved "WOW!" doesn't mean that customers will flock to your business. You still have to market your business. And that's where the "outside perception" comes into play.

The outside perception is how customers and prospects *perceive* your company. The outside perception is developed by all of the interactions people have with your company. Customers will draw on their past buying experiences to form their outside perception.

But even if your customer service is great and your customers love you, none of that means squat to a prospective customer if 1) they don't know you even exist as an option, or 2) they can't distinguish your value because of your inability to market yourself properly. They perceive that you are no better or worse than anybody else. Marketing ineptitude creates a chasm between your inside reality and your outside perception. To your buyers, they are totally different. Take your pride and stick it on the shelf for a minute. Regardless of how good you are or how good your *inside reality* is, your prospect can't figure it out based on your marketing. You appear on the surface to be just another company that sells whatever it is you sell. The prospect will likely be apathetic at best, resistant or hostile at worst.

Ask yourself: "How many competitors, either direct or indirect, do we have in our business?" Whatever that number is, that's how many choices your prospects have, and how many businesses they have to sift through to try to make a buying decision. And that's assuming they want to buy what you're selling! Because of the large number of competitors, marketing has to 1) interrupt the prospect, 2) facilitate the decision-making process, and 3) lower the risk of taking the next step in the buying process.

Have you ever heard the saying, "If you want to know why John Smith buys what John Smith buys, you've got to see the world through John Smith's eyes?" Well, it's true. If you want to know why John Smith buys what John Smith buys, you MUST see the world through John Smith's eyes. Most business owners and managers know how to look through John Smith's eyes. Unfortunately, they don't know how to communicate what makes them good—their inside reality—to their customers. Most businesses are good at knowing what John Smith wants, but because they aren't communications experts, they can't communicate their inside reality to the outside world. They can't take their WOW and lead prospects to the conclusion: "I would have to be an absolute fool to do business with anyone else but you."

How to do that is what *Monopolize Your Marketplace* is all about. Think about your business. Your ability to know what John Smith wants is what has made you as successful as you are now. I'll assume that you have good products or services and that you fill a market need. You've probably been studying your market, your prospects and your business for years, and you have solutions that add value to John Smith's life. Why, then, aren't you making all the money you deserve? Because you're an expert at what you do, not a marketing communications expert. This is a critical distinction.

Now, there are hundreds of books, workshops and trainers that try to help you improve your outside perception. You've got books like *Guerrilla Marketing, Marketing Warfare, and The 22 Immutable Laws of Marketing*. You've got sales and marketing gurus galore who try to help you make your business look good to the outside world. The problem is this:

None of these books or trainers pays any attention
to how good your business actually is.

Advertising guru Rosser Reeves once said, "To be effective, you've got to make the product interesting, not just make the advertisement different." That's something too many of the books, gurus, and agencies don't understand. Visit an ad agency or a media sales rep. They'll say, "Just bring me any product or service and a big bag of cash, and we'll guarantee you that we'll spend all of the money." They put all their creative effort into trying to make the ad different, with no thought for the inside reality of the product or service. Do you think that the "dot-coms" of the late 1990s all failed because of bad marketing? They certainly did have some of the worst marketing in history. But the real reason they failed was because they had stupid business concepts in the first place. Nobody wanted to buy wine from wine.com or pet food from pets.com. But there were plenty of money-grubbing ad agencies and media outlets willing to take those piles of cash that were plundered from stockholders and put them straight into their own pockets.

If you lost money in the dot-com meltdown, guess where the money went? It didn't just disappear! It went from your hands to the dot-com's hands, who took *their* multi-million dollar cut and passed the rest to the ad agencies, who took their 15 percent plus creative fees and passed it on to media moguls who then took it and bought Ferraris, Lamborghinis, Porches, and $10 million homes. So now you at least know where your money ended up! All based on sorry inside realities.

You've got to work on *both* sides of your business—the inside reality and the outside perception. If you concentrate all your efforts on the inside reality but you don't know how to market properly, you set yourself up for frustration and failure. You'll be pulling your hair out trying to figure out where YOUR big bag of money vanished to, or you'll feel like the "best kept secret in town." Or, if you're focusing all your efforts on the outside perception, and your inside reality stinks, then you'll have customers, but they'll hate your guts because you're selling them a lie! You've got to balance both sides of your business.

Here's what we've observed over the last several years: Most businesses could stand some improvement in both areas, but they struggle most with the outside perception. They've built good companies and they offer good value, but they have problems differentiating themselves in the marketplace given today's intense competition. Generally, this is because communication is not their core competency. But that's what the MYM system is all about. It teaches you to improve both the inside reality *and* the outside perception of your company. Part of the system deals with innovation and how to make your business competitive from a product, operations, and management standpoint. Then the system deals with how to communicate through your marketing—whether that be advertising, direct mail, web-based, or whatever—so that it effectively separates you from your competitors in the minds of the prospects.

Business philosopher Jim Rohn summed it up best when he said that in order to communicate powerfully, you have to: "Have something good to say. Then, say it well. Finally, say it often." Chances are excellent that you've already got something good to say (if not, innovation is an inevitable by-product of implementing the MYM system). We help you improve the outside perception of your business. We teach you how to *say it well* and *say it often* so people instantly recognize you as their best choice. You become their no-brainer decision.

Just learning you how to innovate leaves you with a wonderful, innovative company that nobody knows about. Just learning sales, marketing, advertising, or PR techniques will drive in business that won't stick around because they receive no value. You have to consider both the inside reality *and* the outside perception.

MYM is the only program that integrates these two important aspects of growing your business. Stop and think for a minute: What is the inside reality of our business? What is the outside perception?

Although what your current customers think about you is important, what your *prospects* think about you is even more so. Can they perceive that you're any different or any better than their alternatives by looking at your ads? What about your brochures? What about your website? Chances are, they can't. Even though your inside reality is good, the outside perception is average, or worse, non-existent.

Grab your marketing communications. Look at your ads and your website. Is it instantly obvious what makes you better? Can you quantifiably demonstrate what makes you unique and different? Do you show your prospects how to judge your offer, what factors they need to consider when deciding, and how you provide superior value?

If not, you have some work to do: to ensure that your *outside perception* is an accurate reflection of your *inside reality* and to convince prospects that you are the obvious choice to business with.

Chapter 2:

Are You the Obvious Choice to Do Business With?

Do your prospects and customers feel that they would have to be absolute fools to do business with anyone else—regardless of price?

Are you marketing your company in such a way that it is instantly evident that you are the obvious choice to do business with? If not, you need to learn how to make those advantages *so obvious* to your prospects and customers that they quickly and easily draw this one conclusion:

"I would have to be an absolute fool to do business with anyone else but you—regardless of price."

Our program is about getting more results and making more money with the same time, the same capital, and the same effort that you currently put forth.

Suppose that you own a moving company and spend $3,000 a month for a full-page ad in the *Yellow Pages*, and that ad generates 70 calls per month. Is that good? Is that bad? It depends. What if you could take that same full-page ad and generate 955 calls a month just by changing what it says or how it says it? What's more, what if the average quality of the prospect was quantifiably better?

Or, suppose that you're the CEO of an up-and-coming bank that is trying to get a stronger foothold in the small business loan market. You've got 22 retail locations supported by hundreds of thousands of dollars a month in total marketing and advertising expenses for the small business loan program, including heavy telemarketing, direct mail, newspaper, and some radio and television as well as brochures and collateral materials at each sales office. Despite spending a fortune on advertising and marketing, your efforts to generate leads and subsequently close loans are losing money. Over time, the return on investment is getting worse. What can be done?

What if you could change your marketing message in your brochures and collateral materials and:

- Increase the number of leads you generated by 465 percent
- Increase the *quality* of those leads, and
- Increase your closing ratio from a paltry 8 percent to a healthy 31 percent?

You can do this *without* changing how much money you spend. You don't have to hire an expensive celebrity to say he gets his loans from you. In fact, you don't have to do anything substantially different. All you have to do is change *what you're saying and how you say it so that it works better.*

You can use the *Monopolize Your Marketplace* system to leverage what you're already doing, whether you spend $3,000 a month, $370,000 a month, or $3 million a month on marketing. You can get those results for your business by changing the message in your ads, media spots, brochures, websites, trade shows, signage, and everything else. The process for getting these results is systematic, and anyone with a strong business background can understand it.

My purpose is to show you how to change your advertising to leverage your marketing and gain and sustain momentum. I'll teach you how to make more money for the same resources expended.

Many business owners feel that their marketing is under-leveraged. As a result, they're looking for solutions. Maybe that's you. But others don't see their untapped potential. They spend some money on marketing or advertising, get some results, make some money, and then decide that whatever result they are getting is as good as it gets. They figure 70 calls a month on a $3,000 ad is about average; they don't realize that 955 calls for the same investment is even possible.

When you learn how to use the *marketing equation,* you'll get predictable, consistent and much better results every time you do anything called "marketing."

The MYM system is based on a true principle of human nature: *People always want to make the best buying decision possible.* Therefore, marketing's job—your job—is NOT to talk incessantly about how great you are or how low your prices are. Instead, your job is to facilitate the prospect's decision-making process and allow them to feel they're in control of the decision, based on having enough quantity and quality information. The system is a breakthrough in marketing and advertising, yet it's simple and easy to understand. When implemented properly, it works every time, regardless of what business or industry you're in.

Unlike most ad agencies, we reveal our results-getting processes to our clients, so they can evaluate the program for themselves. We show them step-by-step how to make more money every time they run an ad, produce a brochure, create a website, show up at a trade show, make a sales call in the field, or any other sales-generating activity.

We compete head-to-head with marketing consultancies and large ad agencies that take money from their clients with no accountability for results. These agencies hate us because we expose their ineptitude and threaten their existence. They even call us the "anti-agency." This antipathy has earned me the title of "the most hated man in advertising and marketing."

How can we say that everything you've ever learned is wrong? How can we accuse you, without ever having met you, of leaving huge untapped profits on the table—profits that are easily and readily available just by applying the MYM system? How can we say that *you don't know what you're talking about* when it comes to marketing—even though you've been doing marketing for decades and getting what most people would consider good results? The rest of this book will answer those questions.

Our marketing and advertising makes money. Our program has a set of strategies and tactics that can be applied systematically to any business. Our program includes a set of evaluations that allows you to instantly and objectively rate your own marketing and predict the success of a marketing campaign before you spend any money.

This program is exactly what you need to take your business to the next level of profitability and success. We are unique as marketing consultants because we don't specialize in any industry. We've successfully implemented marketing programs in over 400 different industries. In a typical year, our consultants will work with or implement marketing and advertising strategies for more than 10,000 companies. We've completed marketing programs for service businesses, financial companies, retail stores, real estate companies, home builders, restaurants, consultants, software companies, professionals, entrepreneurs, internet companies, manufacturing companies, and anything and everything else. We work with all sizes of businesses from start-ups to Fortune 500's. We're the only national marketing company that has the expertise to consult with the nation's largest companies and the bandwidth to help the smaller companies. We achieve this through the cooperation between our frontline consultants and our corporate staff.

You need to make sure that the person or company you take your marketing advice from knows what they are talking about. Since you invest thousands or hundreds of thousands of dollars a year in marketing, I want you to feel confident that the information you receive is credible, accurate, and effective. We are listed 28th on *Inc.* magazine's annual list of the 500 fastest-growing privately held companies in the country, with a five-year growth rate of 3,300 percent. These numbers show we practice what we preach. Wouldn't you like to know that the company showing you how to grow fast has grown fast itself?

We're growing fast because we walk our own talk. We educate you about how marketing really works. Our clients are people who want their companies to be the best they can be. They have a passion for their customers and for doing things right. They'll do whatever it takes to deserve more business. They can't stomach the thought of a customer doing business with a competitor. If you strive for such excellence, you automatically surpass 99 percent of your competitors because they won't put in the effort.

We spent 10 years perfecting our system so that it's easy to understand and foolproof to implement. I honestly believe that you would be an absolute fool to do business with anyone else but us.

I hope you feel that way about what you are doing. I hope you put that kind of effort into perfecting your craft so that it's worthy of attracting the lion's share of the dollars in your industry. If you don't feel that way, and you're not willing to put in the effort, then give this book to your competitors and get ready to get snuffed out by someone who does feel that way.

Monopolize Your Marketplace will let you quit competing on price and start selling for what you're really worth. You'll drive in more leads and increase your advertising response by two to more than one hundred times. You'll convert a higher percentage of those leads and make your salespeople into superstars. You'll increase the amount of each sale and augment your repeat business. You'll get a bigger bang for your marketing buck.

We'll show you how to build a "profit faucet" for your business—a stream of profitability that you control. Fast or slow, hot or cold, it's up to you. If you start generating more leads than you can comfortably handle or you reach full capacity, just turn down the marketing faucet until you get caught up. Need more business? Want more profitability? Turn up the faucet and let it flow.

Chapter 3:

The Three Purposes of Marketing

Surprisingly few people can even tell you the purposes of marketing, let alone how to achieve those primary purposes.

What is the purpose of marketing? If I ask 100 business people this simple question, I'll get 100 different answers. Some people would say marketing's job is to get your name out in the marketplace. Others would say marketing positions your company or builds your brand name. Most owners hope marketing generates sales. Others would say that marketing's job is to generate leads that are then handed over to the sales department. Still others would say it's to build brand awareness, hoping people remember the name when they go to buy. And there's always the group that just says marketing's job is "to make money."

All of these answers are partially right. All of the answers are results of what happens when your investment in marketing and advertising does what it is supposed to do.

Marketing is supposed to do three things:

1. Capture the attention of your target market.

2. Teach and train people how to make the best purchasing decision by giving them enough information to facilitate their making the best decision possible when buying what you have to sell.

3. Lower the risk of taking the next step in the buying process so you can further educate them.

Effective marketing accomplishes all three objectives. It causes your prospects and customers to conclude: "I would have to be an absolute fool to do business with anyone else but you—regardless of price."

Objective 1: Capture your target market's attention. Although this seems pretty straightforward, there are right ways and wrong ways to do this. I've got a specific formula I'll give you later that ensures you always do it the right way. Unfortunately, it's done the wrong way 99 percent of the time.

Objective 2: Facilitate the prospect's decision-making process. Please understand that you've got prospects who need to buy what you sell. There are plenty of people who are starving and craving information and solutions you can provide. Because they're not experts at what you do, they don't know the benchmarks or the relevant issues surrounding the decision. They don't know how to make the best decision, which gives you an opportunity to guide them through this process. Your job is to share information to help them make the best decision possible. If the best decision happens to be buying from you—and it should be— then that's all the better. You should think of yourself as the "fountain from whence all knowledge flows," at least knowledge relevant to what you're selling.

All business owners and stakeholders want the same things: They want more new customers and less competition, more profitability and less waste, more retention and less turnover among their best employees, better results from their marketing and advertising, more loyalty from their customers, and higher conversion ratios for their salespeople. In short, they want to make more money.

Realize that prospects and customers want the same things. They want to feel confident that their money is well spent and their purchasing decisions are wise. They want to get the best deal, in terms of both price and value. You never hear anybody say, "I shopped eight car dealerships and negotiated the best possible price, then decided to buy where I got the third best deal." No! *People intuitively want to make the best decision possible, and not feel like they have to second-guess themselves all the time.*

So we have two sets of values: The business wants more customers, more loyal customers and higher margins. Customers want to feel confident that they get the best possible deal in terms of overall value. The process and principles that govern the matching of those two sets of values are the same for every business. This is why we can work with thousands of companies a year in every industry. It's simple: As the marketer, *all* you have to do is figure out what's important to your prospects, educate them about what constitutes the best deal in your area, and then provide quantifiable proof that you provide that best deal in terms of price and value. If you communicate that message properly, your customer will pay attention to the message, believe you, and then take action.

Our system is powerful because your prospects get what they want from you. First, they get the best deal in terms of price and value. And they can buy with confidence that they are making the best decision possible for them.

The problem is most businesses don't hold up their end of the bargain. Instead of using marketing to build a case that facilitates the decision-making process, most companies fill their marketing with self-serving hyperbole, fluff and platitudes that are only a thinly veiled way to say, "Buy from me because I want you to give your money to me instead of somebody else." That's why people become jaded and resist marketing. They tend to either dismiss it or become skeptical of the messages. But you don't want to breed skepticism! You want your prospects to say that they'd have to be absolute fools to do business with anyone else but you—regardless of price!

Objective 3: Give your customers a specific, low-risk, easy-to-take action that further facilitates their ability to make a good decision. You can't cram everything that a person needs to know into one advertisement. You have to find a way to give them more information—and you do this via marketing tools— reports, websites, audio CDs, and CD ROMs.

Have you ever bought a new home from a builder? They have lots of ways to advertise and promote, one being the Sunday paper in the New Homes section. But if you look in that section of the newspaper, you'll see that none of the ads there accomplishes the three objectives of marketing: 1) to capture the attention of the target market, 2) facilitate their decision-making process by educating them about what they need to know, and 3) give them a low-risk way to become more educated and take the next step to further the buying process. Those ads don't do this. Instead, they feature beautiful, happy, smiling people, pictures of houses and floor plans, price ranges of homes, and maps to various neighborhoods.

Take a look at the ads on the following page: none of them do what marketing is supposed to do. None capture the attention of the prospective buyer. The ads all look virtually identical and contain similar pictures and words. From the prospect's standpoint, they *are* the same. There's nothing to get their atten-

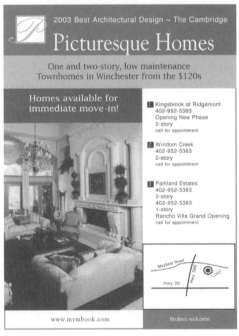
tion, no acknowledgement of what the customer's needs or problems might be. And, there's nothing in any of the ads to educate the prospect. There's nothing to facilitate their decision-making process. There's nothing to show them what they need to know or tell them what issues to consider. How many things do you need to know when buying a new home? Are you an expert on lumber, plumbing, masonry, electrical, insulation, flooring, framing, roofing, finish out, and the 613 other relevant, pertinent issues involved with building a home? Of course not. And you won't be after reading those ads, either.

I'm not saying every buyer wants to know all that stuff; what I am saying is that *all buyers would like to at least be aware of the relevant issues that are at stake*. With these ads, all you know is that smiling people supposedly live there, and they all have floor plans and maps to neighborhoods. All of these ads are ineffective because prospective buyers want and need to be educated—so they can feel confident when making their decision. Nobody is providing this information. The first one who does, wins.

Then there's no low-risk way for the prospect to take the next step in the buying process. The only option these ads give is to come into the model home. You say, "That's low risk." The heck it is! You tell me, if you're just thinking about buying a new home, and the only option is to come to a model home that's 45 minutes from your house, and you know that it will be stocked with starving salespeople who will do everything in their power to force you to buy that home on the spot, is that low risk?

If you think I exaggerate, go meet the salespeople who sit at those model homes all weekend long. Some are wonderful, but 90 percent of them are starving and took the job because it's the only thing they could find that had a $2,000 a month draw. They look at you like a big, thick, juicy steak to be devoured, not a prospect who wants to make the best home-buying decision possible.

All of the ads fail miserably on this level; as a result, they get lost in the shuffle of all the other ads.

There's a better way to handle this situation.

Why do you think that business people always feel forced into a price-competitive situation? If you feel that's the case in your business, it's your own fault. Your lack of marketing ability has led to a situation where there are no distinctions between you and your competitors. You haven't introduced the proper parameters or educated your prospects on the relevant issues. You've made no offers to lower the risk of taking the next step.

If you feel that you're always competing on price, it's because price is the only relevant variable you've given your prospects to consider, and from the prospect's perspective, all things are equal, so they would be fools not to demand a lower price.

Chapter 4:

Why Everything You Learned about Marketing Is Wrong

You have been conditioned to believe and practice
certain things about marketing and advertising
that are all wrong because they can't grow your business.

All you have learned about marketing is wrong because it doesn't allow you to accurately, effectively, and succinctly portray your inside reality to the outside world. This is a product of years of conditioning of marketing the wrong way.

Let me explain how and why you landed in this mess. You'll have a better appreciation for the problem, as well as the solution to the problem, if you know *why* the problem exists in the first place.

In the early days of advertising—the late 1800's and early 1900's—most companies were competing on a local or regional basis. Because of their proximity, competition was fierce. Much of the advertising was comparative in nature. They wouldn't just say, "Hey, we're better." They'd say, "We're better, and here's exactly why based on this, this, this, this and this." They did a pretty good job building a case and helping prospective buyers understand the important issues regarding their particular product or service. This information helped facilitate the decision-making process for the prospective buyer, which is what marketing is supposed to do.

In other words, the ads performed a *sales function*. This highly competitive environment forced advertisers to use their brains when writing ads, and the beneficiary was the buyer. Back in those days, ads were thought of as an "army of tiny salespeople armed with the perfect sales presentation." The result was that the outside perception was generally a fair reflection of a company's inside reality.

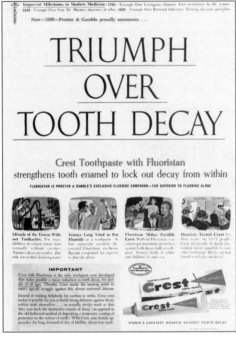

Here's an example of such an ad:

This kind of marketing continued through the end of World War II. Then, everything changed. At that time, Americans had unprecedented prosperity, free time and discretionary income. People were saying, "I'm ready to consume!"

Then the most significant event in the history of marketing and advertising occurred. In 1945 television appeared on the scene, and it changed everything. In 1945, there were fewer than 7,000 TV sets receiving signals from just nine stations in five markets. From there, it mushroomed. By 1951, there were 12 million sets. One year later, in 1952, there were 20 million sets.

Television changed all advertising in a negative way. In the 1950s, the typical family in America had one TV set that received just three channels. The entire family gathered around and watched practically every night. It was very powerful. Some of the biggest companies in the country said, "Hey, here's a relatively low-cost way that we can reach everybody in the whole country with an advertising message."

Until then, national distribution of an advertising message was limited to print advertising in a few magazines or the Sears catalog. Now, corporations could buy a TV commercial and reach just about every living person in the country watching TV for just $4,000 a minute. What a bargain! When more companies began to catch on, the prices for commercials went through the roof. Local and regional competitors quickly lost their ability to buy air time, and soon *only* the largest national companies could afford the huge advertising rates. They gladly paid the money because of the almost instantaneous effectiveness of those advertisements.

As advertising prices went up, the length of the average TV commercial shrank. Instead of one or two minutes per commercial, the networks started selling them in 30-second blocks. This meant that advertisers had less time to sell. Now, there was no time to educate the public about important issues. It was impossible to build a case as to why they were different, better, or unique. Instead, they started using slogans, and the outside perception stopped accurately reflecting the inside reality.

What is marketing supposed to do? First, get the prospect's attention. Even with only 30 seconds, getting attention was no problem. But then what? Marketing must facilitate the decision-making process and make prospects feel that they would be absolute fools to do business with anyone else but that company— regardless of price. Companies and their ad agencies found that this was much harder to do in only 30 seconds. But they also found out that *they didn't really need to do it* because the number of real competitors (those who could actually *afford* to be on the tube advertising along with them) was amazingly, wonderfully, few. On television they could just spend money and win by default because of the limited number of players. The big spenders discovered they could win by being the only one who reached the consumer consistently. Not because their products were better. Not because they had a better inside reality. Not by better advertising. It was like winning a sporting event by forfeit: if the other team doesn't show up, you automatically win! And even if there were two or three major competitors—like Pepsi and Coke—that was fine because there was plenty of business to divide two or three ways. So, because of the the scarcity of options, a company's inside reality and outside perception didn't have to match up.

Because of the limited air time available and scarce competition, all of the focus shifted to the first step—getting attention. Advertising quickly lost its penchant for selling and developed an appetite for creativity. The idea was to get something creative into the consumer's brain that would stimulate them or cause them to recall the product later on when they needed it. Slogans began to rule the roost. "Aren't you glad you use Dial?" "Ring around the collar." "Melts in your mouth, not in your hands." "Don't squeeze the Charmin." Some of those commercials ran for years!

The creative approach soon filtered into other advertising media, including radio, newspapers, magazines, billboards, and *Yellow Pages*. Once the creative message was in place, big companies opened up their checkbooks, spent the big bucks, and basically gave people no option but to remember the message. After 6,722 times of hearing "Plop plop, fizz, fizz," you'll remember it, whether you want to or not! You tell me, how *do* you spell relief?

We call this the *C&R Formula*: *C* stands for creativity and *R* for repetition. Make something creative, spend a billion dollars to ensure repetition, and take your money to the bank.

Does creativity still work? It depends, to some extent, on how much money you have to spend. To test its effectiveness, I'll give you some slogans of companies, and you tell me: a) what company the slogans are for, b) what they do, and c) what you think their inside reality is. I bet you don't get more than one.

The power to know.

Log in and meet.

At your side.

A passion for the middle market.

Instruments for professionals.

Now you're really flying.

Everywhere you go.

I pulled all these slogans from a current major business magazine for major companies with major products or services. They spend a lot of money supporting these campaigns to raise "awareness." But, chances are, none of them have any impact on you at all.

I'm not saying you shouldn't have a slogan. But I am saying that if you're betting on a slogan, you're in trouble. Even if you spend enough money to gain widespread awareness, there's still no guarantee that people will know what your inside reality is and feel compelled to buy something from you. There's a big gap between what the ad agencies like to call "awareness" and what we like to call "selling something."

The Big Brand Era

Creativity and repetition became the calling card of the big advertisers, and their methods trickled down into other media. Then, ad agencies and business schools started to "benchmark" these companies. They did some research and discovered that the big, rich companies were getting bigger and richer by advertising on TV with all this creative, slogan-oriented stuff, spending a bazillion dollars on repetition. This led them to conclude: "That must be how you get rich in business:

You spend more than your competitors on advertising, clog the airwaves, make sure everyone sees your name and hears your slogan 50 million times, and do it all as creatively as possible." For a period of time, they were right.

We call this the "era of the brand builders." Through the 1970s, this was a no-brainer formula for market dominance for companies with the financial resources to pull it off. Large ad agencies started using this formula for all their other clients—even small ones. Business schools started teaching marketing and advertising based on these hackneyed methods, churning out graduates who only knew one way to do "marketing." Brand builder marketing and advertising became the *de facto* standard for "how you do it." After a few decades, nobody even questioned the formula.

You and I grew up in an era where almost all advertising was a product of the "brand builders." We all became conditioned to advertise this way. We all learned the pattern and knew what to put into a commercial. We learned about humorous slogans and jingles. We were taught the *outside perception doesn't have to reflect the inside reality.*

So, now you're in charge of marketing and advertising for your company, and you need to create an advertisement, brochure, or website. You draw on all your collective resources. If you're putting the marketing together yourself, you dredge your mental archives for everything you've ever seen. Maybe you've had a few marketing classes or picked up a few books from Amazon.com on marketing and advertising. Or, you go to an ad agency for advice or hire a marketing expert.

Here's the sad truth. Because these resources are based on an outmoded, antiquated, brand builder, "spend a billion dollars on creativity and repetition" model that doesn't work any more, they won't help. Maybe it still works to an extent for Coca-Cola, who spends over $1 billion annually, and General Motors, who budgets up to $4 billion for advertising each year. They have the money to fund the repetition side of the equation. You throw enough mud at the wall, some of it's going to stick. But even if you have a billion dollars to spend, it still isn't the way to maximize your return.

Institutional or Menu-Board Ads

The current state of marketing and advertising is a mess. Today, generally, the outside perception built by the advertisements and marketing pieces do not reflect or reveal the inside reality of the company. Most ads can be classified into two categories. They are either a) institutional advertising or b) menu-board style advertising. Institutional ads say, "Here's our name, here's our best attempt at being cre-

Creativity, Repetition and Positioning =
C R A P .

ative, and here's the biggest budget we could muster to support this CRAP" (Creative Repetition and Positioning). Almost all big companies and ad agencies—along with many small business and small agency copycats—specialize in institutional advertising. It's what you see in most magazine and TV ads.

Here is an example of institutional advertising. Is this what your ads look like?

Menu-board advertising basically says, "Here's our name and here's a list of what we have for sale." Just like a menu at a restaurant. We have hamburgers, chicken, salads, and roast beef. Maybe there's even a little picture of it. In advertising, it goes like this: "We're a moving company. We load and unload. We move local and long distance. We move houses, apartments and offices. We do commercial and residential moves. We have insurance." Oh look, a picture of a truck! Get the point? Just like a menu at a restaurant, the ad is a simple listing of what's for sale.

Many large companies, and almost all small businesses, specialize in menu-board advertising. If you let the newspaper or radio creative department put your ad together for you, you're almost certain to get a menu-board style advertisement. This advertising does little for you. It doesn't get the prospects' attention, it doesn't facilitate their decision-making process, it doesn't build a case, it doesn't lower the risk, and it doesn't lead prospects to say, "I would have to be an absolute fool to do business with anyone else but you—regardless of price." It just says, "Hey, we have stuff for sale. Come buy some from us for no justifiable, rational reason other than we want your money."

Of course, you're assuming your prospects will see the ad in the first place.

Platitudes Take Over

The final result—whether institutional or menu-board style—is that platitudes dominate marketing and advertising. A platitude is a trite or banal remark or statement, especially one expressed as if it were original or significant. Does this describe *your* marketing and advertising? Is it full of trite words and phrases that are expressed *as if* they were original or significant?

Trite means lacking power to evoke interest through overuse or repetition, and *banal* means drearily commonplace and often predictable. Let me summarize all those definitions into one:

Platitudes are words or phrases that are drearily commonplace and predictable. They lack the power to evoke interest through overuse or repetition—even though they are stated as if they were original or significant.

In marketing and advertising, we see and hear platitudes all the time: "largest selection, most professional, lowest prices, highest quality, best service, fastest, most convenient, largest in the state, more honest, experts in, specializing in, works harder, get the job done right the first time, been in business since 1431 BC"—and all such stuff.

I'm not saying you shouldn't *be* those kinds of things. Those, obviously, are foundations to build your inside reality on, right? So, what's the problem? Where's the disconnect? If my advertisement says that I have high quality and great service, is that drearily commonplace and predictable? Does it lack power to evoke interest through overuse or repetition? Is it nevertheless stated as though it were original or significant? Does the inside reality—what really makes me good—shine through? Can you tell, specifically, what makes me valuable to the marketplace when I say "quality and service?"

No! You can't describe, demonstrate, exhibit, reveal or display your inside reality using platitudes. It's impossible. Platitudes result in an outside perception that you're just like everybody else. No distinction, separation, or differentiation. None. You can't make your inside reality and outside perception match using platitudes.

If you've ever felt like you've got a great business, but you're "the best kept secret in town," you are likely a master of the platitude. I would bet that most of your marketing pieces are littered with platitudes, which is why I can accuse you without ever having met you and tell you that everything you've ever done in marketing is wrong.

Don't you think that the definition of platitudes describes most marketing and advertising, including brochures, websites, signage, on-hold messages, billboards, tradeshow booths, direct mail, and everything else you can think of? All marketing is full of words and phrases that are drearily commonplace and predictable, that lack the power to evoke interest through overuse or repetition, and that, nevertheless, are stated as though they were original or significant.

Almost every ad stinks, almost every brochure is boring, and almost every website is stagnant because nobody knows any better—including you. If you still don't believe me, take three quick evaluations to see if *your* marketing and advertising gets caught in the platitude trap.

Platitude evaluation #1: "Well, I would hope so!" When you make a claim, don't think about it coming out of your mouth; think of it entering your prospect's ears. Then you'll realize how ridiculous these claims sound. Whenever you say something, ask yourself if the prospect will immediately respond with: "Well, I would hope so!"

We do this exercise in some of our workshops. We ask people to write on a piece of paper why a prospect would favor their business over the competition. Here's an answer that a huge printing company gave as its number-one reason to choose its services over the *16 zillion* other printers: "We help the non-professional print buyer understand the various options available." ***Well, I would hope so! You're a printer! Isn't that what you do?*** It's a platitude. The value proposition is drearily commonplace. It lacks power to evoke interest because of overuse or repetition.

Try this one from a management training company: "Our training leads to change! And it will increase productivity, performance, and profit." ***Does anyone hire a management consultant for any other reason than to do those things?*** That's a platitude.

Or, what about an auto mechanic who says, "We're honest. We fix your car right the first time." Well, I would hope so. Is it believable? Does it tell you anything about the company's inside reality?

Here's a clue for you: Companies can easily get away with lying when they use platitudes. What else would you expect the guy to say? "Hey, we're lousy. We'll fix things that aren't broken and make sure the original problem goes unsolved so you'll bring it back so we can fix it and charge you again." Of course not. Everyone's always going to say wonderful things about their company if they can get away with it.

Again, the problem is, if your company has an exceptional inside reality, and you're using all the same platitudes as everyone else, the outside perception is that you are exactly like everyone else. And that's a tragedy. That's why you're not selling as much as you should, even if you're currently selling a lot. You've got to break past the trite and banal remarks and communicate more powerfully!

These platitudinal statements are like the barber telling you that your hair will be shorter after it's cut, or the gas station telling you you'll have more gas after you fill the tank. Duh!

Always use this important evaluation question whenever you make any claim: *Why would anyone choose you over your competitors?*

Answer the question right now. If you can't come up with the answer instantly and articulate it well, you can bet that your customers can't answer it either.

Write your answer down. Now look at your answer. Is it a platitude? Is it a word or phrase that is drearily commonplace and predictable? A phrase that lacks power to evoke interest through overuse or repetition that you stated as though it were original or significant? Honestly evaluate your answer against the "Well, I would hope so!" remark. Does your inside reality shine through?

Next, check out all your advertising and marketing materials. Do they pass the "Well I would hope so!" evaluation? Or, are they full of platitudes too? If they are, then you need to make changes. Or, you had better hope and pray that one of your competitors doesn't get hold of one of our programs!

Platitude evaluation #2: "Who else can say that?" This is also a product of the era of the brand builders. Pay close attention to this one; the question is not who else can *do* what you do. The question is who else can *say* what you say. The answer is usually *anybody and everybody*.

One time we consulted with an auto repair facility that was by far the most awesome business of its kind we'd ever seen. They had 63 bays, 11 mechanics who were fully ASE certified in all eight areas of specialization, twice as much high tech equipment as any dealership, and floors so clean you could eat off them. They turn out 95 percent of all jobs in less than 24 hours and unconditionally guarantee all repairs. If you ever call to check the status of your car, they patch you directly through to the *technician* working on your car via a 900 mhz phone—and he tells you personally how things are going! They have a waiting room that includes a play area for your kids, free drinks and snacks, current issues of magazines, and clean bathrooms. They put competitors out of business every year—and capture market share in the process. Their inside reality was second to none.

Still, they had a big marketing problem: Even though nobody could even come close to performing at their level, their advertising looked virtually identical to all of their competitors. Their *Yellow Pages* ad, for instance, used the same generalities and platitudes as everybody else: "ASE certified mechanics. Foreign and domestic cars serviced." And then there was a long laundry list of services performed, ranging from air conditioners to brakes to transmissions. Get this: They accept Visa and MasterCard! Well, I would hope so! Who else can say that?

We asked the owner and the service manager that very question, and the service manager started to get upset with us. "Nobody can even touch us. The dealerships bring cars to us that *they* can't fix. Our mechanics are the best in the state. Nobody, and I mean *nobody*, can say what we say." I was a little nervous. The guy was so bent out of shape that he was screaming and flailing around.

To prove the point in a civil way, I told the owner to pull out the *Yellow Pages* and see what all of his competitors were saying. After he inspected the section, his jaw hung open for about two minutes. He pointed at the page and said to the service manager, "Look. I know this guy. He's terrible. His ad says the exact same thing that ours does. In fact, I think he copied our layout and verbiage word for word." He looked at the page and saw that all of the ads were virtually identical to his. Remember, it's not who can *do* what you do; it's who can *say* what you are saying.

Companies like to lie with generalities and platitudes. Those platitudes, however, don't allow your business to separate itself from your competitors, and let your inside reality shine through. You need to learn how to communicate your inside reality to your prospects in a compelling way that will build an outside perception worthy of your company that nobody else can copy. Less worthy competitors won't be able to say what you say because of the specificity—they'd be lying if they did—and you'll win every time.

Once a big barbecue catering company said: "The flavor and taste of our quality meats gives you the best BBQ you've ever eaten." That's drearily commonplace. Everyone would say the exact same thing. It wouldn't pass the "Well, I would hope so" test, either.

Guess what industry this is: "Experienced staff; company in business 35 years. Research and development of new technology. Customer service always available. Available to clients after the sale." This could be *any* company in *any* industry. These remarks are all drearily commonplace and lack power to evoke interest through overuse or repetition.

Platitude evaluation #3: Scratch out, write in test. Look at your brochure or advertisement. Now scratch your name out and write in your competitor's name. Is the ad still valid? If so, then you've failed the test. Now, get your competitor's ad and scratch out their name and write in yours.

You'll find that you run high on the platitude meter, and you'll discover that your inside reality, excellent as it may be, is nowhere to be found, lost in a swamp of platitudes, never revealed.

To get the most out of the MYM program, you need to evaluate your own materials against the platitude evaluations: *Well, I would hope so! Who else can say that?* and *Cross out, then write in.*

Here are a few more telling examples of bad marketing:

Let's review these ads quickly. The first one is the ad for the auto repair shop with the phenomenal inside reality. We know this ad didn't do a good job of portraying the shop's inside reality. It's full of platitudes. By the way, what is a Rotech Diagnostic System anyway? And what does it mean to be servicing New R134A? The customers have no idea.

Now look at the ad for the Sharp copier dealer. Get ready to peg the platitude meter. Right there at the beginning, you've got the headline "Sharp Image" with the words "quality and reliability" underneath. Wow, that's original and significant. Then the first line reads, "Sharp copiers and Southeast Office Systems bring a higher level of productivity to your office." Well, I'd hope so. Who else can say that? Do you really believe that? "High-volume performance, outstanding reliability and razor-sharp copy quality keep you ahead of your copying demands." "Sales and service excellence are the cornerstones of our family-owned business... blah blah blah blah blah."

This reminds me of those Peanuts cartoon television specials back in the 1970s with Charlie Brown and Snoopy. Remember what would happen whenever one of the kids would talk to an adult? Whenever the adults would speak, you wouldn't hear the words they were saying; instead, all you would hear was a murmuring sound. That's exactly what this ad—and any ad that's full of platitudes—sounds like.

You will gain a tremendous competitive advantage if you can fix the platitude problem. When we cover the "Marketing Equation" in the next section, I'll show you how to fix this problem and get rid of the platitudes forever. I'll show you how to become a communications powerhouse by making your outside perception a good reflection of your inside reality. Then, you'll start to get the results you should be getting from your marketing.

The Confidence Gap

Around 1980, the proliferation of competition made things in marketing and advertising even more difficult.

The era of the brand builder was a time of consolidation, resulting in relatively few companies offering products and services. Because there were fewer competitors, companies didn't have to offer many choices to their customers. Remember when there was only one phone company, and you could buy the phones for your house directly from Ma Bell? Remember how many different choices of styles and colors there were? You could choose one of two styles—the wall mount or the desk model, and they came in about three colors: black, white, and green. That was it. Grocery stores didn't used to have to be supermarkets because there weren't many brands, styles, and varieties available.

If you were to go to the *Yellow Pages* in a major city in 1980 to find a moving company, you would have found about 30 companies to choose from. Today you'll find over 300 companies listed in a major market.

We call the days of *relatively* low competition *the days of simple selling*. In those days, things were less sophisticated, and it was easier for a company or a salesperson to get an opportunity to sell. Compared to now, there was low competition, low information, low media coverage, and low technology. Those factors all limited consumer selection and increased the power that sellers had over

DAYS OF SIMPLE SELLING

Up Until The 1980's

The straight line represents the seller's ability to get in the door and make a presentation, use some closes, and walk out with a check.

- Fewer Competitors
- Fewer Choices
- Low Technology
- Low Education

- Low Information
- Low Resistance
- Easier to make a buying decision

The Seller Had The Power

THE CONFIDENCE GAP

1990's On...

The Gap in the line represents how hard it is to even get in the door to get a <u>chance</u> to sell.

Because of...
- Increased Technology
- Increased Competition
- More Choices
- Increased Information
- "Entrepreneurial Boom"

THE CONFIDENCE GAP

Leads to...
- Increased Resistance
- Longer Buying Cycles
- Price Competition
- Products are Commodities
- Identical Mktg. Messages

NOW - The Buyer Has The Power
(and the seller is at his mercy)

buyers. Back then, if you wanted a different telephone, which you probably did-n't even think about, you couldn't get one. It simply wasn't available. Complaining to the phone company wouldn't help. The basic attitude of business was, "You know what we have for sale. Take it or leave it. But, if you leave it, you may have to do without. Sorry."

Suppose you wanted to buy a Ford pickup truck in 1975. Where did you go? To the only dealership in town. You couldn't shop on the Internet or go to Barnes & Noble and get 15 magazines that allowed you to compare trucks and their prices. You couldn't drive to 10 different dealerships and get the lowest rock-bottom price like you can now. Back then, you only had one source of information—the sales-person at the dealership. So you went in there, got sold by the salesperson, and bought the truck because it was your only option if you wanted a Ford truck.

Back then, the *seller* had the power, and the buyer was at his mercy. Back then there weren't 5,000 people calling you every day asking you to switch your long-distance carriers, and over 300 different choices in the phone book for a mover. There weren't 31 varieties of pop tarts and 66 kinds of toothpaste.

In sales, you could call a prospect on the phone and say "Hey, I've got this great new gizmo that will lower your operating expenses by 33 percent", and he'd say, "Wow! That sounds interesting. Come on over and show me." And you'd say, "Would tomorrow at 10 or Thursday at 2 be better?" Then you'd go over there, use a bunch of tie-downs, trial closes, hard closes, and walk out with a check. Or, you could slap together a menu-board ad for the newspaper or radio, and you'd generate leads. Any aggressive company that just showed up would be successful. Not any more.

Now there are tons of choices available to the consumer. Today the buyer can go shopping without the fear of being beaten up by the salesman. Now, in today's Internet, instant-information, tons-of-choices marketplace, the *buyer* has the power. Walk into Best Buy, Circuit City, or Wal-Mart, and you might find as many as 120 different styles and brands of telephones. And that's good—for the buyer!

Buyers have the power today, and they simply want to know who offers superior value. So, if you're trying to find ways to sell more, you need to help prospective buyers decide who offers the best value. You don't do that by saying everything with the same meaningless platitudes that don't communicate worthwhile information. We call this condition NOISE—and it creates a huge "confidence gap" in the sales process that alienates the buyer

This "confidence gap" represents the customer's inability to distinguish the difference in quality of any of the products or services offered. Consumers can not tell from the advertising whether the sellers are any different from or any better than their competitors. To the buyer, all things appear to be equal. That's why they end up shopping price; they don't have the tools to decide based on value.

Using the C&R formula results in a glut of platitudes littering institutional and "menu-board" marketing and advertising. With so many competing companies all using the same drivel, you can see why I can say that everything you've ever learned, everything you've ever done, everything you've ever thought about marketing is all wrong. The convergence of these factors over the last 50 years has brought us to a situation where the problem is pervasive, yet unlikely to be fixed, except by the savviest of business people who realize an opportunity when they see one.

Show Us 10 Good Ads

Do you remember the Old Testament story of Abraham and the two wicked cities of Sodom and Gomorrah? God tells Abraham one day: "Sodom and Gomorrah are so wicked that I think I have to wipe them both out." Abraham says, "Wait a second. I know people there. You can't just wipe them out!" God says, "They're so wicked that I've got to do something." And Abraham says, "What about the righteous people? Won't you save the cities to spare the righteous people?" God says, "Abraham, you go and find some righteous people, prove that they're there, and I'll save the cities." Abraham says, "How many righteous people are we talking about here?" God says, "Look, just find 50, and I'll call off the fireworks." Abraham asks, "Perchance I only find 45?" God says, "Fine, find 45." Abraham counters with 40. God says fine. Finally, Abraham gets God down to 10, and he starts to search for those 10. He hunts around, but in the end he can only come up with one, his nephew Lot.

We know the end of the story right? The fireworks were on! God let loose his best show since the flood and destroyed the two wicked cities.

Okay, fast-forward 4,000 years and pick up your local *Yellow Pages* directory. Our *Yellow Pages* book here in Dallas, Texas, is so big that they have two books with a sum total of 2,017 pages.

Here's what I want you to do: Look through the *Yellow Pages* and find 50 good ads—just 50 ads that meet marketing's three basic functions. Can you find 50 good ones? How about 40? 10?

This problem of crummy marketing and advertising spans every business in every industry, and nobody seems to know how to fix it. Unless you know better, you can't do better, so you keep churning out marketing that only works in direct proportion to the sheer momentum of the marketplace. Hey, people must buy something from somebody, and you can get your fair share with marketing efforts that are no better or no worse than anybody else's. If everyone is terrible, you can subsist off the natural momentum. *Even a dead fish can float downstream.*

Monopolize Your Marketplace is not about subsisting off the momentum of an industry. It's about being worth more to the marketplace and, as a result, getting more response from the marketplace.

45

A More Excellent Way

Now that you know what doesn't work and why,
you are primed to learn and apply a better way.

Until this point, we've identified the problems you may be facing and explained how and why those problems exist. We've talked about the history of advertising, the era of brand builders, the proliferation of platitudes, and emergence of the confidence gap. We've identified some key principles and concepts to help you create a vision of how your marketing is supposed to work.

Now I want to teach you how to take your company's *inside reality*—the inside reality that you've worked so many years to cultivate and develop—and effectively expose that to the outside world via advertising and marketing. Then your prospects can instantly draw the conclusion, "I would have to be an absolute fool to do business with anyone else but you—regardless of price."

The key is a fail-safe method called the marketing equation. You might think you're already following the marketing equation. But I can assure you that you don't. If you did, your marketing and advertising would look like ours, it would work like ours, and it would get results like ours. You would already have a *profit faucet* in place making you all the money you could stand.

If you think that you are *already* doing what you're learning here, you will shut down the learning process, making improvement impossible. You need a clear vision of what you need to do to make what you're currently doing even better. I know that this program will work for you, and I know through experience in dealing with tens of thousands of companies that no one implements what I'm talking about here unless and until we teach them our program.

If I sound like an evangelist, it's because we have cracked the code to knowing how to make people buy stuff, and our formula has universal application for all businesses and all products and services. What you're learning will make a huge difference in your business and in your bank account. This is a life-changing message. So, open your mind as I now take you through each of the four components of the marketing equation.

Chapter 5:

The Marketing Equation

The crux of the marketing solution is to take out the mystery and ego-driven creativity and adopt a systematic approach.

The *marketing equation* is the backbone of the *Monopolize Your Marketplace* system. It's your strategic marketing plan, the foundation on which everything else is built.

The *marketing equation* has four main components:

- **Interrupt:** This is simply the process of getting qualified prospects to pay attention to your marketing. Simple to say, but often difficult to pull off, unless you hit their emotional *hot buttons*.

- **Engage:** Once you've interrupted prospects, you need to promise to provide them with information that will help them make the best decision possible. You engage prospects by facilitating their decision-making process.

- **Educate:** After you interrupt and engage your prospects based on emotional hot buttons, you next provide information that helps them understand the problem in a logical way. Then you prove why you can solve it. You do this by providing detailed, quantifiable, specific, inside-reality-revealing information. This transforms an *emotional* sell to a *logical* sell.

- **Offer:** Once you interrupt your prospects, engage them by promising a solution, and provide the educational information that makes your solution real and believable, you offer them a low-risk way to take the next step in the sales process. You do this by offering a free marketing tool such as a report, brochure, seminar, audio or video to educate them even *more*. The goal of this information is to allow prospects to feel in control of the final decision.

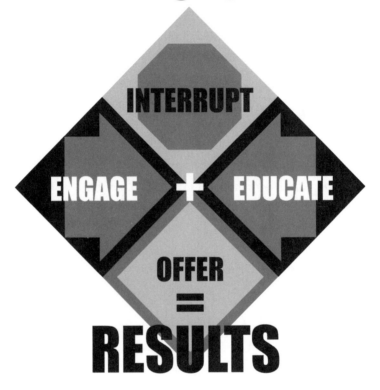

Marketing Equation

Marketing's job is to interrupt, engage, educate, and offer. This *marketing equation* is an easy way to prepare marketing that gets results—and that's what marketing is supposed to do.

Step 1: Interrupt by Hitting Hot Buttons.

The first component of the *marketing equation* is almost always done wrong, and so you may need to un-learn what you know if you want to start maximizing your return on marketing investment.

Big companies and their Madison Avenue ad agencies

like to fancy themselves as the masters of the interruption. We've all seen the Budweiser frogs and lizards and the Whasssuuuup! guys, right? Pepsi does a good job of interrupting us by showing Brittany Spears practically naked. Before that it was Michael Jackson with his hair on fire. Mr. Whipple used to tell us not to squeeze the Charmin, and an old lady used to ask, "Where's the Beef?" They even call this "interruption" advertising; it's explicitly designed to interrupt us while we're doing something else and get us to take a look at what they have to say. Those techniques can work, if you have $100 million to roll out a C&R campaign.

But there's a big difference between interrupting somebody and SELLING something.

The ad agency's C&R formula is not designed to sell anything; instead it's designed to interrupt and then *engrave* that image in your mind. If my formula is interrupt, engage, educate and offer, their standard formula is interrupt and *engrave*, interrupt and *engrave*. But given today's confidence gap, engrave isn't good enough. Engraving a message on people's minds increases the ad agency's holy grail, what they call *awareness*. They define *awareness* as the percentage of people who are aware of the product or the company. Awareness is fine, but our holy grail is sales and profits. Big difference.

We're not the first people to realize there's a problem with traditional interrupt advertising and marketing. There have been so many ineffective advertisements lately, and the creatives have taken a beating from several critics, some of them big-time industry gurus. Recent examples include:

- Donald Deutsch, a former agency big shot who sold his agency for hundreds of millions of dollars, smart-bombed the industry in a speech in front of advertising agency heads and corporate marketing executives. He told them "creative mediocrity" is the problem and suggested their clients shouldn't tolerate the garbage churned out by what he termed "creative retards." Donald's solution is to have better creative people with more business sense.
- Al Ries, author of some of the popular marketing books such as *22 Immutable Laws of Marketing* and *Marketing Warfare*, has a more recent book called *The Fall of Advertising and the Rise of PR*. The book talks about many of the same marketing problems we're discussing. His solution is to use public relations to promote products and services.
- Seth Godin has made a name for himself with books like *Permission Marketing* and *Unleashing the Idea Virus*. He proclaims that mass media advertising is dead and tells companies they have to find a way to get their

customers to willingly accept email advertisements to make an impact.

- Sergio Zyman, the former Chief Marketing Officer for Coca-Cola and author of *The End of Advertising As We Know It*, makes the case that "this crap just ain't working any more." But he only leaves a cryptic solution: "Make sure you do it better when you do it so that it makes you money."

The ad agency formula is interrupt and engrave. That formula is outdated and WRONG. The advertising big wigs know this. But they just don't know how to fix it. Deutsch and Zyman suggest using the C&R formula, just doing it better. Well, that's a good start, but how do you actually *do* it? They might know, but they certainly don't know how to teach you. Ries says, "No, the formula is not C&R, it's public relations." But that's not accurate either. PR is a valuable tool. But Al's theory says that advertising won't work since traditional interrupt advertising isn't working. That simply isn't true. Don't conclude that all advertising doesn't work just because classic interrupt advertising is not working.

Our marketing equation has always worked, still works, and will continue to work. The *marketing equation* goes like this: interrupt, engage, educate, and offer. We didn't invent this formula. It's been around forever. Some of the early pioneers in advertising understood it and used it profitably. But it's been gone for over 50 years. We're finally the ones to restore it.

Godin says sellers should abandon traditional advertising since it doesn't work and turn to email marketing. That's like concluding that because airlines experience delays and flights run late, we should seek out alternate forms of transportation to get from Los Angeles to New York, perhaps taking a train, driving, or riding a bike. I agree that email marketing can play an important role in a marketing program. But marketing is not an either/or game. Others are throwing up the white flag and saying because advertising doesn't work like it used to, it can't work, and won't work. I say that premise is false. Don't believe it for one second.

PR and email each have their place in a tactical marketing campaign. But neither will ever replace traditional interrupt marketing and advertising. Advertising will always be a part of the equation. Television, magazines, radio, and newspapers aren't going away. And if they do, they will be replaced by different media, not by a different incarnation of communication altogether.

Consider the Internet. Gurus claimed it would revolutionize marketing, lure everyone away from their televisions, and render newspapers useless. Yeah right.

Rather than seek a different way to communicate or try harder at outmoded C&R advertising, we suggest that you learn and apply correct principles of marketing—ones that have always worked and will continue to work—and use them within the existing marketing and advertising infrastructure.

Alpha, Beta and Reticular Activators

If you want to know why John Smith buys what he buys, you need to see the world through his eyes, right? If you want to know what John Smith sees, you first must understand how his brain works—and how he makes decisions. To understand that, you need to learn three major concepts that will make all the difference in the effectiveness and profitability of your marketing. The three things you need to know about John Smith's brain are: Alpha Mode, Beta Mode, and Reticular Activator.

Alpha brain waves produce a hypnotic state—automatic patterns that allow your brain to habitually perform tasks without conscious thought. Have you ever driven to work and when you got there you realized that you hadn't noticed a thing along the way? You were in alpha mode. Since driving to work is a habitual pattern, you don't have to think about it. On a conscious level, you can talk on the cell phone, listen to the radio, shave, or put on make-up while your brain drives you to work with no conscious thought. Think of alpha mode as mental sleep-walking. I doubt I am the only person who has put the cereal in the fridge and the milk back in the pantry after eating breakfast!

Here's what alpha mode means in marketing terms: People see and hear ads with their eyes and ears but don't notice them on a conscious level. If you open a newspaper, you may look at 70 percent ads and only 30 percent news articles. But here's the catch—You only see the ads on an alpha level; 9.9 times out of 10 you won't even notice them at all. All you'll see is the news. That's what you picked up the paper for in the first place.

Beta mode is the brain's state of alertness and active engagement. It's like driving to work in thunderstorm. Your hands are firmly gripped at 10 and 2 o'clock and your pupils are as big as dimes. You're sensitive to everything. You're in beta mode when you're watching a movie and the music builds to a crescendo in anticipation of something scary happening. Your heart starts thumping. You can think of beta as "alert mode."

In marketing terms, beta mode is when people consciously notice your ad or marketing piece and become open to suggestions and solutions. Something captures their attention and compels them to keep paying attention.

The key, obviously, is to get prospects out of alpha mode and into beta mode. You want to shake your prospects out of their subconscious haze that never sees your ad or marketing piece and into alert mode where they are fully aware of what you're trying to communicate. Knowing how to do this—and then doing it—is the beginning of your making a fortune in marketing.

Knowing how to move a prospect from alpha to beta mode requires you to learn the third major concept about how the human brain works—the *Reticular Activator*. This part of your brain is on the lookout 24/7—even when you're asleep—for things that fall into any of these three categories: 1) things that are familiar or connected to you in some way; 2) things that are unusual, abnormal, shocking or strange; and 3) things that are dangerous, threatening or problematic.

Whenever your brain detects things that are familiar, things that are unusual, and things that are problematic, it sends a message to the conscious side of the brain and says, "Hey, wake up! There's something you need to pay attention to here." We call those familiar, unusual or problematic things *activators*. Your brain acts like radar on a subconscious level, constantly looking for activators. It's searching for things that are familiar, unusual, or problematic—things that require a conscious response. Whenever it finds one, it snaps your brain out of alpha sleep and into beta alert.

Let me give you an example. I bought a new SUV, a Ford Excursion, a few years ago. Ford stopped making them because there just aren't many people who want to drive a 7,200 pound, 19-foot tank that gets 11 miles to the gallon. At the time, we had just had our fourth kid (I've got six now), and we needed something big enough where we could seat the kids far enough apart so they couldn't touch each other. The Excursion was the only vehicle that could do this. But I'm the kind of guy who doesn't want to have the same car as everyone else. So I called my car guy and said, "I want the Excursion, the green one."

He said, "Oh, you mean the emerald green. That thing is beautiful."

I said, "No, I don't think it's emerald green. I think it's a different shade of green."

He said, "Well, they have this sort of army green looking one, the thing is ugly and nasty looking!"

I said, "That's the one I want—the ugly green one. I don't want anyone else to have one that looks like mine."

So I get this big, nasty truck for my wife to drive. The kids loved it. They called it "Shrek," the big ugly green monster! Guess what I found out? As we started to drive this green monstrosity around, I found that there were other fools who also drive this same big ugly beast! About two months after I got it, I was sitting outside Home Depot one Saturday. My wife went in to grab a few things, and I watched the kids. I saw not one, not two, but three Shreks drive by while I was sitting there for less than 15 minutes!

How is that possible? Well, that's the reticular activator at work. Because I have one, it's now familiar. The green truck has become the activator. When my subconscious radar picks one out of the crowd, it pokes my brain, and says, "Hey buddy, check it out!" Before that, when Shrek wasn't familiar, my brain would still detect another ugly green Excursion on a subconscious level, but it wouldn't notify me. It wouldn't poke my brain. Back then, that truck wasn't an activator because it wasn't familiar, unusual or problematic. It didn't snap me out of alpha sleep and into beta alert. It was just another vehicle.

Have you ever met somebody for the first time, and two seconds later, you realize that you've forgotten their name? It can be embarrassing; I do it all the time. Usually people brush that off and say, "I'm not good with names" or "I have a bad memory." But here's the real problem. When you meet somebody and hear their name, that's an alpha mode activity. Meeting a guy named Fred Jones, Steve Johnson, or Rich Harshaw, for that matter, is not unusual—nothing pokes your brain and says "Huh?" So you never really hear the name in the first place.

Here's my point: Trying to remember Fred Jones' name two seconds after being introduced is like trying to recall the company's ads on the newspaper page that you turned two seconds ago or the billboard that you just passed at 75 miles per hour. You can't remember it because you never consciously noticed it. But what if you meet somebody whose name is Hubert Hinklemier, Elmo Fudrucker, or Cornelius Oglethorpe? Or what if you meet a person named Michael Jordan, George Bush, or Connie Chung? You'll most likely take notice and remember.

I once did an interview in Minnesota with a guy from Russia whose name was Yoseph. When we first met and he told me his name was Yoseph, I thought it was just his accent, so I asked him, "Excuse me, did you say Joseph?" He said, "No, *Yoseph* with a *Y*." I thought to myself, "I've never heard that name before." But, no big deal, I didn't really think twice about it, but I did notice it. My reticular activator heard that name, determined it was unusual, poked my conscious brain, and said, "Hey, pay attention; there's something unusual going on here."

Here's the interesting part. After the interview, I picked up *USA Today*. On the front page was an article about two Israeli youths who had been killed in a car bombing. The first one's name was Yoseph, with a Y. Now how is that possible? I'd never heard the name in my life, but within one hour, I'd heard it twice. Why? Because the first time I heard it, it was unusual or strange to me, so that name took me out of alpha sleep and snapped me into beta alert. My reticular activator detected the disconnect. Now that this name was familiar to me, my brain picked it right out of the newspaper article with ease.

The reticular activator is always looking for things that are familiar, unusual or problematic. In the case of Yoseph the first time, it was unusual. Then, the second time, it was familiar. But each time I had the same reaction, right? I noticed the name. All of this happens on a subconscious level. No thinking involved. I'm sure this has happened to you, too.

In addition to finding familiar and unusual things, the reticular activator is also always on the lookout for things that are threatening or problematic. In my house, this is what wakes mama up in the middle of the night when the baby's crying. Her reticular activator's has its radar going even when she's asleep. She hears the baby cry, and her brain says to her, "He ain't waking up, so you'll have to take care of this." The reticular activator snaps her from alpha sleep mode into beta alert mode when it detects something problematic.

What does all this have to do with marketing? Everything! Understanding the reticular activator is what's going to get us past *interrupt* and on to *engage*. And if we can engage the prospect, we've just increased our chance of selling something by 1,000 times. This is going to solve the problem that Al Ries, Seth Godin, Donald Deutsch, Sergio Zyman, and every other marketer hasn't figured out— how to get the prospect not just interrupted but also engaged. *Not just finding any activator, but finding the right activator.* Marketing's first job is to interrupt the prospect—to get them to "snap" out of alpha into beta—by noticing the things that resonate in the prospects' reticular activators. This snaps them into beta mode.

Actually, this is interrupting, without engaging. It is very easy to do; the monkeys on Madison Avenue do it all the time. They prefer to use activators based on things that are familiar and unusual because they're the easiest to pull off. Have you ever noticed how many different kinds of animals you see in advertising? That's because animals are familiar and likable. The idea is that those animals will interrupt you by poking your conscious brain when your reticular activator detects them. Budweiser has frogs and lizards, Gateway computer has cows, Coca-Cola has polar bears, Energizer has a bunny, Merrill Lynch has a bull, Aflac has a duck, and Microsoft has a butterfly. All of these animals have *interrupt value* based on their familiarity.

That's the main reason why big advertisers use celebrities. Yes, celebrities also lend credibility, but that's not the main reason they are used. People know that the Buick Rendezvous isn't any better because Tiger Woods drives one in the commercial. Everybody also knows that Tiger Woods doesn't really drive a low-end SUV in real life. He probably drives a Lamborghini, Ferrari, or a Hummer. But Buick doesn't care because they know that as soon as your reticular activator detects Tiger's presence, it'll poke you in the brain and say, "Hey, wake up! Tiger's on the tube!" Then you see the Rendezvous. Now Buick is in a position to sell—if they can now move you from being interrupted to becoming engaged (which, incidentally, they don't).

What about activators based on unusual things? That's what creativity is all about. Creativity's main purpose in advertising is to dream up something so weird, strange, shocking, or unusual that it will snap you out of alpha mode and into beta mode, otherwise known as interrupt. If a guy named Yoseph instead of Joseph will do it, just think what Whasssup and dancing babies and an SUV driving up the side of a cliff will do. Then they take something familiar like a frog and make it do something unusual like talk. Now they're doing a reticular activator double whammy: giving your brain something that's familiar and unusual at the same time. It's the creative director's panacea. And what about sex? You've probably heard that sex sells. Right? Actually, it's not true. Sex interrupts. If something sexy is put in an advertisement where you weren't expecting it, then *boom*, you're interrupted, but not necessarily engaged.

Finding the Prospect's Hot Buttons

Once the brain is activated, broken out of alpha sleep into beta alert mode, it wants to be engaged. So it immediately searches for additional, clarifying information. The person wants to know, "What's this all about? How does this affect me? Do I need to do anything about this?" So, the brain goes on a fact-finding mission. The brain wants to know, "How relevant and important is this to me? Should I allocate any bandwidth to this?" So it searches for additional facts. If it finds them, it will become engaged; if not, it will quickly revert to alpha mode.

We call these important and relevant issues *hot buttons*.

How do hot buttons work? If you're a golf fan and your reticular activator detects that Tiger Woods is on the television, it notices that on a sub-conscious level because Tiger Woods is familiar. He's an activator. Then your brain immediately asks, "Why is Tiger Woods driving that car? Is there anything there that's relevant or important to me?" Your brain is looking for a hot button. But what typically happens is your brain determines that the Buick Rendezvous is not relevant or important to you. It doesn't solve any of your problems. It's *not* a hot button, so your brain immediately reverts back into alpha mode.

On the other hand, your brain becomes engaged if it recognizes a problematic situation that's familiar. This triggers a hot button and your brain becomes automatically engaged if additional, clarifying information is present. An *activator* is something that snaps a person from alpha to beta mode, and it's based on something that's familiar, unusual or problematic. But an activator can only also be classified as *a hot button* if—and only if—it's based on something that's important or relevant to the prospect. Madison Avenue likes to use activators based on things that are familiar and unusual. My advice is to focus on things that are problematic to your target market and use those as your activators. Why? Because when you hit the hot button (the problem), your brain is automatically open to a solution.

For example, suppose you own a chain of camera stores and you're promoting digital cameras in your newspaper advertising. What would you say in the ad? Well, you could find a picture of a monkey holding a camera. There would be some interrupt value there. The animal would be the activator. Or you could hire a celebrity to hold a camera. Or a scantily clad woman. All these techniques might work to varying degrees, but they don't address the main issue when it comes to digital cameras. If you use an activator that's not based on a problem, you'll create a "false beta," and the prospect won't become engaged.

What are the main problems facing prospective buyers of digital cameras? The vast majority of them know practically zero about megapixels, zoom lenses, flash memory, and all that technical mumbo jumbo. Always cater your marketing to the "most people" category and not the "exclusive few" who are already "in the know."

Typically you'll see menu-board advertising for products like digital cameras. They'll show you a bunch of pictures of different cameras, and each picture will have a bullet list of all the features of that model—how many megapixels, what kind of lens, and all that stuff—along with the price. The pictures of the cameras will work as an activator for people with an interest in them, but then, when the brains automatically scans for more information, it finds stuff that might as well be written in a foreign language.

The hot button here is uncertainty—most people haven't the foggiest clue about what to buy. Your advertising has to address this issue because it's important and relevant. How about this headline: "If you're thinking about buying a digital camera, but haven't got the foggiest clue what to look for or how to com-

SOLUTION: THE MARKETING EQUATION

Human nature demands that buyers always want to make the best decision possible. Marketing and advertising should get the attention of the target market, facilitate their decision making process, and lower the risk of taking the next step in the selling process. (see page 2!)

The process for accomplishing this is exactly the same every single time for every kind of business. Just like 2 + 2 always equals 4, the marketing equation always produces the right answer.

Interrupt + Engage + Educate + Offer = RESULTS

Interrupt:

Get qualified prospects to pay attention to your marketing. Accomplished by identifying and hitting your prospects' hot buttons.

Engage:

Give prospects the promise that information is forthcoming that will facilitate their decision making process.

Educate:

Identify the important and relevant issues prospects need to be aware of, then demonstrate how you stack up against those issues. Build a case for your business.

Offer:

Give prospects a low-risk way to take the next step in the buying process...put more information in their hands and allow them to feel in total control of the decision.

RESULT:

The Right Answer Every Single Time.

---

pare, then call for our free camera buyer's guide. Learn everything you need to know about megapixals, zoom lenses and flash memory." Add a subheadline that says, "Learn the seven most important features of any camera to make sure you only pay for what you need." With an activator based on the hot button of uncertainty and unfamiliarity, that headline reaps an order-of-magnitude increase over the usual menu-board-style ad. If you've even thought about buying a digital camera, don't you wish you could get that buyer's guide?

Your best bet to successfully interrupt and engage your target market is to identify your prospects' problems, frustrations, and annoyances and then address them in your marketing. Find out where their pain is, identify that pain, and describe situations and scenarios that exemplify that pain. Put this information in your headlines and subheads, then let the prospects' reticular activator take over from there.

The results are inevitable. The things causing their pain, for all practical purposes, are their hot buttons. Tap into problems they already have—there is no need to manufacture problems. Just point out those problems so their reticular activators notice and bring them up on their active radar screens. When you key in on problems, you're hitting the problem button at the same time you're hitting their familiar button. This is a reticular activator double-whammy because everyone's familiar with their own problems.

Now, this program will only work for you if you select activators that are *relevant* hot buttons. If it's not relevant, the activator either won't work in the first place, or the prospect will quickly revert back into alpha mode. *This is a false beta.*

Here's an example of a false beta. You're at the airport in the baggage claim area. You're minding your own business waiting for your luggage to come off onto the conveyor. There are 300 people milling about. With all those people and the sound of the conveyor and suitcases, it's loud. Then, suddenly, from behind you, you hear an unfamiliar voice call out your name above the noise of the crowd. Let's say your name is Bob. "Hey, Bob!" What's your response? Do you turn around and look? Of course you do. You couldn't *not* respond even if you wanted to. The reason why is obvious. Your name is an activator. It's just about the most familiar thing to you. As soon as you hear your name, it instantly pulls you out of alpha and puts you into beta mode. Then your brain starts searching for additional, clarifying information. You wonder: Who is it? Can you identify the voice? What do they want? How urgent did their voice sound?

What happens if you turn around and discover that they are actually calling out to someone else with your same name? You disregard the interruption.

A false beta occurs when you are interrupted, but you don't become engaged because the activator is not based on something that's important to you. It's not a hot button. This is what happens in most marketing and advertising. The marketing interrupts, but it doesn't engage. It captures your attention and interrupts you, but you quickly revert to alpha mode when you find out that it's not based on anything that's important to you. There's nothing relevant to you, nothing that solves some problem you have. Major advertisers keep changing ad campaigns because over time the activators lose their ability to snap you from alpha to beta mode. After a while, Tiger

Woods enters your reticular activator, pokes your brain, and your brain says, "Oh, that's the car commercial again. Don't waste my time." And nothing happens.

But you get action when you use hot button-based activators. Legendary advertising great Rosser Reeves said: "Unless a product becomes outmoded, a great campaign will not wear itself out." A great campaign has to be based on the *marketing equation* and have the right hot buttons for that to happen.

We've been conditioned to believe that as long as we interrupt the prospect, that's good enough. The job is done. But we know if you only interrupt, that's only one-fourth of the *marketing equation*. And here's the bad news: The *marketing equation* is just about an all-or-nothing game. If you get one-fourth of the *marketing equation* right and three-quarters of it wrong or incomplete, you'll still lose! You've got to get all four components—interrupt, engage, educate and offer—to reap the maximum results.

Headline Hot Buttons

When it comes to writing the marketing, we typically like to portray the hot buttons in headlines. The headline is your first opportunity to interrupt the prospect. You've got about one-half of a split second to interrupt the prospect, so you had better make sure the headline has activators in it—activators based on things that are important and relevant—the hot buttons. The headlines must have words and phrases that describe familiar problems that the prospect is feeling, so their reticular activators latch on to them and snap them into beta mode.

In print advertising—magazines, newspapers, and *Yellow Pages* —the form of the headline is obvious. In radio and television, it's the first sentence spoken. In brochures and marketing collateral, it's the first thing they see.

What would you be more likely to read—a brochure from a mutual fund company entitled "Landmark Mutual Funds" or one from the same company that said, "Mutual Fund Investment Strategies: Which Ones Actually Work and Which Ones Are Guaranteed to Drain Your Savings, Jeopardize Your Retirement and Squash Your Quest for Financial Independence?" Does "Landmark Mutual Funds" contain any hot buttons? Does it get you from alpha to beta? No! It leaves your eyes glazed over.

What about a slogan of some sort on the brochure instead? How about "Building your Future on Solid Ground"? You should know by now that that's a major platitude, stated as if it were original and significant. Who else can say that? Does it pass the *cross out, write in test*? No, even though it's the language you'll find in every brochure today. If your brochure has a similar title, you need to change it. What about the other title for a brochure, the one about draining, jeopardizing and squashing? Any hot buttons there? Does it identify any problems or frustrations and imply a solution? You bet it does.

Now, you may say that you would never use such language in your marketing, that it's not very professional. Hey, you can do whatever you want with your money and your brochures. But you'll be the most professional broke guy with his pride intact and his bank account emptied.

The tone and words used in the headline mirror the intensity of the emotional level of the prospect. For instance, when we're talking about investing, that's an important topic to the prospects. So I use words like *drain*, *jeopardize* and *squash* to mirror the intensity of the feelings the prospect has about investing.

Contrast that emotional headline to one that uses words that are less emotionally intense. Compare the original headline: "Mutual Fund Investment Strategies: Which Ones Actually Work And Which Ones Are Guaranteed To Drain Your Savings, Jeopardize Your Retirement And Squash Your Quest For Financial Independence" with "Mutual Fund Investment Strategies: Which Ones Actually Work And Which Ones Are Guaranteed To Reduce Your Savings, Threaten Your Retirement And Postpone Your Quest For Financial Independence."

Changing the words "drain, jeopardize and squash" to "reduce, threaten and postpone" definitely weakens the headline. But it's still not that bad.

Now, how about this headline:

"Mutual Fund Investment Strategies: Which Ones Work and Which Ones Will

Reduce Your Savings, Delay Your Retirement, and Hurt Your Financial Goals"?

What do you think? Notice, I eliminated the word "actually" from the headline, "Which ones actually work?" The word "actually" is important because it implies that many of them don't work without saying it directly. Eliminating the word "actually" reduces the emotional intensity of the headline.

Next, I removed the word "guaranteed" from the phrase "which ones are guaranteed to" and just said "which ones will." Again, I've reduced the emotional value; I haven't fully tapped a hot button inside them that says, "There are a lot of crummy investments out there." I also changed the phrases which started out as "drain, jeopardize and squash" to "reduce, threaten and postpone." Now, I've neutered them clear down to "reduce, delay and hurt." See the difference?

Choosing the proper word is one reason why it's so difficult to put this together and execute it yourself, and why utilizing an experienced professional consultant is probably the best way to go for most companies. Think about it: The meaning of the two headlines is exactly the same, but the power, strength and impact is totally different. It's easy to see and recognize the difference, but writing powerful headlines is not so easy.

The headline must be loaded with problem-oriented hot buttons that trigger the proper emotional response. You must communicate those hot buttons in a tone and with words that elicit the proper emotional intensity from the prospect. When that happens, prospects will immediately search for clarifying information and, if that clarifying information is present, they'll become engaged.

Here are more examples of taking the prospects' hot buttons and putting them into headlines.

3 CRITICAL Characteristics To Demand From Your Attorney

Does Yours Stack Up?

1. Expertise. The key here is not just experience, but ex-experience in **cases like yours**. There are over 60 different broad disciplines, each of which has over 100 sub-categories. We will always find out the details of your case, and assign the attorney with the right ex-perience for **your** case. If our firm doesn't have the expertise, we won't take the case, period.

2. Case Load. Too many irons in the fire is a big problem with many firms and their attorneys. Nationally, the number of cases assigned per attorney could be as many as 40 or 50. That leads to slow response time and in-attention to detail. Make sure your attorney has no more than 10 files at any given time.

3. Fee Policies. Your attorney should help you solve your problems, not be the source of them! Unfortunately, some firms "conceal" certain changes until after it's too late to undo the damage. Request our free report for more info.

Find Out How We Stack Up...Call For Our FREE Report:

Borrowitz & Grubits, LLP
Counselors at Law

2525 Apple Avenue, Franktown, New York
1400 Main Street, Citytown, New York
1000 Franklin Avenue Middletown
402-952-5383
www.mymbook.com

How To Chose The Right Lawyer for Your Case
402-952-5383

Typical menu-style ad.   *A marketing equation ad.*

You can see the advertisement for the camera store that we just discussed. The headline reads, "Thinking About Buying A Digital Camera But Don't Have The Foggiest Clue What You Need.... Or Even What's Available?"

Did you catch how the headline hits the hot button of "uncertainty" and speaks the prospect's language. It hits the right level of emotional intensity when it uses the phrase "haven't got the foggiest clue." You tell me, how would you feel if you were in the market for a digital camera but didn't know the first thing about them? Would you say that you were "overwhelmed by choices?" Maybe. How about "confused?" Possibly. However, saying "I haven't got the foggiest clue" takes the emotional intensity to another level. It makes the headline come alive; it sucks in the reader an even deeper level. And it's all based on the hot button of "uncertainty."

Let's evaluate another ad that doesn't effectively use a headline based on hot buttons.

This ad is for a telephone company that is selling high-speed internet access. The ad has a close-up photo of a frisky dog holding a computer mouse in its mouth. It has a headline that says, "One Dot-Com Minute." The copy says, "Fess Up. Your office needs

beefier internet access. So call Berge. We bundle router, line, service in one package, at frisky rates. We include the router, saving you hundreds. And we back it with 7-day-a-week tech support. Could it be any easier? Call Berge. We'll come running."

Remember this is for a telephone company that is trying to sell high-speed internet service.

What is the activator in this ad? Is it the headline, "One Dot Com Minute?" No, it's the dog. Remember, an activator is what snaps you out of alpha sleep into beta alert mode. If you're interested in dogs, your reticular activator will signal your brain that there's something on the page that's familiar, unusual, or problematic. Most people like dogs, so their brain says, "Hey, look at the cute doggie there on that page." If you like dogs, there's a good chance you will see this picture, and it will pull you out of alpha mode and into beta mode. This happens in a split second, without your being aware. The activator forces you to look at that ad. Then, your brain starts searching for additional, clarifying information. "What's with the dog?" So you'll read the copy to figure out what's going on, and you'll realize that it's an ad for internet access. Then your brain will begin to short circuit. It will struggle to make the connection of why there's a dog associated with internet service. Since these two things don't normally go together, it's a tough connection to make. It's a false beta.

Here are a couple of distinctions. First, people who don't like dogs won't look at this picture no matter what. Their reticular activators won't flip the switch. To them, the dog's not familiar, unusual or problematic, so it's not an activator. Everyone who needs internet access but is not interested in dogs will never be pulled out of alpha into beta mode to see the ad and even have a chance to sell. Why would you put a dog as an activator for an internet service since the only people you are going to reach are people that like dogs? Is it possible that people who don't like dogs need internet service? I think it probably is.

Certainly some people who like dogs will also need internet service, so Berge will have a chance to sell to that subset of people. But why wouldn't you just make the activator based on a hot button—something that's important and relevant to all users, not just dog lovers?

Here's a hot button for internet users: solving all the problems that they may have with their current internet service, or lack of service or tech support.

I know one thing for sure: the dog in this ad ain't the prospects' hot button! Yes, *the dog is an activator, but it's not a hot button.*

I've taken the liberty to write a new ad based on the hot buttons we culled out of the text. Notice how the hot buttons now take the center stage and how the ad follows the formula of interrupt, engage, educate and offer.

Can you tell the difference between an activator and a hot button? *An activator is anything that interrupts—anything at all. A hot button, on the other hand, is an activator that's based on something that's important and relevant to the prospect.* If you interrupt the prospect with something that's not important, you might gain awareness. But awareness is tough to pull off without $100 million, and awareness isn't equal to cash. Far from it. Also realize that you'll get the same awareness you'd get by using the *marketing equation*. But you get one more thing: You get sales, too!

Marketing is an equation. Just like arithmetic demands that 4 X 3 = 12, the *marketing equation* demands *interrupt, engage, educate, offer.* An ad agency says no, the formula is creativity and repetition; they say, "Let's put a dog in the ad and use ridiculous puns in the copy." They think that advertising is an art, not a science. But they are wrong. Hiring an ad agency or anyone that doesn't know the *marketing equation* is like hiring someone who doesn't know math to take a calculus test for you.

Step 2: Engage the Prospect.

Once the activator snaps the prospect out of alpha sleep into beta alert, the brain automatically searches for additional, clarifying information. If the activator is based on hot buttons, the prospect will be mentally prepared to become engaged. At this point, crossing that gap from "ready" to be engaged to "actually engaged" is simple. All you have to do is use a headline or subhead that *promises the readers they will get the information they need to make the best buying decision possible if they keep reading the ad.* Not sales information. Not "here's how great we are" information. They need information that facilitates a decision. So here's the evaluation to determine if a headline has engaged a reader: "Does the headline or subheadline promise to educate the prospect?" That's a simple question, and one that should yield a clear answer.

Here's how this works:

Let's look at the digital camera ad again. The main headline reads, "Thinking About Buying a Digital Camera But Don't Have the Foggiest Clue What You Need ... Or Even What's Available?"

That headline does a good job of interrupting based on the "uncertainty" hot button. But now the brain is awakened into beta alert mode, it will automatically search for clarifying information. That's what the subhead does: "Five Things You Need To Know Before Buying A Digital Camera." It promises readers they will find information that will further facilitate their decision making if they keep reading. It promises to educate the reader. It passes the ENGAGE evaluation because it promises to educate the reader.

I'll give you some more examples of interrupt and engage throughout the book. I'll also share a few case studies that will tie everything together. I'll point out how each component of the *marketing equation* works and how each component works in conjunction with each other.

Step 3: Educate the Prospect.

Now that you have successfully interrupted and engaged your prospect, your job as marketer is to deliver relevant information in a way that's easy to scan and digest quickly—what the prospect needs to know to determine how to buy what you sell. You've got to give your prospects enough quantified, specific, delineated information that they feel they understand the important and relevant issues. This understanding makes them feel in control of the decision and confident that they are making the best choice. The more you educate prospects on what they need to know, what to look for, and what to look out for, the more you'll sell. Education is how you make your outside perception match your inside reality. That's why it's so important.

The information you give to educate prospects is called "control information" because it puts them in control of the decision.

Components 3 and 4 of the *marketing equation* are closely tied, just like components 1 and 2, because, by definition, the offer is supposed to give the prospect a low-risk way to become further educated so he can take the next step in the sales process.

In a small ad or a 60-second radio spot, it's difficult to tell people everything they need to know and educate them about how to make the best decision.

Here's a blueprint of what to do. Have the headline and subheadline interrupt and engage based on relevant hot buttons. Then, give a basic overview of the elements the prospect needs to know about buying what you sell. Finally, make an offer for a marketing tool—a report, video, website, or audio program—that will promise to further educate. The offer is positioned as *risk free*. It's a FREE way for prospects to gain information without sensing that they'll be bothered by a salesperson. If you do this properly, your ads will inevitably pull 10 times more than they do now.

You need to prepare your case as thoroughly as an attorney would prepare a case for court. In court, the attorney's case can mean the difference between freedom or incarceration, between life and death. In your business, your case for your product means the difference between you getting rich and you going broke. Think about your marketing and advertising strategy this way:

Your product or service is on trial. The consumer is the jury. You are the attorney. You must educate the jury on all the relevant issues and prove to them that you offer the best value available. It's a life-or-death sentence. Your job is to define the relevant issues, prepare a convincing argument and produce all the evidence, presenting it in a way that the jury believes you. Remember, your prospects are the jury!

To properly educate your prospects, you need to build a case that gives prospects and customers confidence that they would be a fool to business with anyone else but you—regardless of price. You accomplish this by educating your prospects about what they need know about buying what you sell. You do this by teaching them how to determine value. Once they know the value benchmarks, provide specific, quantifiable evidence that your company, product or service will give them that value.

Most businesses build no case at all. Ironically, most attorneys don't even know how to build a case for their own business. Look at this ad for a law firm. It leads with a non-interrupting, non-engaging, platitude-plagued headline: "When It Comes To The Law,

Close Is Not Good Enough." If that weren't bad enough, check out the platitude-filled control information they offer where they should be educating: "With Borrowitz & Grubitz, you can rest assured we get the details right. Whether it's personal injury litigation, real estate, or business law, our team of attorneys work hard to get the job done right...the first time. Our smart, savvy lawyers love a good legal challenge and thrive on helping our clients seek justice. When you're in need of legal council, call the law firm of Borrowitz & Grubitz." The platitude cup runneth over, don't you think!

Does the ad define the important and relevant issues when it comes to choosing an attorney? Does it build a case? Does it make you believe that they do anything different or better than anyone else? Does it make you think that they offer a superior value? Does it give you any clue as to their inside reality? Does it provide evidence? Does it give the prospect control over the decision of what attorney to chose?

For an example of how to properly educate the prospect, look at the revised ad for the law firm Borrowitz & Grubitz.

3 CRITICAL Characteristics To Demand From Your Attorney
Does Yours Stack Up?

1. **Expertise.** The key here is not just experience, but ex-perience in **cases like yours**. There are over 60 different broad disci-plines, each of which has over 100 sub-categories. We will always find out the details of your case, and assign the attor-ney with the right ex-perience for **your** case. If our firm doesn't have the expertise, we won't take the case, period.

2. **Case Load.** Too many irons in the fire is a big problem with many firms and their attorneys. Nationally, the number of cases assigned per attorney could be as many as 40 or 50. That leads to slow response time and in-attention to detail. Make sure your attorney has no more than 10 files at any given time.

3. **Fee Policies.** Your attorney should help you solve your problems, not be the source of them! Unfortunately, some firms "conceal" certain changes until after it's too late to undo the damage. Request our free report for more info.

Borrowitz & Grubits, LLP
Counselors at Law

2525 Apple Avenue, Franktown, New York
1400 Main Street, Citytown, New York
1000 Franklin Avenue Middletown
402-952-5383
www.mymbook.com

How To Chose The Right Lawyer for Your Case
402-952-5383

You would think an attorney would know how to build a case! But when it comes to marketing and advertising, every company needs to learn this lesson: It's impossible to build a case and expose your inside reality using platitudes!

Remember the OJ Simpson trial? OJ's team of attorneys sold a jury of 12 people a story that got him off the hook despite overwhelming evidence against him. Think what would have happened if OJ's attorneys got up on the stand and spewed a bunch of platitudes, "Come on. He couldn't have done that! He's OJ! The Juice! He runs through airports! He's the 2,000-yard Buffalo Bill! He's a movie star! He wasn't even there that night. He was out somewhere else. He just couldn't have done it." He would have been nailed in two minutes.

As ridiculous as that sounds, that's about as good a case as most businesses prepare to defend and sell their products. They just offer a non-compelling, sur-face-level laundry list of platitudes and hope that someone will give them money. As if just being in business entitles them to our money! Good luck!

What did OJ's attorneys do? They got all kinds of forensic reports, alibis, expert witnesses—everything they could to prove that he couldn't possibly have done it. They defined the important and relevant issues and brought in experts to teach the jury what they needed to know about them. They had a guy who was a glove expert show why the glove couldn't possibly have been OJ's because it was too small! They had blood splatter experts who testified that there's no way that the blood would have splattered the way it did if OJ had done it. After hearing their testimony, the jury felt they knew enough about gloves and blood splatters to let OJ go free. In a trial, that's what matters—if you win or lose.

Here's what you need to do to redesign your strategic marketing plan. Determine the important and relevant issues; these are the points you will build your case around. When the attorney begins the trial, he or she addresses the jury and says: "Ladies and gentlemen of the jury, in this trial, I will prove to you that so-and-so committed such-and-such crime. I will prove to you beyond a reasonable doubt that this occurred, and I will do it based on the following evidence: 1, 2, 3, and 4. I will introduce three witnesses who all concur that it happened in this fashion. I will present two expert witnesses who will testify that these things happened this way. When you have seen this evidence, you will have no option but to conclude that he is indeed guilty." In effect, the attorney educates the jury to know what the important and relevant issues are and then gathers and presents the supporting evidence.

Ultimately, if you present your case in a compelling and convincing way, you'll build confidence with your prospects and bridge the confidence gap. They'll feel like they're in control of the decision. You'll have business coming to you because you will effectively separate yourself from your competition. Just like the jury draws the conclusion of guilt or innocence, so will your prospects. They'll feel like they would be fools to do business with anyone else but you, regardless of price.

Before: Dog as the Activator

71

After: Price as the hot button

How TO Buy SBC's $1,000 A Month 1.544M T1 For Only $399 A Month.

Now You Can Benefit From New Laws That Have Forced SBC To Make Their "Pipes" Available To Other Carriers For A Fraction Of The Cost...

It's True: SBC Has No Choice But To Sell Their Lines For Less Than They Can Charge You. You know that the Baby Bells have enjoyed monopolies on phone service, but did you know that in 1996, a law was passed forcing the Baby Bells to make their lines available to other carries in an effort to promote competition?

What To Look For...
And What To Look OUT For!
Comparing T1's is often like comparing apples to oranges. To make sense of a company's offering, you've got to understand what the important and relevant issues are, including:

1. What is the length of the contract? Most companies charge more money for shorter contracts. We charge on low flat rate, period.

2. Is the router included or not? If not, then the telco manages it for you, which will cost your more. We include the router so your cost is LOWER.

3. How much is the "Loop" charge? This is how much it costs to get the line from the ISP box to your office. With some companies, your Loop Charge can be as much as 25% of the monthly fee.

4. Is monitoring included? Most companies charge more money to monitor your ISP to make sure it's up all the time. We include monitoring even at $399 a month.

How Much SHOULD You Pay For A Good T1?
The bottom line is that if you know how to compare apples to apples, you can get the best value possible. T1's don't have to be expensive, especially if you are educated when you go to purchase one.

Call For Your FREE "T1 Cost Comparison Guide"

Name: _____
Company: _____
Address: _____
City, State, Zip: _____
Phone: _____ Fax: _____
Please Fax This To (402) 952-5383 or Call (402) 952-5383

We've rewritten the Berge ad to show you what to do. Instead of featuring the ridiculous dog, we are going to focus on a major hot button—price.

Normally we don't use price as a major hot button, but in this case we will for a very specific reason. Usually prices are going to be relatively constant across the board within any industry. There may be some companies that have a lower cost of goods sold because they buy larger quantities or because they have created certain efficiencies, which allows them to turn around and sell for less. But even in those cases, my advice would be to add more value and additional services and charge full price and just make more money on each transaction.

But this case is unique because deregulation in the telecommunications industry has forced SBC, which used to be a monopoly, to now make its lines available to competitors like Berge at reduced prices. The new rules allow Berge to sell the exact same product for substantially less money. So, from a marketing standpoint, why not capitalize on that situation and use the *marketing equation* to sell the service?

Note that in the revised ad we've used a headline loaded with hot buttons: "How To Buy SBC's $1,000 A Month 1.544M T1 For Only $399 A Month."

Since the brain will demand clarifying information to answer the question of "How is that possible?," we use a subheadline that reads, "Now You Can Benefit From New Laws that Have Forced SBC to Make Their Pipes Available to Other Carriers for a Fraction of the Cost."

We've interrupted and engaged. Now it's time to educate. It's time to build a case and prove that what we are saying is true. Our case must cause prospects to conclude they'd be fools not to buy from us.

Our special report provides a detailed description of how the regulations have changed and what that means to SBC, Berge and the end-users. Then we go into a detailed comparative analysis of what the components of a T1 are, how much they should cost, and what to look out for. We educate the reader so he knows what's important when buying a T1. We show him what other competitors are offering, and what is good and bad about those offers. We show different options that can change the price. We do this in a compelling way that leads readers to conclude that they might get a raw deal if they buy from SBC.

Step 4: Offer Prospects Additional Information.

Every marketing piece should contain a low-risk offer to encourage prospects to take the next step. Generally, the offer should be to receive additional information so you can further educate the prospect and build your case.

A powerful offer can sometimes increase your response rate by 100 times—all by itself!

The right offer allows you to capture a large percentage of all future buyers in addition to the now buyers. You must realize there is an educational process that the prospect goes through from the moment he begins thinking about buying your product or service to the point when he actually puts down his hard-earned cash. We call this the "Educational Spectrum."

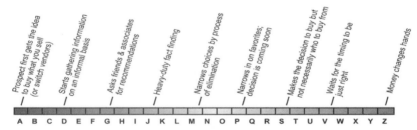

Think of the *educational spectrum* like a straight horizontal line stretching from left to right. At the far left hand side of the line is "Point A." This represents the moment when the prospect first considers the idea of either buying what you sell, or, if they already buy what you sell from another vendor, it represents when they first consider switching vendors. Not the point where they actually switch or buy, but the point where they start *thinking* of switching or buying. At the far right-hand side of the spectrum is "Point Z" where money actually changes hands.

Monopolize Your Marketplace

Many things have to happen between points A and Z. At about Point D the prospect's reticular activator kicks in and he starts to notice ads for the product or maybe starts to browse that product in the store. At about Point F the prospect begins to gather information on a few competitors, either by searching the Web, calling around or visiting stores.

Points L M N O P denote hard-core research and comparison. The prospect might also start soliciting the opinions of friends, family members or co-workers for recommendations. The prospect makes the decision to buy somewhere around Point S. He's at the point where he says, "Okay, I'm going to do it. I'm going to buy one of these." Or, "I'm going to switch who I buy from. I'm not just thinking about it anymore. I'm done talking and I'm ready to start buying." The key here is that the prospect hasn't necessarily decided WHO to buy from and may not be in a position to buy just yet. Around Point V is where the prospect decides to buy a specific brand or do business with a specific company. However, the prospect might not take action if circumstances aren't just right yet. I made a decision to buy a 65-inch Pioneer Elite Series Big Screen High Definition Television from Ultimate Electronics 10 months before I actually bought it. Why? Because I was building a house and wouldn't need the TV until the house was completed. Finally, at point Z all decisions are made and money changes hands.

At any given time there could be hundreds or thousands of prospects at various positions along the *educational spectrum* of buying what you sell. And no sale is complete until they reach point Z and give you money, even if they decided to buy from you somewhere along the way.

Understanding the *educational spectrum* is vital if you hope to outsell your competitors. The vast majority of marketing and advertising efforts are only geared toward the prospects who are hanging out at the far right-hand side of the *educational spectrum*, down past R and S. They have made the decision to buy and are ripe for marketing that can sway them to buy from a given competitor.

But, at any given moment, the number of prospects on the right hand side of the spectrum—*the ones ready to buy right now*—represent no more than 5 percent of all those who are ultimately going to buy what you sell. Up to 99 percent of your prospects are in the "thinking-about-it" or "gathering-information" mode! Most marketers don't give these potential customers the information they need to make an informed buying decision.

This is where the fourth component of the *marketing equation* becomes absolutely huge: Your offer gives you the opportunity to provide additional educational information—control information—to those prospects who are in an information-gathering mode. There's an additional benefit: you're also able to capture valuable information about these people so you can pro-actively market to them on an on-going basis. This allows you to control your target market.

The same rule applies to the ads for home builders. Currently, ads for new homes are full of smiling people, floor plans, front facades, maps to the neighborhoods and price lists. But ads that work need to interrupt, engage and educate the prospect about what they need to know when buying a new home. But here's what they also need: A compelling offer to get more information on a low-risk basis.

Who's looking at those ads in the paper? Prospects at *all points* on the *educational spectrum*—that's who. You've got one group of buyers who will be making a buying decision in the next month. We call them the "now" buyers. They're the ones most likely to respond to any ad—good or bad—because their urgency factor is high. They are willing to drive 45 minutes and subject themselves to the agony of enduring the starving salesperson because they need to buy right away.

Do you think there's anyone else looking at those ads? What about someone who's time horizon might be a little longer? Do you think there are people who are just trying to get a feel for the market, see what's out there, and determine what the price ranges are? Are there any people who may not decide to buy a new home for a year? What about people who aren't ready to

Before: Home-hum!

2003 Best Architectural Design ~ The Cambridge

Picturesque Homes

One and two-story, low maintenance
Townhomes in Winchester from the $120s

Homes available for
immediate move-in!

1 Kingsbrook at Ridgemont
402-952-5383
Opening New Phase
2-story
call for appointment

2 Windom Creek
402-952-5383
2-story
call for appointment

3 Parkland Estates
402-952-5383
2-story
402-952-5383
1-story
Rancho Villa Grand Opening
call for appointment

www.mymbook.com

Brokers welcome

After: Home-run!

The Only New Home Community In Frisco, Plano Or McKinney With Homes From The $180's To $400's That Was Designed Specifically For Professional People With Children.

• 6 Playgrounds
• 5 Swimming Pools
• 4 Community Centers

• 3 Basketball Courts
• 2 Sets Of Hiking Trails

All Surrounding A Brand
New Frisco ISD Elementary School.

Make The Trails of Eastland
The Most Kid Friendly
Community In The
Entire DFW Area.

Trails of Eastland

Mayfield Road

Hwy 121

Trails

**Call To Get A Copy
Of Our FREE Report -**

*Ranking Kid Friendly Communities In
DFW-How They Stack Up & What To Look For*

402-952-5383

move but are having a dream session? How do you capture these people and get them into your sales systems? The answer is *the offer*.

The ad on the following page is for a community with several builders, not just a single builder. So what's the offer in this ad? It's got the obligatory map that shows you where to find the neighborhood and the phone numbers for the individual builders.

What's the next step that you could take in the buying process that's low risk? There isn't one. This ad misses it huge potential. Does it interrupt? No. Does it engage? No. Does it educate? No. Nor does this ad have an offer or any way to get good information. If you're sitting on the *educational spectrum*, anywhere from point A to point L M N O P, your brain will barely get into beta mode, if at all, and it will forget about this ad before it ever sees it consciously. This ad was just a waste of money.

We've revised this ad. Notice that the headline and the subheadline serve to interrupt and engage. The headline keys a major hot button—a kid-friendly community.

"The Only New Home Community In Frisco/Plano/McKinney With Homes From The $180's To $400's That Was Designed Specifically For Professional People With Small Children."

Then, to satisfy the readers' need for clarifying information, we use the sub-headline: "6 Playgrounds, 5 Swimming Pools, 4 Community Centers, 3 Basket-ball Courts, 2 Hiking Trails ... All Surrounding One Brand-New Frisco ISD Elementary School ... Make *The Trails of Eastland* The Most Kid-Friendly Community In The Entire Dallas-Fort Worth Area."

Does that subheadline clarify and give more information? Does it promise to further educate readers if they continue to read? If you were on the *educational spectrum* and thinking about moving into that vicinity, and you had small children, do you think you'd be dialed in to their message? Answer: You couldn't NOT be engaged, even if you tried.

We educated our prospects by supplying more detailed information about the amenities listed in the subheadline and by providing pictures as visual evidence of the quality of the facilities.

What about the offer? Remember, the vast majority of the people who see this ad will be somewhere on the left-hand side of the *educational spectrum*. They'll range from a casual, curious mode to a serious information-gathering mode. Many prospects, favorably impressed with what we've said so far, would be inclined to visit—but not until they get more serious about buying a home. That's why we have the offer. Here, the reader can receive a free report called "Ranking Kid-Friendly Communities—How They Stack Up and What to Look For."

Does this ad hit your reticular activator? Does the headline interrupt and engage? Do you become educated through the information we provide? Might you request that free report? I'm asking you to project yourself into your prospect's eyes and see what the prospect would think. Successful marketers see the world through their prospects' eyes. You've got to see that this set of headlines, case-building information, and the offer are exactly what would get the prospect to take action. And once that happens, we now have a never-ending flow of leads to nurture. We'll talk about how to follow up on those leads later when we get to the tactical part of your marketing plan. I'll show you how to cultivate prospects until they become customers.

One final word about offers. Sometimes people tell us that they do put offers in their ads, what they term "a call to action." These offers are for something like a 20 percent off coupon, or a "buy one, get one free" deal. Sometimes, depending on what you sell, such offers are appropriate. But those are not the kinds of offers I'm talking about. I'm talking about an offer that gives the prospect a low-risk way to become further educated about what you're selling. If your marketing fails to include this type of offer, then you're missing out on an opportunity to start building a relationship with over 90 percent of your potential customers.

By way of review, you might ask yourself these seven basic marketing questions:

1. Who is your target market?
2. Who are your primary competitors?
3. What would cause somebody to want/need to buy what you sell in the first place?
4. What problems, frustrations, annoyances, etc. do people experience when buying what you sell (hot buttons)?
5. What are the important and relevant issues buyers should be aware of when buying what you sell?
6. What are the main advantages of doing business with you?
7. What kind of evidence can you produce to build/prove your case?

Chapter 6:

Two Cases in Point

*Now that you have been introduced to the marketing equation,
you need to see how you, like other companies, can apply it.*

Two case studies tie all four components of the Marketing Equation together.

Case #1: Moving Company

The first case study involves a moving company that increased its monthly lead flow from 70 to 955 without spending any extra money. The success of our marketing program allowed the owner to merge with three different moving companies within six months of implementing the *marketing equation* into her business. She sold out after just 10 months.

The owner was a German immigrant who came to this country with a strong desire to live the American Dream. She married an American, and they looked for a business opportunity. They decided to start a moving company because the service was so bad in that industry they felt could easily dominate just by building a better mousetrap. For 12 months, the owner, her husband, and two of their close friends worked for about 15 different moving companies, filling every position from packer to loader to scheduler to receptionist. They learned what customers liked and didn't like. They saw where other moving companies fell short of customer expectations, and they made notes on things the companies did well.

After a year of in-depth marketing research, they figured out the perfect "inside reality" for a moving company and launched AAbsolute Movers. They named it AAbsolute because the *Yellow Pages* in their area listed companies in alphabetical order.

They launched with high hopes. She intuitively knew that victory goes to the one with superior forces at the point of contact. She correctly identified her battlefield as the *Yellow Pages*. The first thing they did was commit to a $3,000 a month ad. Their original ad—the one they created themselves—was a platitude-filled ad that looked like everyone else's: "Local and long-distance moves. Commercial and residential. Loading and unloading." No distinction, no separation, no inkling as to their inside reality.

After a year, the ad was only generating an average of 70 calls a month. Most callers would ask the dreaded question: "How much do you charge for a move?" Then, if the prospect would let them, they would go to the prospect's house, inventory their stuff, try to explain how wonderful their moving system was compared to everyone else's. After a year, they'd done $120,000 in sales.

By the time we met the owner at one of our *Monopolize Your Marketplace* seminars, she was desperate. Her next *Yellow Pages* ad was two weeks late. If she didn't turn in the ad by 10 a.m. the next morning, she'd miss the book altogether. She had put off writing the ad until she could attend our seminar.

By now you know that platitudes shouldn't go in the ad. You know the *marketing equation* is: Interrupt + engage + educate + offer = good results. How would you write the ad?

Part 1: Interrupt. To effectively interrupt, we first figure out the hot buttons—learn what things are annoying, irritating, frustrating and otherwise problematic for people who move. Once we identify and articulate those problems, we'll flip the switch in the prospects' reticular activator and get them snapped out of alpha mode and into beta mode.

What are the moving hot buttons? First, "Don't break my stuff! And, if you do break it, I expect you to get those things replaced in a timely manner with no hassles." Here's another one: "No additional charges above the original quote." This one happened to me. I had a long driveway on a hill that the trucks couldn't get down, so the movers had to carry all my stuff down this hill. They tried to charge me an extra $1,100, even though their guy who did the original estimate saw the place beforehand. He said at the time that he thought that the trucks could make it down the hill. When they couldn't, the men who did the moving told us we'd have to pay more. The estimator screwed up his job, and now they're charging me extra. When it comes to moving, I know "no added charges" is a hot button.

What about timing? Do you have a problem with a mover who promises to be there Tuesday morning at 9 a.m. but doesn't show up until 2:30 in the afternoon? Of course. These are the hot buttons.

Yet the number one question prospects ask moving companies is: "How much does the move cost?" Is price a good differentiator? Suppose Mover A quotes $1,000 and Mover B charges $1,500. Here's what you don't know. Mover A is cheaper, but they'll also charge you an extra $1,200 after they have already moved your stuff, so the move will cost $2,200. Plus, they're likely to break half your stuff and make you jump through a nasty set of hoops to even file a claim to get it replaced. And if you do get it replaced, you'll be lucky to get 10 cents on the dollar. Mover B, on the other hand, won't charge you more on the backend, and won't break your stuff.

What would you rather pay? $1,000 to mover A or $1,500 to mover B? The outside perception of the two companies is identical. They have virtually the same ad in the *Yellow Pages*. But there are real differences in the inside reality of the two companies, and you can't find that out until it's too late! You say, "Well, I'm smarter than that. I'd ask mover A for references." Great! You can talk to their mother and cousins, and they'll all say good things. Besides 95 percent of customers don't call references anyway.

Here are a few interesting tidbits about the moving industry that will shed some light on the marketing problem our client was having. The moving industry has three kinds of insurance: Number one is called self-insured; it means if they break your stuff, they'll give you a new one—if you can find them and if they have any money left. Good luck. Only about 5 percent of moving companies chose the self-insurance route. About 90 percent have "per-pound replacement insurance," meaning if they drop your television set, they'll give you between 20 and 60 cents per pound, with an average of 40 cents per pound to replace the broken item. Your broken TV weighed 40 pounds; so they'll give you $16 to replace your TV. Then there's the third kind of insurance called actual insurance. Full replacement. If they break your stuff, you get a new one. This is standard procedure for less than 5 percent of moving companies. Our client offered full replacement insurance as a standard practice. Yet in her ad she had the same platitude, "Fully insured." Any mover with any kind of insurance can say "fully insured"—do you see the problem?—and the platitude?

Few of the ads that run in the *Yellow Pages* address any of the hot buttons. One ad has the headline "Starving Students." Do you really want starving students moving your stuff? Does the image of two "starving" kids instill confidence that your stuff will be safe? It says they offer "local, long distance, and office moves." Well, I would hope so! What other moves would there be? I'd say that's drearily commonplace and lacks power to evoke a response.

Most companies ignore everything that's important to customers, only giving them the variable of price to consider.

The next ad is for ATV Moving, which proudly proclaims it is "locally owned and operated." Am I supposed to draw a logical conclusion that because this company is locally owned, it must offer full-replacement insurance instead of rip-off per pound insurance, that they won't drop and break my stuff, and that they won't quote me one price and deliver a final bill with a different price? They do say that there are "no hidden charges." We know better. We know you can lie with generalities but have to be truthful with specifics. Their statement is platitude and puffery 101. They trudge on: "Dedicated to satisfaction. Fully insured. Professional packing service. Full range of materials and supplies. Free estimates." Would you honestly pay somebody $79 to give you an estimate? No. Then there's the real clincher: "Look for the Squirrel."

Now there's a hot button. If the squirrel is your hot button, you've got issues. But wait, there's a second clincher: "We make moving fun." This goes beyond platitudes and puffery. You need hip waders to get through it.

Remember the "find me 10 good ads out of 10,000" challenge? Good luck! You say, "That's just the *Yellow Pages*. Our marketing is better." Well, maybe you don't tell people to look for a squirrel, but you aren't using the *marketing equation*. At least until now. I want you to consider what a huge competitive advantage you gain when you implement this equation into your marketing.

Even though the *marketing equation* sounds so simple, implementing it can be a challenge. Let me ask you this: Where are the headlines that snap the prospect out of alpha and into beta mode? Where are the hot buttons? Where's the talk about not breaking my stuff in any of these ads? Where's the dialogue that talks about replacing my stuff if it does get broken? Where's the discussion about being on time? Where's the iron-clad guarantee that these companies won't charge me more after the move than they quoted before the move? Once again, where are the hot buttons?

Let's fix this ad utilizing what you know. First, we have to interrupt and engage. To do this effectively, we have to write a headline that taps into the existing hot buttons. Because people move infrequently, they know very little about what to look for in a moving company. Less than 5 percent of people know about the particular insurance practices of the moving industry. (And those who do learn this from hard, sad experience!) Less than 1 percent would think to check a company's policy on charging more than the original quote.

When people anticipate moving, they look in the *Yellow Pages* where all the different moving companies appear to be the same. They all have trucks, they all load and unload, they all do local and long distance, they are all family operated, and they have all been in business since 1431 BC.

How would you do the ad differently? You know the hot buttons. But you have one more challenge. How would you know what the problems are unless you've been burned before? You wouldn't. In this case, we've got to bring the important, relevant issues to light for the prospect. We've got to become their advocate. So what about a headline like this to tap those hot buttons: "Last year over 4,350 complaints and lawsuits were filed against moving companies in Dallas."

If you're interested in moving and you open the moving section of the Dallas *Yellow Pages* and see that headline, does that snap you out of alpha mode and into beta mode? You bet!

Advertising isn't designed to get everybody. We've got to tap into the hot buttons that are representative of *most* people. If you were in the market for moving, the headline "Last year over 4,350 complaints and lawsuits were filed against moving companies in Dallas" would get your attention. It would cause you to at least be curious to see what they had to say. This headline has power because it dwells in the realm of quantifiable, objective facts (what most ad agencies and marketing consultants abhor). They prefer their opinions on what's creative, clever or funny.

Part 2: Engage. So, you've read the headline about lawsuits, and now your brain starts to search for additional, clarifying information. We've got to write a subheadline that promises you that if you continue to read the ad, you'll get the information you need to make an educated decision. We'll explain the relevant and important issues to facilitate your decision.

What about this? "Ask these 15 questions to make sure your moving company's policies, procedures, and standards will protect you from an unpleasant moving experience."

Have I given you any clarifying information? If you were the prospect, would you be compelled to keep reading? *Have I promised to educate you?* The answer to all three questions is yes. Note, the answers to these questions are not my opinions; they are objective facts. Notice how the *marketing equation* eliminates the need for subjective creativity by dealing with the issues that are relevant and important to the consumer.

Part 3: Educate. Educate is the third component of the *marketing equation.* It's time to build the case. The purpose of this case was to tactfully expose the lack of integrity in ethics of the other moving companies. We based our case on these five points: honesty, real insurance, no breakage, price, and guaranteed move price. Honesty is a tricky subject. But you tell me. If you get a check for $16 dollars to replace your $400 television set, do you feel like you've been treated ethically? If the quote for the move was $1,000 and the final bill comes in at $2,200, were you treated fairly? Or, does it feel more like you were raped, pillaged and plundered?

For our movers to build their case, they simply had to educate their prospects about potential problems and then assemble evidence proving their performance in those areas. We put together that list with quantified, specific, non-platitudinal information. We did not simply say, "Make sure the company is insured." We explained there are three kinds of insurance and carefully explained how each one worked. Then we shared the specific example about getting $16 for a $400 television set. That's what the list of 15 questions is all about: to allow the prospect to ask any moving company specific questions and then judge their answers according to the standards set.

Part 4: Offer. In this situation, the offer is probably less important that most. Why? Because of the nature of moving, people don't typically start looking until they are about ready to buy. Many of the prospects are on the far right-hand side of the *educational spectrum* because they are ready to take immediate action. That's why we crammed a lot more of the education information into the ad. But we do have an offer that's useful. It's a low-risk way to further educate you and facilitate you decision-making.

What could we offer that would accomplish this? How about this: "Call or go online for a free moving company comparison checklist that helps you judge any moving company before committing to a move or giving them a dime." This checklist is available via their website. Or, prospects can get it by fax or mail. Is that a low-risk offer? Of course it is. And it's convenient to take advantage of,

Let's review the difficult stages of the *marketing equation*:

- *Interrupt*: "Last year over 4,350 complaints and lawsuits were filed against moving companies.

- *Engage*: "Ask these 15 questions to make sure your company's policies, procedures and standards protect you from an unpleasant moving experience."

- *Educate:* Build the case based on the hot buttons. Here's how we fulfill based on those 15 things. For instance, "Here's the kind of insurance that you should have, and here's the kind of insurance that we have. Here's the kind of insurance that most companies have. Make sure you ask." Or, "Here's our policy and written guarantee on the price of your move. Here's what most companies do. Here's what you need to ask to make sure that they don't." These facts educate and build the case.

- *Offer:* Free moving company comparison checklist available via internet, fax or mail.

Here's a copy of the ad as it appeared in the Dallas *Yellow Pages*.

This ad took the company from 70 to 955 calls a month. We produced it in less than *two hours* following a seminar! That is possible when you understand the *marketing equation* and realize that there's only one way to do it right.

Now, you might say, "That's a lot of copy in that ad. No one will read all those words. Some of the text is set in 6-point type." The *Yellow Pages* salesman agreed with you. He almost had a heart attack and argued with us for 30 minutes that nobody would read it.

He was wrong. Flat out wrong. Here's why: If I effectively interrupt and engage you based on hot buttons that are important to you—when it's *your* stuff and *you* are moving your family—you'll read anything and everything I can teach you. You become a relevant-information sponge.

There's been a lot of debate about whether advertising should be based on emotion or logic. You'll see a lot of large, institutional ads that are blatantly emotional, trying to get you to "feel" your way into the store and empty your wallet. We sometimes get accused of using too much "logic" in our marketing, especially when somebody sees an ad like this one. They think it's logic overload.

Every effective marketing piece contains both emotion and logic. Think about it the *marketing equation*. Interrupt and engage based on what? Based on emotional hot buttons. Once prospects become engaged (after we've tapped into that emotion), we educate and build a case founded on logic.

Emotion gives life to the logical argument, and logic gives validity to the emotional one.

Admit it, as I was talking about insurance in the moving industry, you started to crave that information, thinking you'll use that information next time you move. It will be impossible for you not to utilize that information now that it's securely tucked away in your reticular activator. And you're not even moving right now. But here's what I do know: 955 people a month said they would read all that.

Notice how all four components of the *marketing equation* work together. Notice how the type sizes and type fonts reflect the tone of the message. Do you see how the tone of the message is a bit bold? That's because the tone of the ad needs to accurately reflect the intensity and emotion level of the problems discussed. Notice how the layout makes the ad easy to follow and to take action. We lead the prospect from headline to subheadline to the case-building educational information and then the offer.

This ad works. Interrupt, engage, educate and offer. This equation works without fail—you can't mess it up if you try. As long as you're selling something that people actually want, you've got the hot buttons right, and the marketing piece is at the proper point of contact, you will achieve superior results.

Okay, you say, "How will this *marketing equation* help me?" You're convinced that your business is unique or immune to the dictates of human nature and buying behavior. Wrong! It doesn't matter if you're running a bowling alley or doing brain surgery. It doesn't matter whether you've been in business for decades or just getting started. It also doesn't matter whether you're in a service business or sell products. It doesn't matter if you're selling business-to-business or business-to-consumer. It doesn't matter if you advertise on television, on the radio, in the *Yellow Pages*, in the newspaper, on the internet, or on billboards. Maybe you don't advertise at all and only go to tradeshows. Maybe you just have brochures and websites, or you've got an on-hold message or a sign that you stick in people's yards when you fix their toilets if you're a plumber. Regardless of what you do or who you sell to—whether that target market is rich or poor, highly educated or uneducated, the *marketing equation* delivers.

If you've got a business and you want to sell something, no matter what it is, realize that your prospective customers want to make the best decision possible when buying it. They want to get the best deal in terms of price and value. Your job is to:

- Interrupt them based on their hot buttons
- Promise that reading your marketing piece or ad will educate them
- Build a case around the important and relevant issues
- Prove that you offer superior value and then
- Give them a low-risk way to further the education and sales process.

The *marketing equation* allows you to effectively match the outside perception with the inside reality. It always works the same—no exceptions. If you don't agree, it's because your marketing paradigm is so ingrained in your head, your wall is so high, that you're missing the opportunity to do something that will make a measurable difference in your business.

Case #2: Lasik Eye Surgery

Let's go through another case study for a lasik eye surgery center that advertises primarily on the radio. The surgeons had fallen into the normal marketing traps. They were deeply entrenched in brand building. They accepted the advice of the sales reps of the various radio stations that aired their ads. Here's the text of their ad, penned by the creative geniuses at the radio station. (You can hear these ads at www.mybook.com)

(Music playing in background)
Hawaii is one of the most beautiful places on earth no argument there. And it's a wonderful gift that every day you can stare at its lush greenery and magnificent surroundings. The gift of course is good eyesight. Think about that gift now that you've made the decision that it's time to explore lasik corrective surgery.

Well at Walker Eye Care and Surgery they remind you that the gift of eyesight is nothing to tinker with. So speak to the experts at Walker Eye Care and Surgery first. A life without corrective lenses is a tempting option but you need to protect your eyes and that's why you should listen to the Walker experts. For over 35 years they've been a Hawaiian tradition that's meant complete family eye care. Making

sure that you see all the beauty of Hawaii clearly every day and now with lasik corrective surgery Walker offers you pre and post operative care that's unmatched anywhere.
Call 952-5383 today and learn more. That's 952-5383. Preserve your gift choose the best. Choose Walker Eye Care and Surgery.

What did you think? Pretty much the usual stuff you'd expect to hear on a typical radio ad, right? No hot buttons, no information to facilitate decision making, nothing that resembles the *marketing equation.* Did you detect any platitudes? That ad is a platitude fest!

Here's the ad again, with the platitudes in bold:

Hawaii is one of the most beautiful places on earth no argument there. And it's a wonderful gift that every day you can stare at its lush greenery and magnificent surroundings. The gift of course is **good eyesight**. Think about that gift now that you've made the decision that it's time to explore lasik corrective surgery.

Well at Walker Eye Care and Surgery they remind you that the gift of eyesight is nothing to tinker with. So speak to the **experts** at Walker Eye Care and Surgery first. A life without corrective lenses is a tempting option but you need to **protect your eyes** and that's why you should listen to the **Walker experts**. For over 35 years they've been a **Hawaiian tradition** that's meant **complete family eye care**. Making sure that you see all the beauty of Hawaii clearly every day and now with lasik corrective surgery Walker offers you pre and post operative **care that's unmatched anywhere**.
Call 952-5383 today and learn more. That's 952-5383. **Preserve your gift choose the best**. Choose Walker Eye Care and Surgery.

This ad will attract only those prospects on the far right-hand side of the *educational spectrum* who are ready to make a decision on lasik right away. This makes it difficult for the doctor to see the real lack of results. If you were to ask the doctor about the results while he was running that ad, he would say, "We don't get a ton of leads from the ads. But we close almost every lead we do get." Well, of course! This ad will get those people who are ready to buy right now, but no one else. He's missing 95 percent of his prospective customers. Many of these prospects would buy right away if they understood lasik and became educated about the relevant issues. And many more would become ready sooner than later. Finally, the surgeon could control all future marketing efforts directed to them.

The doctor knew that the ad wasn't producing all it could, so he hired a creative agency that specialized in radio jingles to rework the ad. The agency is known for some of the most famous radio jingles of all time, so he felt like the huge sum of money he was paying—about $20,000—would be worth it. Here's what they came up with:

> Come see the people of vision, Aloha Laser Vision, People of vision. First thing that you're going to see, is a vision quality. When it comes to your eye care, you want people of vision there. People of vision can show you how. Come see the people of vision, Aloha Laser Vision. People of vision, listen now, people of vision show you how you can see better you can do it now. See the people of vision (fades out and continues to play as background)

How'd you like that one? This is C&R at its peak. The idea here is to get you to hear that ad enough times so that when you finally decide you need lasik, you think of this company. It has a catchy tune, so there is some interrupt value there. But the interrupt is not based on any hot buttons, so the ad doesn't engage. Of course, there's nothing to educate and there's no offer.

Guess what? This ad didn't work either, even though it probably did get "awareness" up. It probably got a few people who were sitting at point Y on the *educational spectrum* to call. But when the phone quit ringing altogether, the good doctor came to one of our consultants for solutions. We taught him about the *marketing equation* and told him how the ad should interrupt, engage, educate and offer. Well, the doctor is a doctor, not a marketing guy. He wasn't convinced that it would work and reluctantly recorded this commercial. He was so upset that he'd spent all that money on that stupid jingle that he insisted that he use the music as an intro and outro to the new commercial. We reluctantly agreed. Here's the text of the ad:

> (Song playing)
> Come see the people of vision. Aloha Laser Vision. People of Vision
> (Music continues to play without words)

Aloha this is Dr Albert Walker. If you or anyone you know has been thinking about lasik surgery. Call me at 952-5383 and I'll send you my free physicians report called "Candid Answers About Lasik". It will help you understand what the surgery actually is step by step. Will it hurt? How much improvement can you expect and how to choose the right doctor and the right time. So call Walker Laser Vision at 952-5383 and ask for your free physicians report "Candid Answers About Lasik" and we'll invite you to schedule your free screening and consultation with me. Again that's 952-5383 tell my staff that Dr Albert told you to call. Mahalo and I'll talk to you soon.

Here's what happened when this ad ran. The first time it played, the phone rang 25 times. That's 25 people at all points of the *educational spectrum* who were interrupted and engaged, and who wanted to be further educated via the offer for the free Physician's Report. That's 25 identifiable prospects who they can pro-actively market directly to and control over the next several weeks and months. The doctor had never had the phone ring anywhere close to that number as a direct result of radio advertising. In fact, until that time, the office had only a general idea of how its advertising was working. They'd be busy at some times and not at others. They could trace no one directly to their advertising efforts.

When this ad ran and they got the 25 calls, the doctor panicked and immediately called the radio station and said, "Cancel the entire rest of the run of commercials!" Why? Because he hadn't believed that it would work, so he never paid our consultant to write the report for him. They were advertising a report that didn't exist yet, so they had to shut down the advertising while they put it together.

Welcome to the instant profit faucet. Why not make your company the next case in point?

Strategic Marketing

The actual implementation of the Marketing Equation comes with knowing not just what to do—but how to do it.

As we discuss the problems with most marketing and advertising, I hope you come to realize why you haven't optimized your marketing. Perhaps you didn't know a better way to do it. Then we talked about the *marketing equation* and took you step-by-step through each component. You've seen what those ads look like and how powerful they are.

Now we're ready to discuss how to implement the *marketing equation*. It's one thing to know *what* to do; it's another thing to actually know *how* to implement a strategic marketing plan.

Some Assembly Required

I've got six kids; so every Christmas I do the "some assembly required" building of bikes, toys, and dollhouses. Building a bike is like building your marketing program. What I've done so far is this: I've taken the box that the bike comes in, dumped out all the parts on the carpet, and shown you what a bike ought to look like. I've shown you the picture of the bike on the front of the box that lets you know what the finished product looks like. I've given you a detailed description of the individual components of your bike and told you how they all work together. I've also shown you why the bike you're currently riding isn't going to get you where you want to go because it's outdated—it's built on a frame that may get you from point A to point B, but won't win any races if you go up against the new, improved bikes.

But here's what I have not yet done: I haven't shown you the instruction manual. I haven't shown you the step-by-step, here's-how-you-put-this-stuff-together. Why not? Because you need to understand what, why, and how we're doing what we're doing before you can put it together. I don't want anybody to think that putting this "bike" together is an easy process. It's not. We have spent thousands of hours perfecting our system to allow us to put your marketing together *relatively* quickly and easily. What I've done so far is educate you, so you have a clear vision of the possibilities.

However, to fully integrate our system into your business, you may want to meet with one of our consultants. To know for sure whether this is the right route for you, first determine your "marketing risk." This quantifies how much is at stake when you run a marketing campaign. If your company has any marketing risk at all, if you are spending any money on marketing and advertising, whether it's $1,000 a month or $1 million a month, you are doing yourself a disservice to try to put this together yourself. *The cost of doing it right is far lower than the cost of doing it wrong.*

Now in this section I'm going to open the proverbial instruction manual and give you a glimpse inside, so you can understand the specific methodologies we use to get results for you. This will give you a certain comfort level knowing how we do what we do. The way we do things is so different from the typical ad agency way, you need to become an educated *convert* before you're qualified to do business with us.

Our system is composed of *21 steps*. You must complete each one before moving to the next one. (No different than the instruction manual for bikes.) Our professional marketing consultants use these 21 steps over several weeks or months, depending on the scope of the project. We won't go through all 21 steps here in this book. But I do want to give you a quick glimpse into the "manual" so you can get a good feel for the methodology that allows us to consistently achieve outstanding results for all of our clients.

There are two major phases: *discovery* (steps 1-6) and *writing* (steps 7-21). Discovery means gathering information and finding out the prospect's hot buttons. Writing focuses on writing the marketing materials, which allows you to present the case.

Chapter 7:

Five Discovery Questions

Before you race ahead with some shoot-from-the-lip campaign,
discover what your prospects and customers are looking for.

Discovery, the first part of our total marketing system, means gathering information and learning your prospect's hot buttons, developing your case, and uncovering evidence. In this chapter, I'll give you an overview of the discovery process.

We first ask a series of discovery questions to get a good snapshot of your business. We want to know what you do, who your target market is, and what are the important issues in your business.

I'll cover five of the most important discovery questions. These questions help you determine your target market's hot buttons so you can write good headlines that effectively interrupt and engage. They help you pinpoint the important and relevant issues so you can effectively educate and build a case. Answer these five discovery questions, for your business.

1. The qualification question. The first discovery question is the *qualification question.* We want to figure out who is qualified to buy what you sell. Here's the qualification question: ***Under what circumstances do your typical prospects start to think about buying what you sell?***

Let's say you sell wood fences. My wood fence needs to be replaced, and so I'm in the market. Under what circumstances would I start to think about buying a fence? What would cause me to get on the *educational spectrum* at Point A? List as many possibilities as you can think of, without worrying about the order. Here are a few ideas:

- My fence is eight years old and is starting to look run down.
- The posts have become rotten.
- A strong wind is causing one section to lean.
- I'm building a new swimming pool, and the fence is required by law.
- I'm selling my house and want to get top dollar.
- I'm worried about my children's safety with an unstable fence.
- My pets are escaping through gaps in the fence.

Those are things that would give a prospect a glimmer of a thought about buying a fence and put them on the *educational spectrum* at point A. The severity of the situation determines the prospect's position along the *educational spectrum*.

Under what circumstances does a typical prospect start to think about buying what you sell?

Here's another example. The client is an SBA lending bank. The answers to this question might be:

- A company's sales are exploding , and it needs money to buy new equipment.
- A company wants to build a headquarters building.
- A company needs research and development money for a new product.
- A company wants to hire more employees.

Answer these questions for your business. Don't worry about getting the "right" answer. Just list as many things as you can.

To illustrate, think about the reasons why you're reading this book. Perhaps you have marketing challenges. Maybe you've run ads that haven't performed as well as you wanted. So, you start thinking about how optimize those results. Maybe sales are down, so you're looking for solutions. Maybe you're doing well but feel there is still more opportunity to increase sales and dominate your industry. The reasons you are reading this book are answers to the discovery question for me, the author of the book.

What would cause *your* customers to start thinking about buying what you sell?

2. The customer values question. The second discovery question is the *Customer Values* question. Here's what we're trying to find out: *What things are important to your prospects when buying what you sell?*

Let's answer that question for the wood fence contractor. What is important to you when buying a wood fence? You want the fence to: look good, not turn brown quickly, not sag or lean, last at least 10 years, and be high quality. You also have concerns with the fence contractor: You don't want any hidden costs or up charges; you want the fence completed in a reasonable time frame; you don't want workers who are scary drug-users near your home; and you want a reasonable price.

See how easy those answers are? Yet the answers are remarkably powerful. These easy questions give you most of the information you need to implement the *marketing equation*.

Let's do another example. Suppose you loan money to small business owners. What is important to your prospects when securing a small business loan? They want a low interest rate, easy application procedure, few hassles involved in getting the loan, minimal paperwork, fast decision, fast processing, knowledgeable loan officers, and all fees disclosed on the front end.

Now it's your turn. Answer the *customer values* question for your business. *What things are important to your prospects when they are buying what you sell?*

By asking and answering these first two questions—the qualification question and customer value question—you identify your prospects' hot buttons. You create a list of what prospects want when they decide to buy what you sell.

Now, make sure what *you* think is important reflects what *prospects* and *customers* think is important. If you see things on the list of customer values that you currently don't do, then you have some *innovation opportunities*. If the customer wants something and you don't do it, then just start doing it. Find out what customers want and give it to them. Of course, innovations come at a cost. You'll need to analyze the costs connected with that innovation with the benefits in terms of increased business it will bring you.

For example, if you're in the moving business and determine that better insurance will cost your company an extra $8,000 a month or $100,000 a year, you may decide not to offer it. But let's say that currently your average move is $2,500, and you do 40 jobs per month for total monthly revenue of $100,000. If you add full coverage insurance, giving your customers what they want, and then market your business using our system, you could now get $3,000 for the same service. Right away, you'll make $120,000 a month, leaving a $12,000 a month profit even after the increased insurance costs. Then factor in what happens when the number of leads and closes goes up to just 50 jobs a month. Now you'll gross $150,000 a month, a full 50 percent more by only increasing the number of jobs by 20 percent. In that case, the increased profits justify the cost of the innovation.

You could grow your business by 50 percent in just a few weeks. That's what happens when your outside perception accurately reflects your newly revamped inside reality. In that case, the cost of the innovation is justified by the increased profits.

Knowing what its *customers value* helped innovate a company that distributed and installed cabinets in new homes. The business was grossing $8 million a year on the sheer momentum of the marketplace. But the owner was frustrated because sales had stagnated for 18 months.

In a post-seminar consultation, I asked him the *customer values* question, but he couldn't come up with any answers, only platitudes. All he could say is that his customers were only interested in getting the lowest price. After a couple minutes of this sniveling, I told him, "If you want to grow and compete with the big boys, you'll have to innovate your business. You'll have to build a superior inside reality so you deserve the extra business."

Without thinking, the owner responded: "We can't innovate. We sell the exact same cabinets as all our main competitors. And the builders know it. Cabinets are a commodity. We've just got to be the lowest-priced supplier."

I refused to believe his story. "If you really believe that your product is a commodity in a price-driven market and that there is no other means of competing except on price, quit. There's no chance to grow, so don't try." Of course, I also told him that I've never seen any business like that.

Here's what we did. We surveyed his current clients, customers who had switched to another vendor, and prospects who never became customers. We asked them the *customer values* question. We wanted to find out what was important to them when dealing with a cabinet supplier and installer.

Here's what we learned: Builders are always pressured to finish their houses by a certain date, and they almost always lag behind schedule—and those delays impact a dozen subcontractors. Since cabinets are one of the last things to go in a new house, when the job runs behind, scheduling snafus become a major problem. The new home owners expect to close the deal on Monday and move in on Tuesday. So the builder may blame the delay on the cabinet installer. This happens all the time.

The cabinet installers then complain and counter that it's really the builder's fault. They're right when they say those builders should get their act together. But I like what Jim Rohn says: "Don't wish it was easier. Wish YOU were better!" Our client could *wish* that builders would never fall behind and blame their tardiness on him. But they do!

The innovation strategy was obvious to us. Find a way to give home builders what they want: cabinets that can be installed any time they want on a moment's notice, so they can finish houses on time.

What would it take for our cabinet man to be innovative? Scheduling flexibility—perhaps offering a two-day window for installation or guaranteeing the builder he only needed three days notice. That's not too bad, but why not take it even further?

Here's what we told the cabinet installer to do to create a total breakthrough: "First, work a deal with suppliers to have the 30 most common styles of cabinets in stock all the time. Next, hire a crew of installers that works strictly on call. These tradesmen can show up at any given house in the area within 60 minutes. That way the builder won't have to worry about falling behind schedule. An installer can be available any time at a moment's notice, even at 2 a.m.

When I told this to the cabinet guy, he about had a heart attack. "Do you know how much it would cost to have a crew 'on call' full time? Do you know the cost to inventory all those different cabinets? Impossible! It can't be done!"

Although I don't know how much it would cost, I had a good idea how much it would cost *not to* do it. At my insistence, he asked one of the builders he had been chasing for months—the area's second largest homebuilder—this question: Would you give us your cabinet business, at least guarantee us a certain percentage of your jobs, if we could supply you any cabinet you needed and have a crew out on the job site installing those cabinets within 60 minutes after your call?

The builder said he would be willing to guarantee in writing 100 percent of his cabinet business.

Our program is called *Monopolize Your Marketplace* for a reason. It's about owning the market, not about being an also-ran, staying small, getting kicked around by the big guys, or being satisfied with whatever marketshare you get.

To *monopolize* your marketplace, you've got to innovate—to create the inside reality— so people conclude: I would be an absolute fool to do business with anyone else but you, regardless of price.

So, are there things that are important to your customers—things they need or services they would value—that you currently do not offer? If so, here is your opportunity to innovate. I encourage you to get together with your team members and brainstorm ideas for innovation. Ask them: "What do our customers and prospects want that is not currently available in the industry?"

3. The need-to-know question. The *need-to-know* question identifies the things prospects need to know to make the best decision possible when making a purchase. So, ask: ***What do your customers need to know to buy what you sell?***

Remember, marketing's main purpose is to facilitate the prospect's decision-making process. So you'll need to uncover possible pitfalls or buying traps that they aren't necessarily aware of when they hop on the *educational spectrum*. For example, if you are moving, you need to know about the three kinds of insurance and the difference between the price quoted and the price charged. These are things that most prospects would not even think to ask a mover. Those are "need to know" items.

You must evaluate each of your *customer values* to determine what your prospects need to know that they may not be aware of when starting the buying process. Answer this question as if you were giving advice to friends looking to buy what you sell. You wouldn't "sell" your friends; instead you would *teach* them the important and relevant issues.

For example, if you are buying a wooden fence, what do you need to know? We know from the customer values question that quality is something you want in a fence. But let me ask you this: do you even know what constitutes a "quality" fence? Chances are excellent that you *don't*. You need to know about pressure treating wood to prevent rotting, sagging and warping and to prolong the fence life as much as 10 years. Most fence companies use non-pressure-treated wood to save money unless you tell them otherwise because they have the misguided belief that all their customers care about is the lowest price. You also need to know something about different woods that make a difference in the quality of the fence. Do you realize that cedar lasts 50 to 100 percent longer than pine? You should also know that an eight-foot tall gate requires four hinges, not two hinges like a six-foot tall gate, to avoid sagging within six months.

So, if you simply ask the fence company how much the fence costs, they won't tell you what you need to know because they assume that if it costs more, you won't buy it. The "lowest price" factor is almost always fostered more by competing companies than it is by customers!

No matter what business, industry, or profession you are in, I can promise you this: If you have poor marketing you will get beat up on pricing—and it's your own fault. Can you see now why you almost always get crummy service and products? Because every industry is full of people who don't know how to do marketing. They only know how to sell based on price. And the only way to get the lowest price is to cut corners on quality.

When you implement the *Monopolize Your Marketplace* system, you'll innovate your company, if necessary, to give your customers what they want. And you'll give your customers what they *would* want if they knew to ask for it. Knowledge will make your customers feel that they would have to be absolute fools to do business with anyone else but you, regardless of price.

You will be able to charge a premium price once your business improves because innovation becomes profitable. The one who innovates the most wins.

Note: the innovation strategies are sitting right in front of you—just ask your customers what they want and then give it to them! You know what else? You'll find that once you get good at marketing, you'll become a savvy shopper as well, because you'll look for this kind of information.

By asking and answering the question "What do my prospects need to know to buy what we sell?," you can identify their hot buttons and use this intelligence in writing headlines that attract them and in creating copy and content that educate them in need-to-know areas.

What are the *need-to-know* items if you are getting a small business loan? You need to know the experience of the loan officer, how your loan gets approved, how long the process takes, what is the approval criteria, what financial records you need to pull together, how best to present that information, how banks "package" loans, how to qualify for low-interest rates, how to avoid big packaging and application fees, and how to avoid delays.

What do *your* customers need to know? List your answers now.

4. The case-building question. Now it's time to build the case for doing business with your company. Here's the question: **What do you do to give customers what they want?**

Go back to the *customer values* question and consider each of the points you listed there. What do you do to give customers what they want? Answer this question on a value-by-value basis. And again, if what you do is not yet up to par with what your prospects want, there's an innovation opportunity.

The *need-to-know* question focuses mainly on what a prospect needs to know about buying what you sell—it is not specific to your company. It's the pure education of the prospect. The *case-building* question, conversely, is all about *your* company. If your company is innovative, there will be a positive correlation between the answers you give to both questions. Your answer to the *case-building* question should mirror your answer to the *customer values* question. If the answers to these two questions don't match up, then you need to seriously consider innovating your offering.

Our program is all about being on the customers' side and giving customers what they want. It's about creating the "ultimate business" within your industry. If you want to monopolize your marketplace, you have to offer quality products and services (innovate your inside reality) and know how to use the *marketing equation.* Otherwise, you'll run the same platitude-filled ads as everyone else; but you'll get worse results because you'll still be trying to sell at a premium price. When people call you and ask how much your product costs, you'll tell them: "Because of our high quality, our prices are higher." And the natural response is, "I'm not going to pay for it!" Then you'll get frustrated and feel that you have to cut your prices to compete. Eventually, you can't provide high quality and exceptional service, and so you offer the same sorry crap as everyone else for as cheap as possible. This is the rule. High quality companies that persist at a higher price point are the exception. And this whole scenario is all *your* fault because your outside perception and inside reality have nothing in common.

Once you understand this *marketing equation,* you know how to provide higher value. You know how to interrupt your prospects based on their hot buttons. You engage them, educate them, and make a low-risk offer. Then your ability to charge more money for your product or service increases dramatically. Profits go up. Everyone's happy (except your competitors).

Our clients can charge 10 to 20 percent over the industry average price for their products and services and still out-sell their competitors 10, 20 or 100 to one.

Think of the moving company. The owner grew her business by 1,000 percent in 90 days and sold out for millions within 10 months by having full replacement insurance, not adding hidden charges after the move, and charging $500 more than the competitor's bid! Because when you interrupt and engage people based on their hot buttons, when you educate people about what they need to know, they say, "I'd be an absolute fool to buy from your competitor, regardless of price." Giving customers the best products and services possible allows you to *monopolize your marketplace.*

5. The evidence question. As you build a case to educate your prospects, you'll need to provide evidence to back up everything you say. The evidence allows you to break past the platitudes; it gives everything you say substance and power. So here's the question: ***What do your prospects need to see to feel that they have enough information to make the best decision possible?*** What evidence do they need to feel that they are in total control of the buying decision?

You've already identified several hot buttons and *customer values* in the first four discovery questions. Now you need to add the evidence that will validate those points in the prospect's mind. Remember, in marketing, emotion gives logic life, and logic lends validity to the emotion. So, validate the emotions you tap into.

For example, if the wood fence company wanted to validate the *customer value* of quality, the owners might put together a list of standards that all reputable fence companies adhere to. Where does such information come from? Straight from the *need-to-know* question.

Then, the fencing company must provide evidence that those standards are true standards. How? Imagine you are in the court room. You are making claims, and the jury—in this case, your prospects and customers—want proof. If you say that you should use pressure-treated posts and rails, what evidence can you produce to prove that point? You might use photos of various fences that have the right and wrong standards and what those fences look like after 12, 24, and 60 months.

How about a list of appearance, behavior, and performance standards for your workers? What about a letter from your bank confirming that you've never bounced a check? What about a letter from your materials suppliers saying that you always pay your bills fast? Would those things make a difference in the minds of your prospects? Would they convince the jury that you're both competent and of high character? You might get a third-party expert and put on a demonstration to impress the jury.

Let me ask you this: Have you impressed your jury? What forms of evidence are you providing? What about a list of names, addresses, and phone numbers of 500 recent customers? What about photos of dozens of other projects you've done for customers whom your prospects can identify with? What about testimonials from some of those customers?

What should those customers say in those testimonials? Well, first, they shouldn't be spewing platitudes. They shouldn't be saying "Superior Fencing is great. They gave us good service at a low price!" Such platitudes don't play well in court. In a court of law, if a witness said "low price" and "good service," the attorney will ask, "What? How low? Compared to what? Let me see the invoice. What do you mean, the service was good? Give me specific instances." And that's good advice for you: be specific.

Your testimonials need to utilize the same information you use to write your marketing. Find customers who fit the profile of those who come from your *qualification* question. Invite them to write testimonials so your prospective customers can identify with your marketing statements. Use multiple testimonials so that you get a diversity of customers to identify with you.

What would those customers say in those testimonials? They would talk about all the things that build your case, and then add how they've been completely thrilled with the results.

With evidence, it becomes an absolute no-brainer to choose you. If you first provide all that evidence, and then tell the customer your product costs $500 more, would your customer care? Maybe a few would, but you'll win the rest of the business. And, how easy do you think it would be to get referrals from customers who had heard your case? Do you think they would tell their friends? You bet!

What about your business? What would a prospect need to feel confident? What evidence could you provide? Are there articles written about you? Are there charts you can put together? Are there comparisons that you can draw? Are there tests you can provide? Make a list. Remember, the jury won't believe platitudes and generalities.

Answer the Five Discovery Questions

1. Qualification Question: Under what circumstance do your prospects start to think about buying what you sell?_____

_____

_____

2. Customer Values Question: What things are important to your prospects when buying what you sell? _____

_____

_____

3. Need-To-Know Question: What do your prospects need to know when making a decision?_____

_____

4. Case-Building Question: What do YOU do to give your customers what they want?_____

_____

_____

5. Evidence Question: What do your prospects need to see or hear to feel that they have enough information to make the best decision possible?

_____

_____

_____

Evidence Questions

Evidence Type	Specific Evidence You Can Gather
1. Articles & Press Stories	
2. Associations	
3. Awards	
4. Books	
5. Charts & Graphs	
6. Client Lists	
7. Comparisons	
8. Compliance Checklists	
9. Earnings Reports	
10. Endorsements	
11. Examples of Savings	
12. Expertise Tests	
13. Facts & Figures	
14. Performance Audits	
15. Photos & Videos	
16. Product Demos	
17. Quotes	
18. Standards Lists	
19. Statistics	
20. Technical Drawings	
21. Tests & Lab Results	
22. Testimonials	

Chapter 8:

Now Write Something

You've done the research,
now it's time to present your case.

Remember, there are two parts to building a case: discovery and presentation. Similarly, when putting together a strategic marketing plan, there is the research and the writing.

If you try to write ads or marketing pieces without first going through the proper discovery process, you do about as well as an attorney who just appears in court without having researched and prepared his case. The attorney won't know what questions to ask. He won't know the relevant and important issues. He won't have any evidence to back up his claims, and he'll come off looking foolish.

So, before you write the actual marketing pieces, you need to do the discovery. Only then are you in a position to write effective advertising and marketing.

Keep in mind the *marketing equation*. First, *interrupt* based on hot buttons that *engage* your prospects. Then, promise them that the marketing piece contains information that will facilitate their decision-making process. Those two steps, interrupt and engage, hit on emotional issues that will poke the prospects' reticular activators and get them in a state of readiness to be educated. Use headlines to interrupt and engage prospects. The headlines draw heavily from the information you gather during the discovery process in the *qualification* question and the *customer values* question.

Next *educate* prospects and make them an *offer* after you have interrupted and engaged them with your headlines. You do this by building a case, using the information that you've gathered during the discovery process in the *need-to-know* question, the *case building information* question, and the *evidence* question. Your logical case will validate the emotional chords you strike in the headlines. You'll put that quantified information within the text of the marketing piece and also into various marketing tools that you will distribute as offers.

How To Write Powerful Headlines

Headlines are tools we use to interrupt and engage prospects. We call headlines "the ad for the ad." Every ad or marketing piece in any medium must have a headline. It should be an activator that paints a mental picture and interrupts the prospect. It needs to be oriented around hot buttons. Subheadlines promise to further educate engage prospects.

Now I'll show you how to write effective headlines using three main techniques:
• Say it in plain English.
• Use headline starters.
• Borrow from our "Headline Bank."

Using plain English means just that. Just say what you have to say, and it formulates a headline. Here's the easiest way to pull this off. Take the answers to the first and second discovery questions—the *qualification* question and the *customer values* question—and use them to make a simple statement.

For the fence company, a plain English headline might go like this: "If Your Five-Year-Old Fence Is Looking Weathered and You're Worried About the Safety of Your Children...."

That headline is the answer to the qualification question. It's powerful because those scenarios are familiar to your prospects. Then we continue the headline with some problematic hot buttons that would further stimulate the reticular activator: "And You'd Like to Build a High-Quality Fence That Won't Droop, Sag, Lean, Rot, Disintegrate, Teeter, or Fall Over for 20 Years...."

Did you catch all the hot buttons there? They all came straight from the *customer values* question. We've interrupted the prospect with this headline, and all we've done is say, in plain English, what the deal is.

You might think, "Geez, that's a long headline. Will anyone actually listen to or read all that?" That's a fair question, but the answer is, "Absolutely." If people are on the *educational spectrum* with regard to fences, they will be searching for educational information. That will get them into the headline, and the hot buttons will keep them there. Worry more about whether a headline has the right hot buttons than about the length of the headline.

Now our prospects have seen our plain English headline that interrupts and prepares them to become engaged. Their brains will search for additional, clarifying information that promises to educate. If their brains find such information, they will become solidly engaged and eagerly read the rest of the ad.

What could we say next to promise to educate prospects? We've just told them that they can build a quality fence and avoid all the common pitfalls—no more drooping, sagging, leaning, rotting, disintegrating, teetering, and falling over. Now we write a subheadline that *promises to educate*: "Make Sure Your Fencing Company Does These Three Things to Ensure Your Fence Lasts 20 Years."

This subhead passes the *engage* evaluation because it promises to further educate the prospect. That's what writing headlines in plain English is all about.

Let's write a headline in plain English for the bank that specializes in small business loans. You answer the *qualification question* for the bank by saying a company gets on the *educational spectrum*—they start thinking about a loan—if they are expanding and need money to buy new equipment, add new buildings, buy more inventory, take on more employees, or develop a new product. Let's narrow this down and say that this bank specializes in loans for equipment, buildings and inventory.

Here's a headline that works: "If you're a successful business owner, professional or entrepreneur looking to expand your business and need to secure a business loan to finance new equipment, more land, or more building space...."

We've interrupted everyone who fits that category by touching a problem that already exists in their reticular activators. To finish the headline and engage people now that they've been interrupted, we would use values from the *customer values* question. How about: "I'll show you an easy way to get a small business loan with no hassles, no hidden costs, and in half the time."

We've engaged our readers and promised that if they continue to read this ad, they will get information that will facilitate their decision-making process. Yes, the headline is long, but we can now take that headline and use it as the introductory sentence in a sales letter.

Headline Starters

Have you ever gone camping and tried to start a fire with just sticks and matches? I have. It is easy if there are a lot of dry sticks around. But often I'd find myself in a downpour with wet matches and wet wood. In those cases, no matter how hard I try, I can't start a fire.

Luckily for Boy Scouts and other campers, there is something called a fire starter. It's a little wax mini-log that's been soaked in kerosene. To use it, you find a little shelter from the rain, light it on fire with your match, and it will stay lit in almost any condition. You can then use it to light sticks and paper. The "fire starter" is like a super match.

Headline starters are like fire starters. They work the same way. Whenever you're in a situation where your mind goes blank and you just can't think of a headline, use the headline starters. They'll give you a spark and a light. Basically, headline starters give you ideas to start your headlines even if you are having a mental stupor of thought. Once you catch your headline writing imagination on fire, you'll find that it heats up and headlines start to flow more easily.

Headline starters are simply headline categories, such as: news, inflammatory, how-to, questions, testimonials, guarantees, comparisons, bold claims, solutions to problems, numbers, and offers. Headline starters help you get started writing headlines in plain English.

For any given project, I recommend you write anywhere from 20 to 50 headlines before deciding which one to use. That's right, 20 to 50. For our consulting clients, we will usually write at least 100, sometimes as many as 200. Write them using all three of the headline writing methods—plain English, headline starters, and the headline bank.

The reason you need to write so many is threefold. First, usually you must write a lot of headlines to find the few that are really powerful. If you write a lot of headlines, you'll likely come up with several good ones. The second reason is that you'll need a bunch to complete all the different marketing pieces you'll need to create. You'll need headlines for lead generators, for reports and for hopper systems. You can use the same headline more than once, of course, but over an entire marketing campaign, you'll need several. And third, having many headlines allows you to mix and match and see which ones go well with each other. You may find that you've got a certain headline that you really like, but then when you pair it with another headline, it becomes even more powerful. You'll find that some headlines interrupt, some engage, while others do both. You'll need to have a full quiver of headlines to come up with the optimal usage.

As you're reading the headline starters for our fence company, think about your company. Can you formulate some good headlines based on the headline starters? Don't forget. The headlines need to hit hot buttons to tap into existing emotions and interrupt your prospects.

News. To write a good news-style headline, you'll need to use words like *new, finally, introducing, at last.* For the fence company, we might say, "Finally, A Company That Builds a Fence That Doesn't Look 15 Years Old After Just Three Years."

For the bank, we might write: "Introducing the 'Doesn't-Take-Six-Months, Doesn't-Cost-You-A-Fortune-Just-To-Apply, No-Chance-of-Getting-Rejected' Small Business Loan." That headline hits a few hot buttons, wouldn't you say?

Inflammatory approach. What we're trying to do here is gain maximum interrupt value by saying something that's borderline shocking to the prospect. There's no need to be crass, rude or obnoxious. Sometimes being inflammatory works real well. Don't make headlines inflammatory just for inflammatory's sake, though; you still need to make the headline hot-button based.

Here's a pretty inflammatory headline for a fence: How To Keep Your Fence From Falling Over And Squashing Your Kids.

Would that headline interrupt you? Does it hit the hot button of a person who has an old fence that's leaning and who has kids?

Here's one for the bank: "Getting A Small Business Loan? Find Out How Most Banks Legally (But Not Ethically) Plan To Steal $1,500 From You." The word *steal* is pretty inflammatory in that headline, and certainly has a good reticular activator pull to it.

How-to. This is easy to implement: "How To Ensure You Won't Be Buying Another Replacement Fence Less Than Five Years From Now" or "How To Eliminate The Six-Month Lag Time, The $1,500 Non-Refundable Fees, And The 34 percent Chance of Rejection On Your Next Small Business Loan." Note that how-to headlines are good at both interrupting and engaging because they promise to educate the reader.

Comparison. Here's a comparison headline: "Most Fences Only Last Three to Four Years Because of Poor Quality Materials and Shoddy Workmanship. Our Fences Are Guaranteed to Last At Least 12 Years, and Most Won't Need Replacing For 20 Years." Notice that I added a second headline starter, the *guarantee.*

Here's a comparison headline for the bank: "How Much Would You Rather Pay To Process The Paperwork For Your Small Business Loan? $1,500 or $0 dollars and 0 Cents?" Again, that headline contained two headline starter elements, the *comparison* and a *question.*

Testimonial. "After Six Years, My Fence With Pressure-Treated Posts and 3 x 4

Rails Still Looks As Good As The Day It Was Installed." This testimonial hits the hot buttons and gives specific, quantified information. Here's a *testimonial* headline for the bank: "Last Time I Applied For A Small Business Loan, I Got Charged $1,640 in Packaging Fees ... THEN My Application Got Rejected! I Wish I Knew Then About First Commercial Bank's No-Fee Guarantee."

Did you notice how all of the headlines were full of hot buttons that addressed relevant and important issues? Do you see how those headlines work on the prospect's reticular activator and force the brain to snap out of alpha sleep into beta alert mode?

Try this exercise, to come up with headline starts for your business.

For even more examples, you can go to MYMbook.com.

The Headline Bank

The basic concept of the headline bank is to emulate existing headlines to create powerful new ones. Our headline bank contains over 175 headlines written both by us as well as some of the greatest copywriters of all time. Our consultants use the entire bank when creating headlines for their clients.

Here's a pared-down headline bank; it contains 15 headlines, enough to make the point. We call this subset of the headline bank "universal headlines" because they can be used by practically any company in practically any situation. They're essentially "one size fits all" headlines.

1. The Three Biggest Problems You'll Have With Most Plumbers, And How Mr. Burrows Overcomes Them All.
2. What The Eye Surgeons Don't Want You To Know.
3. Major Diet Plans: Which Ones Actually Work ... And Which Ones Are Guaranteed To Torture You, Cost A Fortune, And Leave You Fatter.
4. Three Fairy Tales You'll Hear From Brokers ... Even Honest Ones.
5. The Most Common Tax Mistake (You're Probably Making It Now).
6. A Dozen Dirty Tricks Of New Car Dealers. Most Are Totally Undetectable—Unless You Know What To Look For.
7. Four Critical Characteristics To Demand From Your Skip Tracing Agency ... Does Yours Do These?
8. Of Course You've Heard Of Laser Vision Correction. But Have You Heard Of AFFORDABLE Laser Vision Correction?
9. If Your Pharmacist Goofs, You Could Be Dead. How To Protect Yourself—Takes

Just Three Seconds.
10. How Much Should You Pay For A Good Pair Of Binoculars?
11. Something You Probably Didn't Know About Rolex Watches.
12. A Little Mistake That Cost A Farmer $3,000 A Year.
13. A Challenge To Women Who Would Never Dream Of Serving Margarine.
14. The Most Common Goof In Buying A House.
15. Every 15 to 25 Years, A Major Innovation Completely Changes The Face Of The Copier And Printing Industry. Guess What?

These headlines are full of hot buttons, and they interrupt and engage prospects. All you have to do is modify the content to fit your situation. Just read the headline and see if you can mold your business situation into that headline.

Headline 1 says: "The Three Biggest Problems That You'll Have With Most Plumbers, And How Mr. Burrows Overcomes Them All."

Applying this to the fencing company, we could write, "The Three Biggest Problems That You'll Have With Most Fencing Companies, And How Superior Fencing Overcomes Them All." This headline interrupts based on the problems and promises to educate all in one sentence. For all practical purposes, this headline interrupts AND engages. Could you rewrite that headline for your business as well?

Let's say your company produces premium corporate videos that are streamed to clients over the internet. Try using this headline: "The Three Biggest Problems That You'll Have With Most Internet Streaming Video Services, And How JVC Video Overcomes Them All." Now, you could easily come up with copy for this ad, couldn't you? All you'd have to do is a) identify the problems, and b) tell how you overcome them. Easy enough, wouldn't you say?

For the bank, this headline is: "The Three Biggest Problems Most Small Business Owners Have When Getting a Loan for $50,000 to $2 Million ... And How First Commercial Bank Overcomes Them All."

Did you notice that I added some qualifiers? I identified the target market— small business owners— and I specified loans from $50,000 to $2 million. Those words hit the reticular activator with more force and power and are more likely to interrupt and engage.

How about the second headline in the bank: "What the Eye Surgeons Don't Want You To Know."

That one's easy also: "What Most Fencing Contractors Don't Want You To Know."

For the bank: "What The Small Business Lending Banks Don't Want You To Know."

Monopolize Your Marketplace

With this headline it would be important to come back with an engaging sub-headline promising to educate the prospect if he keeps reading the ad.

Maybe you could then use Headline 4 as a subheadline: "Three Fairy Tales You'll Hear From Brokers... Even Honest Ones." That's a great headline for just about any business to emulate. But for the bank, after the main headline: "What the Small Business Lending Banks Don't Want You To Know,"

Here comes the subhead: "Three Fairy Tales Every Banker Will Tell You About The Loan Process... Even Honest Ones."

This subhead totally engages the reader, compelling him to continue reading to find out what those fairy tales are. For the wooden fence company, we could say: "Three Fairy Tales You'll Hear From Fence Companies... Even The Largest Ones." This would effectively interrupt and engage just about all prospects.

Okay, we skipped Headline 3. It reads: "Major Diet Plans: Which Ones Actually Work, And Which Ones Are Guaranteed To Torture You, Cost You A Fortune And Then Leave You Fatter." You've already seen that headline before. Remember the mutual fund company? We wrote: "Mutual Fund Investment Strategies: Which Ones Actually Work, And Which Ones Are Guaranteed To Drain Your Savings, Jeopardize Your Retirement And Squash Your Quest For Financial Independence."

This headline is pretty easy to reword for the fence company too: "Fence Building Methods: Which Ones Actually Work, and Which Ones Are Guaranteed to Leave You With Rotten Posts, Sagging Gates, and Warped Rails... and Force You To Pay For Another New Fence In Less Than Five Years."

This headline is full of hot buttons that interrupt and engage. See how the information from the discovery questions, particularly the *customer values* and the *need to know* questions, give us guidelines to know what to write?

You already know the hot buttons for the small business lending bank, so this headline is easy: "Small Business Lending Banks: Which Ones Will Actually Work For You And Which Ones Are Guaranteed To Promise You Whatever You Want To Hear, Hammer You With $1,500 In Hidden Fees, And Spit Your Unapproved Application Back At You Six Months Later."

Hot buttons! They're in there! How about Headline 6: "A Dozen Dirty Tricks Of New Car Dealers. Most Are Totally Undetectable—Unless You Know What To Look For."

The fence company would say: "Three Dirty Tricks of Wooden Fence Contractors. Most Are Totally Undetectable—Unless You Know What To Look For."

The bank would write: "Six Dirty Tricks of Small Business Lending Banks. Most Are Totally Undetectable—Unless You Know What To Look For."

How about Headline 10: "How Much Should You Pay For A Good Pair of Binoculars?"

The fence company would ask: "How Much Should You Pay For A Quality Wooden Fence That Will Last More Than Five Years?" And the bank would write: "How Much Should You Pay To Have Your Small Business Loan Packaged?"

Or Headline 14: "The Most Common Goof In Buying A House."

The fence company would say: "The Most Common Goof In Buying A Fence."

The bank would write: "The Most Common Goof Small Business Owners Make When Getting A Loan."

These headline bank headlines are already set up to force you to put the appropriate hot buttons in the appropriate places. The only way to mess them up is to have the wrong information from the discovery questions (which is possible if you have no experience doing this). So again, be careful. This sounds so easy, and it is for people with experience. It's easy for us because marketing is our business. If your marketing risk is high, I recommend you leave writing to professionals. But hopefully this section has at least given you a good understanding of how and why we do what we do.

Now, practice writing headlines for your company. If you're not sure you're doing it right, submit your headlines via email to headlines@mymbook.com and we'll get them out to a consultant in your area who would be happy to give some guidance.

Chapter 9:

Strategic Marketing Communications

Writing a master letter, creating advertisements, and pre-evaluating the effectiveness of what you have crafted is all part of strategic marketing.

Before we jump headlong into writing, I want to first review the difference between your strategic marketing plan and your tactical marketing plan. Strategic marketing has to do with what you say, how you say it, and who you say it to. It's the content of your message and positioning of your brand, company, or product. Your tactical marketing program has to do with the execution of that strategic marketing plan as far as generating leads, placing media, and implementing a follow-up system. We call the tactical marketing program "Franchising Your Sales System" because we show you how to systematize the entire process so that your marketing program is easy to implement and always consistent.

Right now, writing headlines and putting the information we gathered from the discovery questions into an attorney's case format is the strategic side of your marketing program. We're still trying to find the best way to state your company's inside reality, both in terms of what to say and how to say it.

The Master Letter

To that end, the next step in this process is to write what we call the "master letter."

The *master letter* is like a case briefing. It's a snapshot of your strategic marketing plan that utilizes all the information gleaned during the discovery process as well as the headlines you write. The *master letter* should follow the *marketing equation*—it should interrupt, engage, educate and offer. And, as the name implies, it's done in the form of a letter.

We call the *master letter* "the most important letter you'll ever write for your business even if you never send it to anyone." Why? Because once you write the *master letter*, you will have all of the information at your fingertips in a well-written, powerfully stated format that you can easily draw on to write any other piece of marketing you need. Need to write an ad for a magazine? No problem. Just adapt the *master letter*. Need a *Yellow Pages* ad? Same thing. Want to send a postcard? The words are right there in the *master letter*. Need content for your website? Guess what? It's in the *master letter*. Need to put together a marketing tool to further educate your prospects? The basic outline for that report can be found in the *master letter*.

Let's take everything we've gleaned about the bank and the fence company and synthesize them into *master letter.*

Here's the master letter for the bank.

First, note that, although this looks like a letter, there is no set format. Sometimes we'll put the headline on top so it stands out more, like on the fencing company *master letter*, and sometimes we'll make the first sentence of the first

paragraph the main headline, like on the bank's *master letter.*

Let's examine this *master letter* quickly. You'll find all the elements in a nice, tight package.

This *master letter* starts with the first sentence of the first paragraph like it's headline. It reads: "If you are a successful business owner, professional or entrepreneur, and are looking to expand your business and need to secure a business loan to finance new equipment, more land or more building space..."

Do you remember that headline? That's the headline we wrote using the plain English exercise. The hot buttons came from the answer to the first discovery question, which was the *qualification* question. In the *master letter*, the first paragraph continues,

"I would like to show you an easy way to get a small business loan with far less hassles, no hidden costs, and in less time than you could expect from traditional banks."

Boom: hot buttons. Right up front in the first paragraph, which in this case, doubled for the headline. All of this came from our plain English headline exercise.

The *master letter* continues: "My name is Ken Krovinas. I am the Vice President of First Commercial Bank. We are the largest small business lender in the state of Texas. And we do something that is unique to this industry in that we eliminate many of the problems small business owners traditionally have when trying to secure a loan to expand their businesses."

We've interrupted, engaged, and given the reader the promise that if he continues to read he will find information to help facilitate his making the best decision possible when it comes to getting a loan.

The letter now can shift into *educate* mode. The next paragraph tells about a survey that revealed frustrations in the industry and then previews the free report that we'll use for our *offer*.

After that paragraph, you'll see one of the headline bank headlines, which reads: "Three Problems Everyone Has When Trying To Get A Small Business Loan For $50,000 to $2 million."

That headline is straight from the headline bank. It engages by promising to educate the reader. Under the headline, we list each of the three reasons and a brief explanation. We don't go into all the detail we possibly could here; we'll leave that for the report. Remember, this is a case *briefing*, not the entire case!

Underneath those points, we move into the offer with a headline: "Don't Even Start The Loan Process Until You've Read This Revealing Report, What Every Business Owner Needs To Know About Getting A Business Loan." This headline allows readers from all points of the *educational spectrum* to gather more information without feeling threatened by high sales pressure. The rest of the letter then goes on to describe the report and how to get it.

Everything in the *master letter* is a compilation of the work we've done up to this point. The discovery questions and the headlines allow us to know what to say to interrupt and engage, as well as how to educate, and what to offer. It's easy to understand, but writing a master letter can be tough to pull off in real life. That's why I strongly recommend you consider hiring a professional marketing consultant if your marketing risk is high.

There is no set length or format for the *master letter*. If your case is detailed and there are multiple education points, then your *master letter* might be two or three pages long. Cover everything that needs to be covered. When you finish your *master letter*, you will often find that you could send out as a stand-alone letter. That was the case with the bank's master letter. We sent it as-is, and it generated 465 percent more leads—and at a fraction of the cost.

Sometimes you won't send the *master letter* out, but instead will only use it as a basis for creating other marketing pieces. That is the case with the fencing company's master letter. The main source of leads for the fencing company was the *Yellow Pages*, so we adapted the following letter into an advertisement:

Notice how we pulled the verbiage and headlines from the *master letter*. Now you can see why we call the *master letter* "the most important sales letter you'll ever write for your company, even if you never send it to anybody."

Creating An Advertisement

Now you're ready to put your marketing into an "ad" format. There are many ways to design, create and lay out advertisements. But let's start simple by using a basic advertising template. You may think that the ad must be "super creative" and "slicked out" to work. That makes our advertising template look "plain Jane." But even in black and white, this ad will work gangbusters because the *marketing equation* trumps all that other stuff. Here's the template.

HOT BUTTON- LOADED HEADLINE
That Interrupts Goes Here.
The Main Headline Above Along With This One Here Should Both Interrupt and Engage.

Engaging Headline That Promises To Educate Goes Here.

Type in your *Control* information here that helps support and build your case. Get info for these paragraphs from your Discovery Questions. Use as much specific detail as possible; but don't worry too much about the text because your **headlines and offer will pull most of the weight.** Your average paragraph should be *about this long*. A little longer won't hurt.

Continue To Hit Their Hot Buttons. One Line Or Two Is Fine.

Make sure that as you write your text that you remember to use the writing guidelines. **Write like people talk**; it makes you seem more relatable. Use *simple words* and *short sentences*. For example, instead of saying 'with regard to,' just say 'about.' Don't attempt to be cute; it won't work. And most of all...**DON'T try to be an English professor!**

Tagline or Logo Here.

This Headline Should Let The Reader Know That There's A Low Risk Way To Get More Inforamation.

Now you're in the home stretch! Make sure that all of your text supports your case... and remember to **quantify all of your claims**. Also, *use emphasis tools and punctuation*; there's several examples in this letter. But don't overuse them. Oh yes, one other reminder. The word **YOU** is the *second* most powerful word in marketing. *Use it!* (The *first* most powerful word is FREE).

☑ **FREE!** State Your Offer (with handle) For FREE Stuff

Name:_____
Company: _____
Address: _____
City, State, Zip: _____
Phone: _____ Fax: _____
Please Fax This To (555) 555-1212 or Call (555) 555-1212

Writing the Body Copy

Now we'll discuss how to write the *content* of your marketing communications so that your materials are easy to read, compelling, and powerful. Much of the impact of your ad must come from the headlines and the format that's based on the *marketing equation*. Many advertising and direct marketing gurus, however, treat writing the body copy as the most important aspect of getting results in advertising. The fact that I address this topic after covering the marketing equation should tell you something about how important I feel it is. The body copy is important. But unless you plan on becoming a professional marketing copywriter, you just need to learn the fundamentals to know if the copy is any good. You need to know what to look for to spot what's good and what's not. Actually doing it is a task that you may want to defer to others.

Let me give you some guidelines on how to write all of the stuff in between the headlines, sub-headlines and offers.

First, make sure your writing style is simple and conversational. Don't write like an English professor; instead, write the way you talk. This is the biggest trap for most people. They start writing, and all of a sudden big, fancy, flowery words start coming out. They use words they wouldn't normally use in everyday conversation. Complicated sentences and long words make it sound like you're intelligent, but they don't compel people to take action.

Rosser Reeves, one of the great advertising minds of the early 1900s, said it best when talking about the advertising copywriter's fondness for writing flowery prose instead of straightforward copy that sells. Reeves gives this analogy:

"Let's say you've got $1 million tied up in your company and suddenly, for reasons unknown to you, your advertising isn't working and your sales are going down. And everything depends on it. Your future depends on it. Your family's future depends on it. Other people's family's futures depend on it. I walk into this office and sit down in this chair to write your advertising. Now, what do you want from me? Fine writing? Do you want masterpieces? Do you want glowing things that can be framed by copywriters? Or, do you want to see the blankety-blank sales curve stop going down and start moving up?"

In advertising, make your writing style simple and conversational. That's the bottom line here.

Let me give you a better idea about writing in simple terms. I speak fluent Mandarin Chinese. Some people think that if you, as a North American, can speak fluent Chinese, you must be really smart. After all, Chinese is one of the most difficult languages in the world, right? Well, that's right and wrong. It's true that learning to read and write all those strange little Chinese characters is very difficult. But speaking Chinese, learning how to say the words and sentences, on the other hand, is surprisingly easy.

So what does that have to do with your marketing and advertising? The elements of Chinese that make it easy to learn to speak—once you understand them—will help you become a better writer of English. If you could apply the Chinese way of talking to our own language, without much effort you could form the habit of simple, clear, picturesque talk. Ultimately, your simple, Chinese-like writing will help you make more money.

I'll assume that right now all you know about Chinese is Kung Fu and chow mein, and you're not interested in adding to your Chinese vocabulary. So we'll do the next best thing: we'll study Chinese from the outside and get a basic idea of how it's put together. Chinese, to you, is an exotic language, written in weird Kanji characters and spoken in a sort of sing-song. It's true that the meaning of spoken Chinese words depends on musical "tones," which does add one element of difficulty to learning spoken Chinese. But if you look closer, you'll find that Chinese is really simple. Elements that make other languages difficult—conjugations, irregular verbs, subjunctives, genders and a host of other grammatical nightmares—are completely absent in Chinese.

Chinese is known as a "grammarless" language. It has no inflections, no cases, no persons, no genders, no numbers, no degrees, no tenses, no voices, no moods, no infinitives, no participles, no gerunds, no irregular verbs, and no articles. There are no words of more than one syllable. Every word has only one form. All you have to learn is how to put these one syllable words in their proper order. To make it still easier, this proper order is the same as the usual order in English: subject, predicate, object. You may wonder how it is possible to talk in such a language so that other people understand you; and maybe you think this must be the most primitive, uncivilized language of the world. That would be a common error: up to about 100 years ago all language experts agreed that Chinese is the "baby talk of mankind." They were wrong: it is the most grown-up talk in the world. It is the way people speak who started to simplify their language thousands of years ago and have kept at it ever since.

We know now that thousands of years ago the Chinese language had case endings, verb forms, and a whole arsenal of unpleasant grammar. It was a cumbersome, irregular, complicated mess, like most other languages—including

English. But the Chinese people, generation after generation, changed it into a streamlined, smooth-running machine for expressing ideas. It's just like the camera—remember the commercial? It's so advanced, it's simple. The main principle of modern Chinese is exactly the same as that of modern machinery. It consists of standardized, prefabricated, functionally designed parts.

In other words, Chinese is an assembly-line language. All the words are stripped to their essential meaning and purpose and put together in a fixed order. Word order is as important as the order of operations on the assembly line: if you line it up in any other way it doesn't work. If you wanted to say, "I am going home" in Chinese, you'd say "WO HWEI JYA" which means, "I go home." That's it. You wouldn't even have to say "I" because it would be understood. You could just say *"HWEI JYA"* or "Go home." And everyone would know exactly what you meant. See, there are no filler words. If you wanted to say, "I will be going home," You'd still just say, " *HWEI JYA.*" If you wanted to say, "She has six books" You'd say *"Ta you leo ben shu,"* meaning, "She have six book" What's more, the *she* doesn't even mean she. In Chinese it could mean he or she or it. There's only one word for all three of them. Meaning is determined by context.

The Chinese have stripped all the words to their bare meaning and put them together in a simple, predetermined order. They've lost most of the filler words that don't mean anything. In English, the most frequently used words are filler words. According to a study conducted by the British National Corpus and prepared by the Information Technology Research Institute at the University of Brighton, the 10 most frequently used words in English account for 25 percent of all words! Ten words account for 25 percent of our language! Those 10 words, in order of frequency, are: *the, at, of, and, a, in, to, it, is, was.* In English we spend a lot of time, effort and energy saying just about nothing!

How you can use the "It's so advanced, it's simple" lesson in writing your advertising? When you're talking to your prospects, you can't bog them down with all the flowery jibber-jabber and filler fluff words that just take up time, make them use extra brain power, and don't add meaning. You've got to use plain talk to clearly, concisely and quickly communicate your point. It is essential to powerful marketing communication that you "say it well." Use plain talk and you'll be well on your way to doing just that.

Here is a list of suggestions:

1. Use plain talk. Don't try to be an English professor. Write like people talk.

2. Use short sentences. The average should be about 17 words, 25 max. Don't try to stick two thoughts into one sentence. Use two short ones instead.

3. Use simple language. Use:
- A familiar word instead of a far-fetched one.
- A concrete word instead of an abstract one.
- A short word instead of a long word.

Instead of this...	Use this...	Instead of this...	Use this...
Encourage	urge	As to	about
Prior to	before	Continue	keep up
For the reason that	since	With regard to	about
Supplement	add to	In order to	to
Accordingly	so	Acquire	get, gain
In the event of	if	Likewise	and, also
Along the lines of	like	In accordance with	by, under
Nevertheless	but, however		

4. Use personal references: Examples: names, pronouns and human interest words. The best word you can use is *YOU*.

5. Use live words–verbs. Most writing contains nothing more than nouns and adjectives, glued together with the prepositions *is, was, are, and were.* Here are some examples of better verbs to use:

Bear	Blow	Break	Bring	Call
Carry	Cast	Catch	Come	Cut
Do	Draw	Drive	Drop	Fall
Get	Give	Go	Hang	Hold
Keep	Lay	Let	Look	Make
Pick	Pull	Push	Put	Run
Set	Shake	Show	Skip	Slip
Split	Stand	Stay	Stick	Strike
Take	Talk	Tear	Throw	Tie
Touch	Turn	Walk	Wear	Work

6. Evaluate all claims. Be specific and quantify everything:

Writing Evaluations:	Quantification Helpers:
Well I Would Hope So...	What Specifically?
Who Else Can Say That?	Why Specifically?
Well, Whoop-Dee-Do!	How Much Specifically?
Do You Really Believe That?	Typically?
Prove It.	Where Specifically?
What Conclusion Do You	When Specifically?
Want Me To Draw?	Compared To What?
Cross-Out / Write-In	According To Whom?
	Give Me An Example...

Six Things To Avoid At All Cost:
- Cute: "Cute" copy turns ugly when you get no response.
- Play on Words: Play on hot buttons, not on words.
- Company Name: Nobody cares who you are; they care what you can do for them!
- Profound: If you go too deep, your prospects will drown.
- Snoozer: If you snooze, you lose.
- Ego: Don't boast—just state the facts.

7. Use powerful headlines: Use headline starters or the headline bank.

8. Use the word FREE effectively. Don't give away your product, but do offer a FREE (but high perceived value) incentive or educational report.

9. Use short copy vs. long copy. Say as much as needs to be said, then quit. A good, easy-to-read format allows you to use more text. Use video or audio to say what might be too burdensome to read.

10. Talk features vs. benefits. Talk about benefits as much as possible. For example, a #2 pencil should give you some perspective on this:

Features:	Benefits:
Six inches long	Lasts an average of five months
Clay/Graphite composition	Lead won't break, even under high pressure
Pre-fired graphite	Produces dark, legible line

"E-Z-rase" additive	Easily readable, yet won't smudge
Core-locked	Lead won't break inside of pencil
Hexagonal shape	Won't roll off a desk; easy to hold
Lead is cradled evenly	Sharpens quickly and reliably
Bright yellow paint	Easy to see / find
Both paints are non toxic	Can chew without danger of poisoning
Silver-embossed pencil name	Easy to remember when reordering
Silver-embossed manf. name	Reinforces brand awareness
Silver-embossed hardness #	Won't use wrong pencil on test
Silver-embossed lettering	Nice to look at; reasonably classy
"Core locked USA" embossed	Encourages ordering American made
Grooved in two directions	Easy to hold while erasing
Seamless aluminum construction	Prevents nicking / snagging on seam
Bonded to wood w/pressure molding	Eraser is secured, stays rigid
"Flex-o-rub" composition	Erases quickly & cleanly

11. Use emphasis tools. Allow the reader to "hear" your voice tone and inflection while reading:

-**Bold**, *italics*, <u>underlined</u>, ALL CAPS, (parenthesis)

12. Use punctuation. Allow reader to "hear" your pausing and pacing while reading:

Pause	Between words	Between sentences
Normal pause	White space	Period
Shorter pause	Hyphen	Semicolon
Longer pause	Dash	Paragraph

Marketing Evaluation Worksheet

We created an important tool to help you answer one of marketing and advertising's most important questions: "How do I know if what I've written is any good BEFORE I run it?" I can promise you this: There's nobody who hates losing money on marketing that doesn't work more than me. We developed the Marketing Evaluation Worksheet to answer this question.

The worksheet is a way to evaluate and ensure that you're correctly implementing the *marketing equation* into your ads and marketing pieces. The worksheet has two sections. The top section has five parts to help you grade individual components of your marketing. It uses a scale of L-0 to L-5. (The L simply stands for "Level.") What we're gunning for is L-5 materials. The bottom section is where you tally your results and predict the performance of the ad as a whole. Notice that the worksheet follows the *marketing equation* for the first four parts:

- Interrupt for evaluating your headlines;
- Engage for determining whether your ad promises to educate and facilitate the prospect's decision;
- Educate for assessing whether you have built your case sufficiently;
- The Offer, evaluating whether you've sufficiently lowered the risk of taking the next step in the sales process.

Interrupt: Headlines

Points

_____

- L-0: No headline at all
- L-1: Company name or play on words; does nothing to beg the reader to continue
- L-2: Headline exists; ACTIVATORS are not HOT BUTTONS; False Beta Alert!
- L-3: Hot Buttons Activated; not articulated well; but still interrupts
- L-4: Good headline; interrupts prospect; work on intensity and tone to make it more powerful
- L-5: Powerhouse! Headline has proper intensity and tone and hits the right HOT BUTTONS

Engage: Promise To Educate & Facilitate Decision Making

Points

_____

- L-0: If Headline score is L-0, L-1, or L-2...then automatic score of L-0 here.
- L-1: Nothing in ad to make reader want to continue listening... no sub-headlines; no add'l info at all
- L-2: Contains sub-headlines that are NOT ACTIVATORS... reader gives up
- L-3: Reader can tell from scanning ad that there may be decision-facilitating to be found
- L-4: Use of ACTIVATOR-based sub-headlines gives reader promise of useful info in the ad
- L-5: Engaged! Reader quickly scans and becomes enthralled based on excellent sub-headlines

Educate: Building Your Case

Points

_____

- L-0: No case building materials present; maybe cute or institutional
- L-1: Some features generically listed; not quantified, not compelling; perhaps menu-board-style
- L-2: Relevant and important points at least listed but not developed; poorly quantified
- L-3: Relevant and important issues listed with some quantification; educates on a basic level
- L-4: Relevant and important issues detailed; educates prospect; builds a good case
- L-5: Educates as to relevant and important issues; then builds solid, well-quantified case; prospect truly controls information and says, *"I would have to be an absolute fool..."*

Offer: Lowering The Risk

Points

_____

- L-0: No offer at all
- L-1: Contact info present; nothing specifically mentioned as an offer
- L-2: Tells prospect to call for more information or to speak with a representative
- L-3: Offer easily detectable; no handle, offer not as motivating as it should be
- L-4: Good offer, gets prospect to take action—still does not capture widest possible audience
- L-5: Excellent offer with handle that draws in all NOW and FUTURE buyers; causes prospects on all points of the Educational Spectrum to take immediate action!

Interrupt & Engage: Format

Points

_____

- L-0: A total mess; try again
- L-1: Does not flow, no logical reason for any placements; haphazardly done; not professional
- L-2: Basic structure is in place; lacks power due to poor articulation, spacing, thought flow, etc.
- L-3: Structurally sound, flows reasonably well, some parts are still done poorly
- L-4: Proper use of type fonts and sizes on headlines, sub-headlines; spacing well done, etc.
- L-5: Reader can quickly scan and understand main points; knows exactly what action to take

---

Total Number Of Points: _____   **Divided By 5 =** _____ **This Is Your Marketing Writing Level: (L-** _____ **)**

What Your Score Means:

- L-0: Totally wrong concepts, try again. This is a waste of your money.
- L-1: Low interrupt value (False-Betas); does not engage, will get average situational results. Most ads are L-1.
- L-2: Interrupts, hot buttons possibly present but not well articulated; will get good situational results.
- L-3: Interrupts and engages; important and relevant issues defined; lacks power in articulation. Good results likely.
- L-4: Interrupts and engages; important and relevant issues defined; articulation is good. Great results likely.
- L-5: Well articulated, powerhouse ad interrupts and engages, gives reader control, leads to immediate action.

This worksheet not only lets you know whether the ad will work, but it also points out exactly which components of the ad are not working. This information allows you to fix those specific parts. The worksheet allows you to audit each individual component and find out why. Did it interrupt? Did it engage? Did it educate? Did it have an offer? You might discover the ad did interrupt, engage and educate. But there was no offer. Well that's why you didn't get the responses.

Now look at your marketing. Take what you have created (either on your own or with an ad agency) and evaluate it based on the *marketing equation*. I can guarantee that just about everything will come out at L1 or L2. With your new knowledge, you should be able to push that up to L3, good enough to leverage your marketing dollars and get you closer to creating a profit faucet. Our consultants can write L4 and L5 materials, which can put you on top of the heap.

But also do this: Grade your competitors' marketing materials using the Marketing Evaluation Worksheet. You'll discover they are in the L0/L1 situation as well, which gives you a huge competitive advantage if you utilize our program. What if you're advertising side-by-side with your competitor? What if your *Yellow Page* or newspaper ads share a page? What if you were on the same radio or TV station? Do you know what will happen if your stuff is L3 or L4 or L5 and their stuff is L0 or L1? Do you see what a difference that would make?

The moving company discovered this economic truth. The company went from 70 calls a month to an average of 955 calls. Do you think that was because there were more people in the *Yellow Pages* looking for movers? Or, do you think it's because more of the people who were already there looking are now calling our client and not calling the competitors. That's what L4 or L5 will do for you.

Understanding marketing gives you the ultimate power in the marketplace. It allows you to give and take life in business. If you are receiving 10 times more calls and your competitors are not getting those calls, you will benefit—they will suffer. This program is about winning in business!

Chapter 10:

Marketing Strategies

By following a few guidelines, you can learn to apply
the marketing equation to any business or industry.

To wrap up the "Strategic Marketing" section, I want to talk about general guidelines to help you implement the *marketing equation* for various businesses within certain industry categories.

We've identified six major industry categories; within those industry categories, the strategies are similar. Here's a quick list of six industry types with a rundown of the strategies for each.

- Trade service providers
- Professional service providers
- Mass retailers
- Specialty retailers
- Companies that sell to resellers
- Products sold to end-users. These can be split into two categories: products with a defendable position, and products with no defendable position or a "phantom position."

The industry category dictates which strategies you should use.

1. Trade service providers. What I'm talking about here are things like plumbers, roofers, funeral homes, copier repair, pest control, movers, landscapers, auto repair, hair stylists, printing companies and so forth. The reason the *Industry Category Strategies* work is because the hot buttons—the problems, frustrations, annoyances and situations—are common across the board within each service category. In the case of service providers, the hot buttons all revolve around one central theme: the lack of knowledge of what constitutes a good deal.

Remember: If you want to know why your prospects buy what they buy, you've got to see the world through their eyes. When it comes to buying your products or services, they are not experts on the subject. They don't know much about wood fences, auto repair, carpet cleaning, air conditioner service, or computer repair. So, you need to educate them what they need to know, what the standards are, and how to judge quality and value.

Service providers need to use the "Standard Bearer" strategy. This scares many service providers because they know that doing this will expose their crummy inside realities, or the fact that they don't provide fair value for the money. We say, "Good. Either go out of business and stop ripping people off, or start complying with high standards of doing business."

One time when working with a roofing company, we used the Standard Bearer strategy to educate consumers about how to judge a roofing company. In order to comply, a roofing contractor would have to produce for the customer 21 written statements and documents that prove that they are an elite company in terms of reputation, stability, workmanship, and professionalism. Our client was one of only a handful of roofing companies complying with all 21 standards. These standards included supplier lien waiver letters, certified installer licenses for all installers, 17-point sub-contractor agreements, comprehensive directories of past clients, letters of recommendations from banks, and liability insurance certificates.

Your strategy does not have to be that detailed. Sometimes, just producing a checklist of standards is enough. One time we worked with a "skip tracing" company that tracks down cars that are supposed to be repossessed by the bank, but the person "skips" with the car. This client had a good inside reality. We produced a checklist for its prospective customers to use when judging a skip tracing companies. We called the list the "17 Point Assured Recovery Checklist." It taught the banks everything they need to know, including what percentage of cases should be collected and how fast, the importance of liquidation reports, how many files an individual investigator should handle, how often files should be reassigned in the event of non-settlement, database searching capacities, access to credit reporting agencies, the need for trap lines, and insurance requirements. The checklist allowed them to *educate* their customers and prospects and capture 88 percent more business within nine months.

You can make this strategy even easier. Remember the headline bank headline for a plumbing company: "The Three Biggest Problems Everyone Has With Their Plumber, And How Mr. Burrows' Plumbing Overcomes Them All." That headline effectively interrupts and engages. But the ad copy needs to educate. What do you suppose goes in the copy—the three biggest problems everyone has when hiring a plumber! Those three problems are:

1. The plumber never comes when he says he'll be there, so you have to sit and wait.
2. They always charge more than they say they would over the phone.
3. They don't fix the problem right the first time.

See what we've just done? We've just set the standard for plumbers and told the customer that he should insist that any plumber comply. That's the easiest ad in the world to write, and it works about five times better than the average plumber ad!

One client used the same headline, word for word, for his copier repair company: "The Three Biggest Problems Everyone Has With Their Copier Repair Company And How ABC Copiers Overcomes Them All."
Guess what the three problems were? That's right: 1) The copier repair man never comes when he says he'll be there, so you have to sit and wait. 2) They always charge more than they say they would over the phone. And 3) They don't fix the problem right the first time.

How about an auto repair facility? Could you write that headline and ad: "The Three Biggest Problems Everyone Has With Their Auto Mechanic And How Cotton's Garage Overcomes Them All."

Now, you need to identify what those three problems are for the auto repair industry. But couldn't you agree that "repairs cost more than the quote" and "it doesn't get fixed right the first time" are ranked high! Within the service industry, the hot buttons tend to translate well from one kind of company to the next.

So, use the marketing equation: interrupt, engage, educate and offer. It works for all companies in all industries all the time. When you do your marketing this way, using MYM formulas and strategies, you can compete effectively in the marketplace, regardless of your size or years in business. Your customers won't care about how big you are. They *will* care about your ability to solve their problems.

Suppose a national chain of auto repair facilities runs a platitude-filled, menu-board style ad in the *Yellow Pages*. They fix brakes and transmissions and accept Visa and MasterCard and all the usual stuff. If we write an ad with our headline and educate prospects with need-to-know information, I can guarantee you that the ad will pull 5 to 10 times more calls than the menu-board style ad. Imagine what difference that would make in your business if 10 people call instead of the one who was calling before. Good marketing absolutely allows David to beat Goliath. Winning in business is a numbers game, and we don't need all the numbers to win.

2. Professional service providers. Professional service providers include people like financial planners, accountants, consultants, doctors, attorneys, and anyone else who sells their expertise. Most professionals mistakenly think that their marketing job is to convince prospects that they're the best because they've got the most experience, qualifications, or training, which makes them the most qualified to do the job. But that's not what marketing is supposed to do. Marketing is supposed to get the prospect's attention, facilitate their decision-making process, and give them a low-risk way to take the next step in the sales process.

Here's a scenario to help you understand how professionals *should* facilitate the decision-making process. I recently did a consultation with a tax planning expert. His firm worked with high-income individuals and figured out ways to reduce their tax bills every year. He told me that he wanted to do more business with dentists because they were notorious for being poor money managers. If you're a dentist, don't get mad at me—that's just what he told me.

He had been running an ad in an industry journal that went out to about 6,000 dentists in the region. His ad was the normal, platitude-filled crud you'd expect, and it pulled two leads a month. I told him that he wasn't seeing the world through a dentist's eyes. Imagine a dentist working on a patient, drilling and filling, but he is thinking about his finances, wondering what he might do to lower his taxes. He doesn't really know enough about the subject to draw any conclusion. He tells his patient to spit. He knows there must be some way to do it, but how? Go to a seminar? Buy a book? Hire a professional? He's definitely on the *educational spectrum,* but he doesn't even know where to turn for reliable information.

This is why professionals generally do so well with referrals. Since nobody understands what professionals do or how they do it, they default to hoping that a friend who's had a good experience can make a recommendation. That's all fine and dandy, unless you're the professional service provider who's trying to find new clients and who can't afford to sit around and hope your clients bring you referrals.

Later in the book I'll show you how to systematize a referral process, but first you need to know how to generate fresh business from scratch. Instead of running ads that extol how great you are because you've been in business forever and handled 50,000 clients and have all these degrees and credentials, you need to educate your prospects about *what you do* and *how you do it*. Teach your prospect how you get your results. Teach them what to look for, and put that information in a format that's easy for them to understand.

We call this strategy the *"Cliff's Notes"* strategy because you give the prospect a quick overview of your professional field. The idea is to download a condensed version of what you know into their brain. So they too can understand what you do and how you do it. They don't want to become experts, but they do want to understand what they are buying. All prospects want to know that they are dealing with an expert, right? All those sheepskins on the wall are external proof of expertise, but why not give them internal proof? Educate them as to what you know in an abbreviated format. Spend much of your time and ad space downloading your knowledge in a format that's easy to understand. Give them enough information to feel that they are now experts on our subject. That's marketing.

This approach is very powerful. And all other professional service providers can do the exact same thing. If you sell investments, tax planning, insurance, or any financial product, use this strategy to win new business. If you're a consultant, use this strategy. It's the only strategy that makes any sense.

Professionals are often scared to use this strategy because they think it will reveal their "secrets" and then their customers won't need them anymore. They'll start doing it themselves. That's false. Prospects don't want to do it. They just want to know that the professional they hire knows what he's doing! It's all about confidence, and there's no better way to instill confidence as a professional service provider than revealing your methods, procedures, and processes in a marketing tool a la *Cliff's Notes.*

How might a tax planner for dentists use the *Cliff's Notes* strategy? Suppose we use the headline: "Tax Planning Strategies For Dentists: Which Ones Actually Work And Which Ones Are Guaranteed to Send You to Prison, Deplete Most of Your Personal Profits, and Keep You Chained to Your Dentist's Chair Until Age 65 or 70." Any hot buttons there? Inside the report, define the investment strategies that work well for dentists. Show them the ins and outs. Show them how it works. Let them in on your little secrets. Give them a Cliff's Notes version of the inner workings of your brain, and your success is all but certain. What do you think this book, *Monopolize Your Marketplace*, is about? It's nothing more than a condensed version of what *we* know that will allow you to understand not only *what* we do, but *how* we do it.

3. Mass retailers. This includes retail stores that carry merchandise that's basically the same everywhere. Like the Ford dealership that has the exact same makes and models as the other Ford dealerships in the area, or a fitness store that carries basically the same brands, styles and models of treadmills and recumbent bikes as other similar stores. Most of the major national retailers are mass retailers—everyone from Wal-Mart and Target to Circuit City, Best Buy and Toys R Us. They're all mass retailers because they basically carry the same inventory as their main competitors.

But the definition of a mass retailer isn't limited to huge national companies. It could be any company of any size that carries inventory that is not unique and that is generally available at other stores. Either way, big or small, national or local, when developing a strategy for mass retailers, you can't simply build a case based on their inventory because there's nothing unique there.

Instead, we use a combination of two strategies. The first is called the "Consumer Reports" strategy where you help your prospects compare and contrast products on a brand-by-brand, side-by-side, head-to-head basis. See how that facilitates the decision-making process? You become the source of research for your products, so prospects don't have to do it themselves. The second strategy is called "Value-Added Services," meaning you've got to find ways to give more service or more value than your competitors, but at the same price as everyone else.

Let me show you how these two strategies would work for a mass retailer. Let's take the example of a fitness equipment store that specializes in treadmills, bikes, stair steppers, and weight sets. First, the store needs to implement the "*Consumer Reports*" strategy. The store owners would research, evaluate and investigate the various brands and styles of equipment for the consumer, then compile that information into an easy-to-read report.

For instance, if you want to focus on treadmills, you would research every treadmill on the market. You say, "Well, that's too many. I only want to evaluate the models that we carry." That's the wrong conclusion. Think about it from the prospect's viewpoint. How often does he or she buy a treadmill? Answer: Not that often! So, what do these prospect know about treadmills? Answer: Not that much! They might know the difference between the cheesy flimsy one for $200 and the more substantial one for $1,200 at Sears. But how can they tell the difference between the $800 one and the $1,200 one? And what about the one that's the top of the line at Sears for $1,499 that seems to be exactly like the low-end model at the specialty fitness store that costs $2,199? How do these compare that to the so-called "health club quality" model at that same store for $3,999? What's the difference? Your prospects can't tell. There's no way for them to know without walking into the store and being bludgeoned by the salesman.

I walked into one of these specialty retailers a few months ago to buy a recumbent bike. I found one at Sears for $400, but it was out of stock. I thought, "No problem. I'll run over to this little specialty store I had seen at the plaza shopping center just outside of the mall and see what they have." I found out that their lowest price model was $1,200, their mid-range was about $2,000, and their high-end models were priced at $3,000. The one from Sears appeared to have the same functionality as their mid-range, $2,000 model.

So tell me, why I should pay an extra $1,600 for this model? The salesman actually told me that "higher quality" and "better service" made it worth the extra money. Anyone's platitude meter getting into the red zone? I asked him what was "higher quality" about it. He couldn't say for sure. All he could say was that it would last longer. I asked him how much longer. He said at least double. How many years? He couldn't say. I said, "Wouldn't it be a better investment to just buy the less expensive model, and replace it as necessary? He had no answer. See how the customer feels here?

The *Consumer Reports* strategy is very simple. Research all the important and relevant issues regarding the product in question and compile a report. A good part of the information would come from the "Need To Know" question from your discovery process. Tell the prospect exactly what constitutes good quality and good service. Talk about the motor, the belt, the surface area, the controls, the display console, the functionalities it provides, its programmability, safety issues, response time, smoothness, comfort issues, warranty issues. Educate customers on all these issues and then rate every model according to all the issues. Figure out a way to tally the ratings into a master rating. Then compare the rating to the price of a given model and make recommendations for your customers in various price ranges. Tell them exactly what to buy and why.

What if you became their buying advocate? Say you rated 55 treadmills and, out of those, you picked 11 that you thought were the best buys, and you divided those 11 into three major price categories (like $400 to $600, $600 to $1,000, and

$1,000 and up.) Within each category you showed your winners and losers and then explained that you only carried the top 11 models that you found to be best buys.

Think about advertising treadmills in terms of the *marketing equation*. Instead of the ridiculous menu-board style advertisements that everybody else puts out there, you put an ad with the headline: "Compare And Price Out All 55 Treadmills On The Market Without Setting Foot In A Showroom And Without Talking To A Salesperson." With an engaging sub-headline that read: "Only 11 Models Passed Our Stringent Testing Procedures To Be Rated A Best Buy." Run that ad in the paper or on the radio or television and see what happens to your lead count and sales.

You'll catch everyone who's on the *educational spectrum* with this ad. You'll solve the prospect's biggest problem, which in this case is unfamiliarity which leads to uncertainty. You'll rack up marketshare like it's going out of style. You

would need to create the same type of report for all of the different categories that you sell. In the case of the fitness store, that would include treadmills, bikes, steppers and weight sets. And how about a section of each report that helps you decide which type of equipment is best for you

in the first place? It would be important from an advertising standpoint to use separate advertisements for each product category to get the full impact. That's the *Consumer Reports* strategy for mass retailers.

Now let's talk about the Value-Added Services Strategy. Simply put, you need to find ways to give your customers more than they would normally get for their money when buying from your competitors. Think of all the things that your customers need to buy in conjunction with what you're selling or things that they would have to pay extra for and might decide to do without. Identify these things and give them away for free as an incentive to buy from you. Depending on what you sell and your margins, this can be a quick and easy way to separate yourself from the pack.

Think about the fitness store and the treadmills. Let's say that the average gross profit for a treadmill was 30 percent. That means that for a treadmill that runs $500, there's $150 of gross profit. For a $1,000 treadmill, there's $300 gross profit. The idea is to think of related products and services that would make sense as a free bonus at the time of purchase.

Can you come up with a quick list of value-added products or services you could give away with the treadmill that would have a high perceived value but a low actual cost? Here's my quick list: Exercise books or videos, Walkmans or MP3 Players, running shoes or apparel, a three-month supply of Gatorade or bottled water, a subscription to a fitness magazine, health foods or supplements, passwords to a special Web site that allows customers to track their progress on an online journal, motivational posters, free weights, and a monogrammed sweat towel.

If you don't want to stock the gift, at least provide gift cards or certificates for them. Just put your brain into gear and see what you can come up with. Package some of these things together as part of your standard deal and you'll see how powerful this simple strategy is. In the section on Marketing Tools, I'll give you a specific example of how a piano retailer used a combination of the *Consumer Reports* and *Value-Added Services* strategies.

4. Specialty retailers. Unlike mass retailers, specialty retailers can concentrate on building a case for their unique products. Here's a quick example: We had a client who ran an upscale consignment furniture store that only carried nice stuff in excellent condition. They spent almost $20,000 on radio advertising that was junk: "We have sofas, bedroom sets, and lamps. We only sell the finest stuff. We're committed to pleasing our customers. Blah, blah, blah. Our store is located at such-and-such shopping plaza. We're open from 10 to 6 every day." The lack of results proved that this advertising was horrible. Like many business owners, the boss concluded that "radio advertising does not work for a furniture store."

But the problem wasn't the tactical deployment of a radio ad. It was his poor strategy. First, he hit no hot buttons. He didn't say a word about the uniqueness of the items. He did not tell the story of how the richest people in the area, people who have over $2 million in net worth, changed their furniture every two to three years instead of every seven to 10 years like everybody else, explaining why his second-hand stuff was extremely high quality and in almost-new condition. He never mentioned that 70 percent of his inventory changed every two weeks so there was always something new to choose from. He never educated and told his story. He assumed that using platitudes to tell people he had nice stuff would be enough. He assumed that the next step in the buying process was for the prospect to come into the store and browse. Sounds reasonable, right?

The second problem was, he was missing a step. He assumed that everyone was just waiting to hear his ad so they could finally find a place to empty their wallets. Wrong. Since *nobody* had ever heard of this store, they needed a low-risk way to find out more about it before they would even invest the time to check it out. He needed an offer to capture a larger percentage of the people on the *educational spectrum*.

We helped him implement what we call an "Inventory Update List," a document he printed every week listing everything new that arrived in that seven-day period. Then, on the radio ad, after telling his unique story, he offered customers a low-risk option. They could call and request a free Inventory Update List. The ad did not emphasize actually coming to the store.

The results? Walk-in traffic tripled, and his staff took over 30 calls a day from people who just wanted to be on the Inventory Update list. Once they got someone on the list, they had the ability to contact them as many times as they wanted with an opportunity to sell. For the specialty retailer, the *Industry Category Strategy* defines your specialty position, then builds a case for it.

Specialty retailers would include just about all restaurants. The reason to go to a particular restaurant is that the food is unique, the atmosphere better, the selection different, or the prices are higher or lower. Every restaurant has its unique position, and the marketing for each restaurant must build a case to defend that position and explain why people need to eat there, not somewhere else. Same thing would go for health clubs, spas, golf courses, and other entertainment venues.

If you fit into this industry category, stake your unique position in the marketplace and then build a compelling case to prove to your customers and prospects that you are truly unique. Specialty retailers also can utilize the mass retailer strategies of *Value-Added Services*, and *Maximizing and Optimizing* strategies that I will discuss later.

5. Companies that sell to resellers. In general, I am talking about manufacturers; however, many manufacturers also sell directly to the end-user. So, I'm talking about any company that makes something and sells it through an external distribution channel. (Manufacturers who sell directly to consumers need to use the end-user strategy that I'll touch on next.)

The industry strategy for manufacturers that sell through distribution is called *Make More Money*. When manufacturers are selling to a distributor, they need to know that only one hot button is of any real importance to a distributor—making money. Most manufacturers, however, rely on poor marketing that focuses on how great the products are. I guess this is because the manufacturers are very proud of those products. But the distributors only care about making money. So, the marketing program that is directed to those distributors should focus on how they can make more money. All of the great features of the products only serve to support the theory that end-users will want the products, so the distributor will make more money!

At the end of this book, I'll give a detailed example showing how this strategy helped a company that manufactures coin-operated pool tables, air hockeys, foosballs, and video-game cabinets go from near bankruptcy to industry leader.

6. Companies that sell products to end-users. I'm not talking about retailers here; instead, I'm talking about the merchandise being sold, either by a retailer or directly from a manufacturer or a distributor, to the end-user. The key is that the advertising message is geared toward the end-user. In the case of the car dealership, the dealership would be a mass retailer, and would need to use the appropriate strategy. The manufacturer of the car, however, would need to run advertising under the model of *Sells to End-User*. If a manufacturer sold through distribution and advertised to end-users to stimulate sales, they would have to use one strategy to recruit resellers (the make-more-money strategy I just described) and another one to convince end-users to buy those products.

Most of the consumer advertising we see on television and in magazines is for products that fit into this category. Think of all the ads for cars, beer and soft drinks, food, and cleaning products. The key to getting the strategy right is to know whether the product has a defendable position in the marketplace, or, if the product has to make up a position. Let me clarify the difference.

When I say a product has to make up a position in the marketplace, I'm talking about products like soft drinks, toothpaste, laundry detergent, gasoline, and other consumer products and packaged goods that you simply can't build a bona-fide case for because there is no foundation for building a case. The strategy here has to do with creating a position for that product and advertising as though the attributes being promoted were real.

For example, take Pepsi Cola. There is no bona-fide, defendable position for Pepsi since the only attribute the product has is taste, and taste is a subjective thing. Back in the 70s, Pepsi tried to build a case based on the Pepsi Challenge and convince people that Pepsi was the preferred taste, but nobody believed them because they knew that Coke and Pepsi tasted basically the same, and that's why nobody could win the challenge.

So, Pepsi gave up the Challenge in favor what we call a *Phantom Position*—a position that doesn't really exist. The Pepsi phantom position is that Pepsi is for young people and for people who want to act or feel young. Pepsi is for the rising generation—the Pepsi Generation. They attach this position to their product and then work on building a case based on hot buttons that exist in people's minds, but that their product, in reality, can't solve. A can of sugar water does not make you feel younger or more hip.

That's why we call this the *Phantom Position* strategy. It is impossible to build a case to prove that Pepsi makes you feel younger than Coke. You just can't do it. But Pepsi spends over a $1 billion a year with Britney Spears or the celebrity of the moment to convince you otherwise. This is where institutional advertising comes from. Attach a feeling to a product and hope people will buy it. This is the realm of C&R advertising. If a company has $2 billion to make people believe their product is a solution to the hot buttons they've pushed, then it can be very compelling.

If you're selling a product without any defendable position, then this strategy might work for you. Here's the problem. Few companies in the world sell such products. So few, in fact, that there's a 99 percent chance that this strategy doesn't apply to you. Most companies that sell to end-users have products that do have a defendable position, and yet they still advertise and market using the *Phantom Position* strategy.

You can stake out an actual *Defendable Position* for everything from computers to pianos to cars to cruises to watches—even for products that are less sophisticated like shoes, furniture, lawnmowers, bug killer, pens and books. Many companies mistakingly use the *Phantom Position* strategy and churn out institutional ads whose main purpose is to instill a feeling when the *Defendable Position* strategy would be more appropriate.

In the case of a *Defendable Position*, the strategy is simple: Identify the hot buttons and build a case. That's it. It's the essence of good marketing. All advertising and marketing efforts need to follow the *marketing equation*. A good example of doing this *wrong* is a recent advertising campaign for Hewlett Packard. These ads are C&R at its pinnacle, with a tagline that simply reads: "Invent." I found one of its print ads in the copy of *Inc.* magazine—it's an ad for one of HP's multi-function business machines that prints, scans, faxes and copies. The ad shows a picture of the machine, which is helpful for people who are in the market for a copier, because their reticular activators will hone in on the picture. It will motivate those people who are already on the *Educational Spectrum* to go from Alpha Sleep to Beta Alert mode.

Then, as soon as the brain starts to search for clarifying information, HP drops the ball. The copy is small, hard to read, and full of platitudes. "Wouldn't it be great if a single decision could solve multiple business problems? It can, if that decision is to buy an HP Multifunction Printer. If you need a business machine that can print, color scan, copy and fax, an MFP is the answer. It can even scan documents. . .blah, blah, blah. Factor in HP's reputation for reliability and support, and the decision's a real no-brainer. To find out more, call…." Then HP has its little logo with the word "Invent" under it.

This specific product is called the 9000 MFP. In my office I have what's known as a Brother MFC 9600. HP can't even come up with unique names for this stuff, let alone unique products that warrant the tagline "Invent!" Not only is the copy full of platitudes, the offer is horrible. This ad only caters to urgent buyers who are on the far right-hand side of the *educational spectrum*, the ones in so much pain they'll buy the first thing presented as a solution. Think about it: If you were in the market for one of these types of machines, would the HP ad do what marketing is *supposed* to do—facilitate your decision-making process and lower the risk? No way.

Now I can guarantee you this: By the time this ad ran, multifunction machines like the one described in this ad have been around for years! Every manufacturer makes them. So let me ask you this: Does this ad build a case that supports the word "Invent"?

The obvious idea here is that the folks at HP are innovative and invent cool stuff. In reality, HP is a very innovative, forward-thinking company. Its engineers push the technology envelope and are responsible for many new and outstanding product developments. Its inside reality for quality, innovation, and leadership is solid. But you can't tell this by looking at these ads. Instead, HP opted for the *Phantom Position* of "Invent" for an institutional ad. HP's inside reality and the outside perception don't match up. If instead, the company built a case and demonstrated the inside reality, the brand image that it's trying to promote would clearly shine through. As it is, from the prospects' standpoint, there's no proof that HP does anything different or better than anybody else. All things appear equal. Guess what this leads to? Price shopping.

If a company is marketing a product with a defendable position, then its strategy should be to build a case for the inside reality of that product. Its executives should identify hot buttons and articulate a quantified, specific case with evidence to back up all claims. When you build a case properly, you automatically build a brand image based on your actual, legitimate inside reality. In other words, if HP wants people to think of the company as innovative, don't spew platitudes and tag the ad with the word "invent." Instead, build a case for HP's unique and innovative products, and let the case speak for itself. Then the tagline "invent" becomes the flag on top of the mountain called innovation. It becomes a symbol of everything HP's inside reality is about. It means something.

As the ad stands now, there's no proof that the company is inventive. So, the prospect discounts everything the ad says. "Invent" is a flag, but it's not on top of any mountain! Any idiot can have a flag. It takes some serious marketing prowess to set that flag on top of the mountain.

And what if a product that *should* have a defendable position is not particularly different than its competitors? What if you *can't* build a case that warrants separation, distinction, and leadership? Then the product does not *deserve* special attention, *deserve* to lead its category in sales, or *deserve* to have its flag on top of any mountain. If that's your product, then you need to go back to the discovery questions and innovate your product and your company to offer something that is worthy of praise, attention, and dollars.

If you're selling beer, soda pop or shampoo, then you might have to invent a *Phantom Position* —and plant that flag on top of a mountain that doesn't exist and spend lots of money to convince people that there is a mountain there. On the other hand, if you are marketing a product with a defendable position, then build a case for that product based on its unique and innovative inside reality. That unique and innovative inside reality will build a brand image that's fitting. That car manufacturers don't do this—and instead opt for institutional, phantom position ads—is a testament to how messed up marketing is.

Remember that these *Category Strategies* are guidelines. If you need help figuring out where your company fits, give us a call. Also remember: The Industry Strategies are just strategies, not complete marketing plans. They still have to be tactically executed and implemented, which is what I'll address next. Every company needs to implement *Maximization and Optimization* strategies as well. This section is not your marketing plan. It gives you guidelines to help you devise your strategy that will anchor your entire marketing program.

Tactical Marketing Program

At some point you have to execute your strategic plan.
Here's how to do it—and do it right.

In this section, I'll talk about your tactical marketing program, what we call *Franchising Your Sales System*. I'll give an overview of the importance of systemization. Then, I'll cover the principles of lead generating, marketing tools, hopper systems, and knock-down lists. I'll also discuss what we call *maximizing and optimizing* your marketing program, which are more advanced tactical execution strategies.

There's an old Chinese saying that says, "Victory goes to the one with superior forces at the point of contact." We've spent the first part of this program talking about your strategic marketing plan. In the context of the ancient Chinese saying, we've been making sure that you have superior forces.

Now, you need to make sure that your superior forces are at the proper point of contact—at the right place at the right time. Your strategic marketing plan has to do with what you say, how you say it, and to whom you say it. Your tactical marketing program, on the other hand, has to do with the execution of that strategic marketing plan to generate leads, place media and implement a follow-up system. We call the tactical marketing program *Franchising Your Sales System* because it has to do with systematizing the entire marketing and sales process so that your marketing program is consistent and easy to implement.

Chapter 11:

Franchising Your Sales System

*If you don't have a system to your marketing, you'll be stuck
in a hit-and-miss mode that wastes time, talent, and money.*

Franchising your sales system has everything to do with systemization. You make decisions ahead of time and put a mechanical process in place that eliminates the need for constant, crunch-time decision making. This system allows you and your people to produce at peak levels.

Think about the way a McDonald's is set up, and you'll understand the great power of systemization. There's a reason McDonald's is the biggest company in the fast-food industry. And it's not because they have the best food. It's because they have, by far, the best systems for doing everything from operations to sales. It may not be the greatest hamburger in the world, but at least it's consistent. When you go into any McDonald's, you see the menu with pictures of the food in case you can't read. You just look at the picture and tell them what you want. It's idiot proof. The system sells the food. You don't have to rely on employees to tell you about the food. They just ask you the magic question: "May I take your order please?" and then add, "Would you like an apple pie with that, sir?" It's all scripted.

The grills and ovens at McDonald's have two preset positions: on and off. They don't leave it up to employees to figure things out. They've got French fry measurers, automatic timers, and automatic soda pop machines. Last week I got a drink at the drive through and looked at the cup and thought, "Amazing! There are lines on the back of the cup to tell the guy how much ice to put in it."

You don't have to be systematized to that degree, but you can learn from the power of a system. For example, a martial arts master doesn't have to think what punch to throw or how to react to the opponent's move. Thinking wastes valuable time and gives an opponent an advantage. A master is already programmed what to do. It's automatic. He makes it automatic by predeterming every move, every strike, and counterstrike. He knows how to react to anything his opponent throws at him. He programs his mind by practicing every day, week after week, year after year, until it's automatic.

Remember the movie, "The Karate Kid?" The old Japanese master was trying to train the kid's brain and body to react automatically. Remember he had the kid wax the car and paint the fence. "Wax on. Wax off. Wax on. Wax off. Paint up. Paint down. Paint up. Paint down." He had the kid condition his mind and body so that when it came time to fight, he didn't have to think. His hands automatically did what they needed to do.

That's really what I'm talking about when I talk about *Franchising the Sales System*. I want you to figure out, in advance, all the situations that could arise, and then set up your marketing system to handle them.

You need to put systems in place to:

- Generate the leads.
- Follow up on those leads immediately.
- Educate the prospects via marketing tools.
- Use a hopper system to continually follow up on those leads.

You can systematize far more than you even thought possible. You can systematize the follow-up letters and procedures, the phone scripts, the element of "surprising" your customers, the "thank- you's," problem handling, lead generation— everything. You can even systematize the passion. Hey, you're the eagle in the business, right? Not the duck. You're the leader, and you're in charge. You've got to find a way to get your people to deliver the passion that you have for the business.

Obviously, at some point there will be a sale made, many times by a salesperson, sometimes by an order-taker. It depends on your business. Make sure that every step of your marketing program facilitates the decision-making process of the prospect so that the actual close becomes easy. We let the "franchised" marketing system do the heavy lifting in the sales process, and let the salesperson wrap up the details. The key is to get each component of the tactical system right.

This includes the lead generators, the marketing tools, and the hopper systems. Let's discuss each one.

Lead Generators

When it comes to generating leads for your business, you must first determine whether you're selling to a defined or a non-defined target market.

A defined target market means that you can identify and list your target market. You can obtain this list and cost-effectively market directly to them all via mail, email or fax using a hopper system. This is an important distinction, because you won't need to spend money on lead generation using radio, television, newspapers, and billboards to reach this group because you've already got the entire list of prospects available at your finger tips.

Why would you spend money to try to find people who are somewhere on the *educational spectrum*, then get them out of alpha mode and into beta mode, and finally have them respond to an offer to become further educated, when you can just gather a list of everyone who could possibly buy what you sell and market directly to them on an on-going basis?

Just treat the entire target market like hot prospects. For example, if you sell a water treatment device to dentists within a certain geographic area, you can identify and obtain a list of dentists and market directly to them. If you sell coin-operated pool tables to amusement operators and know that there are only 5,000 of these amusement operators in the country, again you can identify these people and obtain this list. Or, if you own a staffing service that provides IT professionals to companies with over 1,000 employees, you can pinpoint these companies and obtain a list.

Obviously, once you market directly to those prospects, you will identify some who are not on the *educational spectrum*—prospects who don't have the problem that you solve. There are dentists who don't need or don't want water treatment devices. There are amusement operators who don't want your pool tables. There are large companies that don't need your IT employees. Maybe they already have a relationship with another supplier. So it might seem like a waste of money to send marketing materials to prospects who don't want or need what you're selling.

But, think about the alternative. Any lead-generating activity you do—for instance, placing an ad in the regional trade publication looking for prospects who have a certain hot button in their reticular activators—will likely cost a lot more money than going straight to your target market. Any lead you generate would ultimately be on the list of prospects that you could obtain anyway. If that list contained every single prospect within that geographic area, you don't need to generate leads. Instead, just go start using marketing tools and hopper systems to harvest sales out of your defined target market.

Here's the advantage. If you go straight to your list of prospects and send them a mailer, an email message or a fax and you do it consistently, then you can increase sales. You'll sell to those already on the *educational spectrum*. And you will also push several more onto it by bringing up problems, frustrations, and annoyances that they may not have realized. If you send marketing pieces to prospects and talk about the dangers of a problem they are experiencing *and* how your solution eliminates it *and* you build a case for how your machine works *and* how every other solution falls short *and* you bombard the prospects 78 times a year with well written, *marketing-equation*-based, strategic marketing pieces, how can they ignore that message? Some prospects will get something stuck in their reticular activators and become interrupted. It's impossible for this not to work, assuming you've formulated your strategic message properly.

We once consulted with a company that sold car batteries to auto parts stores and mechanics' shops in seven states. We discussed their strategic marketing plan and then shifted to tactical implementation. He was afraid we might propose an expensive and comprehensive media plan. I said, "Let's think about this, Jim. Would the most effective way to reach these mechanics and store owners be to run TV commercials?" He looked confused. I said, "Of course not. Why would we spend money on TV to find these guys?" What about radio? We could buy up time on 100 stations in the seven-state region and get the message to the target market that way." He was starting to catch on. So I continued, "What about newspapers? We could put a full page ad in the *Dallas Morning News* and catch some of those mechanics there."

Then I asked the magic question. "How many mechanics and auto parts stores are there in the seven-state region? He said about 12,000. More than 2,000 of those were already in their database, and we could easily and inexpensively identify the other 10,000. At that point, we bought a list, used some parameters like annual sales and number of employees and number of locations to cut the list to about 5,000 prospects and then launched a hopper system. It worked like a charm. The owner enjoyed a huge return on investment. Welcome to the defined target market.

So, next question: What's a *non-defined* target market? You have to rely on a lead-generating strategy to reach this market. Simply put, you've got a non-defined target market if:

1. You cannot identify, pinpoint and obtain a comprehensive list of your target market or

2. If that list is too huge to manage in a cost-effective way. If there are 1.8 million people on that list, you'll probably need to look into using the media to generate leads.

Here are a few examples to clarify the difference:

- You sell insurance to high-risk drivers in a major metro area. Industry statistics show over 1.3 million drivers fit your profile. That kind of a list is just too big to manage. You'll have to advertise to find the ones who are on the *educational spectrum* and sell to them.

- You sell computer training to people who are making a career change and entering the IT field. There's no way of knowing who, specifically, is interested in changing careers, so you cannot pinpoint this list of people. You'll have to advertise and generate leads.

- Look at us. We sell marketing consulting services to businesses. Businesses of all sizes are good prospects for us, from start-ups clear up to Fortune 500 companies. There are over 13 million businesses in the United States alone, not to mention tens of millions more world-wide. That list is just too big to manage. So we run advertising, generate leads from companies who are somewhere on the *educational spectrum,* and then focus our marketing efforts on those prospects.

Look at your target market and decide whether they represent a defined or a non-defined target market. If the target market is defined, there is no need to read the lead generation section that follows. You can go straight to the sections on marketing tools and hopper systems.

Determine Which Media to Use

If your target market is non-defined—if you can't pinpoint, identify and obtain a list of prospects—you've got to figure out the most cost-effective way to generate leads through advertising.

How do you determine which media to use to generate a lot of high-quality leads? Remember the saying, "Victory goes to the one with superior forces at the point of contact"? All we're doing here is trying to determine what those points of contact should be.

Often our clients will feel overwhelmed at the thought of lead generation since there are so many media choices. But if you break the media down into major categories, you see that there are basically only *10 ways to generate leads*: television, radio, newspapers, magazines, telemarketing, Internet, signs, trade shows, directories (like the *Yellow Pages*), and mail.

You can break these 10 categories into sub-categories, of course. Television comes in two flavors: broadcast or cable. The newspapers category includes local dailies, national, specialized and free distribution. Internet subcategories are banner ads, search engines and email. You can send letters, postcards, oversized, card decks, piggyback mailers, among others in the mail category. Signs include billboards or the message on the little stick that separates your groceries from the next guy's at the supermarket checkout.

But there are only 10 major categories, and this is good. Here's why. There are only a few kinds of media that make sense for *your* business. If you run the local dry cleaners, you probably don't need to run a Super Bowl ad. Let's take the example of the moving company. Advertising on television probably isn't the way to go. Neither is the newspaper or the radio. Why? Because people usually aren't even on the *educational spectrum* until they're close to making the selection decision. And when they do make that decision, they usually go to the *Yellow Pages*. It is *possible* to find prospects who are on the *educational spectrum* on TV, but why not go directly to where most prospects are? I always suggest fishing where there are the most fish. It increases your odds dramatically. Then, if you have the most appetizing bait, you'll catch the most fish. The strategic marketing plan is all about having the most appetizing bait.

Casting Your Line

Now, where do you cast your line? Here's a simple four-step formula to use: 1) think, 2) ask, 3) check, and 4) survey. Sadly, few agencies use this simple formula. Big ad agencies wouldn't dream of using it because it would prevent them from wasting enough of their clients' money.

Here's what the formula means.

First, think about what advertising media will likely work best. Here's an annotated list of the media.

✔	R.I.		✔	R.I.		✔	R.I.	
		Newspaper - Local Daily			Telemarketing			Mail - Letters
		Newspaper - National			Internet - Search Engines			Mail - Postcards
		Newspaper - Free Distrib.			Email			Mail - Piggyback
		Radio - Local, Spot			Signs - Trucks, Movie Screens, etc.			Mail - Card Decks
		Radio - National Network			Billboards			Yellow Pages
		Television - Broadcast			Cross Promotions			Other Directories
		Television - Local Cable			Flyers, Doors Hangers			Other
		Classified Ads			Trade Shows			Other
		Magazines			Trade Journals			Other

Notice we've broken each category into sub-categories so you'll have everything you'll need. Next to each listing you'll find two boxes. Put a check in the first box if you think that media would be a good fit. You may already have a good idea; if you are just starting out, trust your gut feel. Don't worry about whether you're right or wrong. This is only the first step out of four! Nobody's telling you to spend a fortune on your gut feel! Just check everything that seems appropriate. If you're not sure, but it seems like a definite maybe, go ahead and put a check.

The box next to that rates the relative importance of each of the media you've checked. If you think a particular medium is a sure hit for your business, then rate it a 10. If there's another medium that you think you ought to be using, but you're not sure, maybe that rates a 5.

Rate these media as to their usefulness. If you've used television with great success in the past, and you've used direct mail with great success in the past, you can rate both of those as 10s. If you have an idea that online advertising would work for you, but you've never used it, put that as a 2 or 3.

Second, ask your customers which media they access. Just ask your customers:

- What magazines do you read?
- What radio stations do you listen to?
- Do you read the newspaper? Which one? Which sections?
- Do you use the Internet?
- Do you have email?
- Do you attend seminars?
- Do you read books?
- Do you read faxes?
- Do you use the *Yellow Pages*?

Ask anything that would be helpful in your situation. If you think that the newspaper is a good place to generate leads, you can then ask them specifically what they think. They can then either confirm or refute your thoughts.

Sadly, most businesses are just too lazy, apathetic, or ignorant to do this. They would rather gamble their budgets on their own personal opinions about what their customers will respond to. Your opinion is the place to start, yes! It allows you to know *what* to ask your customers. But then it is much better to deal with facts. Don't assume that your customers listen to a certain radio station or read a particular magazine. Ask the customers, and then listen closely.

We had a client that manufactured rubber stamps. He felt being in the *Yellow Pages* was a good point of contact, and we agreed. His dilemma, though, was which section should he put his ad? Would you put it under R for "Rubber Stamps" or just S for "Stamps" or O for "Office Supplies"?

His ad had run in the "Rubber Stamp" section the previous year and got poor results. So, we helped him rewrite his ad and create a better strategic marketing plan. We had someone on his staff randomly call 150 businesses and ask this simple question: "If you needed to order a rubber stamp, the kind you would use to stamp a return address on an envelope, what section of the *Yellow Pages* would you look in?" Almost 75 percent said they would look under "office supplies." The total time investment was four hours, but those four hours made a big difference that next year.

Take the time to ask and save yourself a lot of headache.

Here's another example. Before we came on the scene, a Lexus dealership signed a contract to buy $47,400 of ads each month on an "easy listening" station that supposedly reached people with a lot of money. However, the platitude-filled ads didn't pull in many prospects. After a year of placing these bad ads on this station, they decided to poll their customers and find out if they heard their radio ads. Only six out of 458 people surveyed ever listened to that station! And none of those six remembered hearing their ad! As it turned out, the people they were selling cars to listened to hip hop music, country music, and classic rock. Remember, victory goes to the one with superior forces at the point of contact. You've got to make sure you've to the right point of contact!

Third, check those media to see if any companies similar to yours are already advertising there. Remember, the formula says, "think, ask, check and then survey." Take the answers and conclusions from the first two steps and check into the media that seem like they're a good fit.

Here's what you're looking for: You want to see if similar businesses are advertising there already. If not, be wary—there is probably a reason. Don't ever assume that all your competitors must be stupid to not have figured out to advertise where you're about to advertise. Don't think, "Wow! Great! I'll get all the business because I'm the only one!" It rarely works that way. Instead, it is more likely that other people have already tried unsuccessfully and quit before they lost all their money.

Here's another story from the same stamp manufacturer. The owner had been looking for some other media outlets that would drive in more business besides the *Yellow Pages*. Soon media salespeople started showing up on his doorstep by the droves. One of them was the salesperson for *The Thomas Registry of Manufacturers*, a comprehensive directory of North American manufacturers primarily used by industrial buyers to source products and parts. It's a wonderful place to advertise for many manufacturers, but not for those in the rubber stamp business.

The salesperson was persistent: "You're a manufacturer. You really ought to be in there. One small ad (five inches tall by one inch wide) is only $3,200 for the whole year. Besides, you'd be the only one with a space ad in the section. Everyone else in the section just has a line listing. Anytime anyone went there to find a stamp manufacturer, you'd be sure to get all of the business."

Don't bite on that hook. There's a reason nobody else's ad is there—they've tried it, and it didn't work! Unfortunately, the stamp guy bought the ad anyway, and nobody called. And since he was the only one with an ad in the book, it's a safe bet that zero people had looked there for their rubber stamp needs.

Sadly, the second year, he renewed the ad and managed one call.

What was the main problem? People who buy rubber stamps have never even heard of *The Thomas Registry of Manufacturers*! They either call their office supply company or look in the *Yellow Pages* under "Office Supplies." In this case, the customer told him that they wouldn't look in *The Thomas Registry of Manufacturers* for stamps. You see, they voted with their dollars. But he didn't figure it out until he wasted over $6,000.

When it comes to advertising, being one of the pack is often better than being the lone dog. While this is not always true, this guideline can help you make the best decisions most of the time.

Car dealerships understand this principle. For all the goofy, weird stuff they do, they do understand the principle of being one of the pack. They clump all their ads in one section of the newspaper because they know that this method is more likely to increase the number of people who see any given ad. They get all the car-buying eyeballs directed to just one section of the paper. In addition, the dealerships like to locate next to one another. They figure that if they can attract all the possible car buyers to one part of town, they might sell more cars overall. They clearly understand this principle: Become one of the pack.

Do a quick search of the media you're considering and see if anyone else has already walked down that path. Generally, the more footprints, the better. If the medium you are considering has no other businesses like yours anywhere to be found, be wary.

Once you determine where there are other ads, move to the fourth step:

4. Survey other businesses that are advertising in the medium you are considering and ask how it's going for them. Ask them:

- How long have you been advertising here?
- Does the investment pay for itself?
- How many inquiries, leads or sales do you generate from these ads?
- How long do you plan on staying with this particular medium?

You don't need to talk to all of the advertisers. Some of them won't share that information. But enough will so you can get the real scoop on the true performance of the medium. If you can't reach some of the advertisers, you can do an indirect survey by checking the history of the medium to see how long their advertisers have been with them. This is easiest if it's a printed medium, like magazines, newspapers or *Yellow Pages*. Just save the back issues or research them at the public library or at a university.

We've created a worksheet to help you do this.

Company	Ad Size	Lead Flow	Conv. Ratio	% of Business	Comments
1.					
2.					
3.					
4.					
5.					
6.					
7.					
8.					
9.					
10.					

Summary / Notes: _____

I encourage you to use this worksheet to evaluate the media.

Most people just don't go through the effort to do it right. Then they wonder why it feels like they're throwing their advertising money down the toilet. You'll find that this little formula—*think, ask, check and survey*—will tell you with a great degree of certainty what has worked and what hasn't worked for others before you. So, do a little investigative work before you plunk down your cash.

Dealing With Advertising Sale People

Now let's talk about a person who can be one of your biggest allies or your No. 1 enemy in deciding which media to use. It's the advertising sales rep. Unfortunately, many businesses don't know how do deal with advertising sales reps and, as a result, the sales reps take advantage of them.

A little education here can go a long way. First, understand that advertising salespeople make commissions on the ads they sell you. So, they'll try to load you up with as much as possible because it makes their commissions bigger. They might try to sell you more than you actually need to get the job done. So, you need to understand what you're buying so you can know if they're loading you up with too much.

Buying advertising is *not* like buying a suit. You walk into the suit store; you need to buy one suit. If the guy in the suit store tries to sell you four or five suits, you smile politely and let him know that you only need one suit. If he becomes pushy, you tell him to back down because you're sure that you only need one suit. See, if you know you only need one suit, you just buy one suit; maybe two if he's really pushy.

But how many radio ads do you need to make an effective campaign? That's harder to say. What stations should you be on? Some are more expensive than others. How do you even know what you need to buy? How big should your newspaper ad be to maximize effectiveness? What section of the paper should it be in? Which days should it run? It's not easy to know what you need to buy in the first place, and that's what makes it so difficult to know whether the ad sales rep is proposing what you really need. That's why you need to have a working knowledge of how advertising sales works. If an ad sales rep had a brain, he'd create a *Cliff's Notes* version of what he knows and educate you on your various options.

Here's a quick disclaimer. If you're spending a lot of money and there's a lot riding on the results, I strongly recommend you hire a professional to help you get those results. You will earn back any money you pay them (assuming they are competent) by the money you earn due to their expertise. If you have any questions at all about choosing the right media, or any other aspect of your tactical marketing plan, I suggest you get in touch with one of our marketing consultants.

Here are some guidelines to help you evaluate various media. Use them to test your advertising sales reps. These questions will help you determine if they're trying to maximize the effectiveness of your budget or just maximize their commission checks. Before you ask these questions, draw your own conclusions about the best way to buy that particular medium—and then ask the sales rep these questions:

Question 1: What media mix would you recommend? Tell the sales rep you have a certain budget for your advertising campaign. Give a specific amount, like $25,000. The number isn't important. Just tell them what your budget is for your entire campaign—not just their station, newspaper or billboard. Then ask this magic question: How would they spend your $25,000 if they were in your shoes? Which stations, newspapers and billboards would they buy? Again, make sure you've researched the answer ahead of time so you have a good idea of the correct answer. Their answer won't mean much if you don't at least have an idea. Once you do know, their answer could be very revealing.

Let's say you've determined that you should spend $5,000 of your $25,000 budget on one particular radio station, and as much as $7,500 would be within reason. Then you ask the sales reps how would they spend your budget if they were in your shoes. They suggest that you spend at least half your budget on their station, and only $3,000 on the other station that is their major competitor, and the rest should go to print ads, direct mail and Internet efforts.

That answer throws up a big red flag, doesn't it? You've determined that they should get 20 percent of your budget, and they're gunning for 50 percent. Now don't misunderstand. I'm not faulting the guy for wanting half the budget. I'm just making this point: Now you know that you can't trust his opinion.

Question 2: How much should I budget? Here's another way to test the trustworthiness of your advertising sales rep. In this scenario, you don't reveal your entire campaign budget. Instead, you tell the sales rep how much you want to spend. Make sure the number you give is 50 to 100 percent higher than you actually *intend* to spend. If you plan on spending $5,000 on his station, tell him you want to spend $10,000. Low-end sales reps will lick their chops and tell you that you're an advertising genius as they try to take your money. You might find out, however, that they try to steer you in another direction.

We do this sometimes for our radio clients. We tell the sales rep that we want to spend $10,000 in a week, knowing that $5,000 is plenty to get the frequency and gross rating points we want. Sometimes the rep will fax over a proposed schedule with $10,000, even though that inflated budget would be overkill and a waste of money. About half the time the sales rep will say, "Hey, that's just too much money to spend in that short time. You need to either cut your budget or extend the run of your ads." That answer makes you feel more confident in that sales rep. If they don't say that, then you know not to trust that person.

Question 3: What about competing media? Here's the third thing you can ask sales reps to find out if their opinion is worth*while* or worth*less*. Ask them about specific competing media. Again, do your homework and form your own opinion about the competing media before you ask. If you've concluded that a competitive radio station or the other daily newspaper would be a good fit for your campaign, and the sales rep only has negative things to say about it, that throws up a red flag. Here's a sales rep with one thing in mind: Fattening his commission check. Steer clear. Ask for a new rep that's more objective.

If the sales reps don't know, they are not familiar with the industry. If the Ford Explorer salesman can't tell you how that vehicle is better or different than a Jeep Grand Cherokee, you'd be concerned. Expect at least that much knowledge from a media sales rep.

Question 4: How long have you been selling advertising with this particular media? The longer someone's been around and the longer they've been with their current company, the more likely they will be objective. If a guy hops around from radio station to radio station every six months, that person is more likely to tell you whatever he thinks he needs to get the sale…because he's probably starving! Longevity is usually a decent measuring stick.

Why evaluate your sales reps? Because the ones who are good, who have your best interest at heart, can be a good source of information. They can give you helpful suggestions and steer you in the right path when you don't know the best way to proceed. Usually, these reps will work with you even if you're not buying anything for them at that time. They know that if they help you now, you are likely to buy from them when it is appropriate. This goes for ad agencies too. From a *tactical* standpoint, there are good ones and not-so-good ones out there (strategically, they *all* stink). Wouldn't you like to know which is which? Use these tips to find out.

Chapter 12:

Return on Marketing Investment

Any dollar spent on advertising and marketing should come back to you—and bring some friends with it. But how can you know in advance?

Now let's talk about how to figure out how much *money* you should spend on advertising. People always want some magical formula; they'd like to know that in their industry, their ad budget should be 4 percent of sales. Or for retail, your advertising budget should be 10 percent of sales minus the rent.

I think your advertising budget should be *as much as possible* as long as it's making you money. But you've got to *think* a certain way to pull this off. Most people worry too much about budgets and industry standards and *not* worry enough about monopolizing their marketplace. I put together a budget and the client says to me, "This advertising costs too much!" They are shocked when they see how much the advertising for certain media in certain markets will cost them. It is easy to get sticker shock when you see a single 60-second radio commercial on a popular Los Angeles station costs $1,000. Or when you realize that all the dot.com businesses in Silicon Valley made radio spots on top stations in the San Francisco market that cost as much as $2,500 a minute. Or when you hear a six-inch newspaper ad in your local paper costs $2,000.

It's easy to conclude those ads are pricey. But ask yourself: Does the ad *actually* cost too much? A savvy advertiser will tell you that the cost of the ad is not the issue. What's important is the return that ad will bring. If you paid $40,000 for a 60-second radio commercial that generates enough sales to make a $50,000 *profit*, would the $40,000 be a lot of money? The answer is "No, of course not!" You'd be a fool not to beg, borrow, or steal the $40,000 so you could make the $50,000 profit! Heck, I'd spend $40,000 a minute to make a $2,000 profit. Can you get those returns in the stock market? No way! Getting rich in business is easy to do when you learn how to harness the potential of marketing and advertising leverage.

Determine ROI

You've got to figure out how much money an ad will make before you determine whether it costs too much. So how do you do that? Here's a simple process for determining the return on investment (ROI) of an ad.

First, you've got to know how much *profit* you make on each sale. For instance, if you buy something for $50 and sell it for $100, your gross profit is $50.

Next, figure your *closing ratio*. If, on average, you close one sale for every four people who inquire, that's a 25 percent closing ratio. If 9 out of 10 end up buying, then your closing ratio is 90 percent.

Now, figure what your *break-even* is. Do this by taking the cost of the ad and dividing it by the amount of gross profit per sale. For example, if the ad cost $1,000 and your average gross profit is $50, that means you've got to make 20 sales to make back the $1,000. That's your break-even point.

Finally, figure out the *number of leads* you need to generate from the ad to break even. To do this, you've got to know your closing ratio. For example, say your closing ratio is 25 percent. If you close 25 percent and you need 20 sales to break even, then you would need to generate 80 leads to break even on a $1,000 advertisement.

In this example, we calculated you would break even if a $1,000 ad could generate 80 leads since you need 80 leads to make 20 sales. With $50 profit per sale, that would make you $1,000. That's a ROI of 0. I realize that you are in business to make a profit. But let's *start* with breaking even; that's the bare minimum you can accept when running an ad. At least you didn't come up with a *negative* ROI!

Now say you want to double your money. What would have to happen to your numbers? You'd have to double your lead flow, or, in this case, generate 160 leads instead of just 80. That means that if you generate 160 leads, you would generate a profit of $1,000 on $1,000 spent. In other words, you've doubled your money. Your ROI is 100 percent. Pretty impressive!

These are the important numbers to know: What's your gross profit per sale? What's your closing ratio? How many sales do you need to break even? How many leads do you need to generate to make enough sales to break even? What's your ROI on any given number of leads that you generate?

I've created a worksheet to help you keep track of all these numbers.

Advertising Return On Investment (ROI) Worksheet

Average Sale Price	$			
Gross Profit	$			

Advertising Medium				
Cost of Advertising	$	$	$	$
Closing Ratio	%	%	%	%
Sales Needed to Break Even				
Leads Needed To Break Even				
Cost Per Lead	$	$	$	$
Sales Needed To Double Ad Cost				
Leads Needed To Double Cost				
Cost Per Lead	$	$	$	$
Profit Goal: Sales Needed To Reach Profit Goal				
Leads Needed To Reach Profit Goal				
Cost Per Lead	$	$	$	$

The worksheet describes the information you need and shows you how to do the math. Or, check it out online at www.mymbook.com.

Now you know how to figure out how many leads you need to generate to break even on the cost of the advertisement. You can calculate the ROI for each ad you place.

Next, let's figure out the *lifetime value of a customer.* Say your average customer generates a $50 gross profit per sale. Is that the only time that customer will buy anything from you? How many times does that average customer come back in a year? If your average customer shops with you once a month and produces $50 of gross profit every time, that customer is worth $600 a year in profit. And if you know that your average customer stays with you for three years, now that $50 a month client is worth a tidy $1,800.

So, now how much would you spend to obtain that client? What if those were your average numbers, $50 a month for three years. Using our earlier example, we broke even with 80 leads and just 20 sales. Now those 20 customers would be worth $36,000 over the next three years. And it only cost you $1,000 worth of advertising. Now your break-even looks much better, doesn't it? If you could accrue a $36,000 annuity every time you ran $1,000 worth of ads, wouldn't you mortgage your house and spend as much money as possible on advertising! You would when you understand the numbers.

When you are figuring your ROI for advertising, first estimate your numbers conservatively, on the low side. Always figure on getting a lower number of leads than you're expecting. Always count on a lower closing ratio than you're used to. If you calculate your numbers using conservative figures, then you'll do fine if your results are actually lower than projections, And, in the event you do as well as you had initially hoped, you'll just make more money than you expected.

For example, we once worked with a company that promoted seminars. At the seminars, they tried to sell a service that cost $8,000. When they started to promote these seminars, they wondered how much they should allot to the ad budget. They wanted to fill seminars about one week after starting the advertising, so we suggested radio advertising would be the best way to get the message out quickly. The client agreed and gave us a budget of $5,000 a week for five weeks. We asked them how many sales they planned on generating. They believed they could sell at least 100 packages in that five-week period.

We told them they would need to budget at least $20,000 a week—a total of $100,000—to generate the number of leads required to sell that many packages. That number—$100,000—sounded huge. It caught this CEO off guard. His idea was to spend $5,000 a week. Welcome to "sticker shock."

To take the emotion out of the process, we figured the ROI. First, we calculated gross profit per sale to be about $3,500. Second, we tabulated the closing ratio. He thought his would be about 20 percent. Knowing the formula, how many sales would he need to break even on a $100,000 advertising expenditure? We divided $100,000 by $3,500 gross profit per sale and figured about 28 sales.

If his closing ratio were just 10 percent—only half the 20 percent he claimed—he'd have to generate about 280 leads to break even. He needed 280 leads on $100,000 worth of radio. That's easily attainable.

Finally, we figured out how many leads he'd need to reach his goal of 100 sales. If his closing ratio were 10 percent, he'd have to generate about 1,000 leads. On $100,000 of radio, that was reasonable. He'd generate a total gross profit of $350,000. If you subtract the $100,000 advertising cost, that's still a healthy $250,000 gross profit. His attitude toward the $100,000 changed instantly!

See how that works now? Run through your numbers, and you'll know how much money is a lot of money when it comes to advertising. The key is to do the math and know the numbers. Too often, people skip this step and just cross their fingers. When done properly, marketing is a science, not a dice game.

The next thing to master is the science of testing. Testing allows you to prove your numbers in the real world before spending much money on marketing. For example,. I would never dream of allowing our seminar client to blindly roll a $100,000 on the radio just because the ROI worksheet said it would make him money. You have to test the process first!

Chapter 13:

Testing Before Investing

Never make a major marketing mistake again. You can stick with hunches and opinions and market by the seat of your pants, or you can test to know *which approach is best.*

In his classic book *Think and Grow Rich*, Napoleon Hill says that one of the major causes of failure is that people "prefer to act on opinions created by guesswork or snap judgments rather than facts." Advertising decisions based on what you *think* will work rather than what the marketplace wants is the main reason ads don't work—and businesses fail. Your livelihood depends on your ability to determine which messages will effectively attract new customers and entice your current customers to come back for more.

You can make these determinations by putting every important marketing and advertising question to a vote by the only people whose ballots count: customers and prospects. These people "vote" in the form of small, inexpensive tests. An advertising test is different than a questionnaire, survey, or focus group. These things don't necessarily reflect your prospects' willingness to spend their money; the results are usually skewed toward what the participants *think* you want to hear or what they think they *might* do. Testing, on the other hand, tells you which headlines, offers, and prices the market will respond to—and cause them to buy—*before* you spend a fortune on advertising.

Monopolize Your Marketplace

You can test the effectiveness of certain parts of your ads on small representative samples of your market to learn what works. The results are reliable because each advertising question is answered with cash, check, or a major credit card. The purpose of testing is to demand maximum performance from every marketing and advertising dollar you spend. You will find that one approach often substantially out-performs the others. *But unless you test, you won't know which approach is the best one.*

You would think that everyone would test their advertising before running it. Are you doing it? Are you testing your ads or just running them and hoping for the best? Most businesses haphazardly run whatever ads "seem to be pulling well lately." If you methodically test and calculate your advertising efforts, you'll shred your competitors' advertising to pieces and win *their* customers in the process. In short, you must test every aspect of your advertising. That includes the advertising media, placements, headlines, prices, offers, packaging, formats, type fonts, and sales pitches—everything.

By testing, you ensure that you will never make a major marketing mistake. If an advertisement or promotion fails in a small scale test, you either adjust it and test again, or scrap it for something different. By testing, you take the guesswork out of advertising. You should be scientific with your marketing—keep experimenting until you find what really works.

For example, one man who, after 25 years in the retail jewelry business, retired and sold diamonds at wholesale prices directly to the public from his home. Because his prices were so low, he managed to sell several diamonds a month solely on word-of-mouth advertising. But he was clueless about advertising.

One day he hatched a brilliant idea. He decided to start a company to sell lower-end jewelry and collectibles nationwide using ads in *Parade Magazine*. He placed ads that looked exactly like the Franklin Mint's ads; the only difference was his company's name and address at the bottom of the ad. He figured that if his ads could pull just six responses out of every 10,000 readers, net profits would triple the ad cost. He could break even if he could muster just three responses per 10,000 readers. Hey, if Franklin Mint could do it, why couldn't he?

On the strength of projections and his reputation in the community, he raised over $200,000 from local investors to launch the first product, a gemstone ring. The initial ad cost over $60,000 for complete coverage in the *Parade Magazine* circulated in the *Los Angeles Times*. Since the paper was delivered to several million homes, he expected to be extremely rich soon.

To make a sad story short, the product bombed. He tried a different product the second time and still another after that. Finally, he had to quit after he depleted all of his capital. His investors were not happy.

How could this have happened? All he needed was a measly six responses per 10,000 readers. Instead of blowing the whole budget on a couple of unproven ideas, he should have run some tests in similar magazines with smaller circulations. These inexpensive tests would have told him which ad concepts worked, which prices pulled the most orders, which terms his customers found most convenient, and everything else he needed to know before rolling out an expensive campaign.

It's better to learn what works and what doesn't *before* investing $60,000 in advertising. Testing will ensure you never make a major marketing mistake again.

Test both the strategic and tactical parts of your marketing campaign. On the strategic side, when you test one marketing variable against another, you will find that one always out-pulls all others by a measurable margin. A price of $39 may out-pull $49 by three times. A certain headline in a newspaper ad might out-pull another one by as many as *5 or 10 times*! That's means five or 10 times the results with no increased expense! Advertising and marketing offers your business the greatest source of leverage, but you have to test to take advantage of that leverage. As you test different approaches, carefully analyze and tabulate the results. When you find something that out-pulls everything else, that becomes your "control." Once you know what works best, you can test other variables in your advertising mix.

Once you find a headline that works well in a magazine ad, you can then test it in different magazines, or different placements in the magazine or in different sizes. Just be sure not to test more than one variable at a time or you won't know what effect changing each variable has. If you change the headline, the publication and the format of the body copy, you won't know which component accounted for the difference in results.

On the tactical side, you can test one radio station against another. You can test radio versus television, newspaper or direct mail. You can test one section of the newspaper against another. You can run your ads on the same station but at different times of day. Put every strategic and tactical part of your marketing program on trial and let the marketplace decide what they will respond to!

Another wholesale diamond seller found that his business became increasingly profitable the more he tested his advertising. His main selling point had always been lower-than-retail pricing. He successfully ran ads in the local university newspaper with the headline "Wholesale Diamonds" for several months in a row. He then decided to test three or four other headlines based on low prices, including this one: *"If you're planning on spending $2,500 on a diamond engagement ring, I'll send you home with either a ring worth $3,800—or $1,000 still in your pocket."*

This simple re-articulation of the selling point "low prices" graphically illustrated just how low the prices were. It brought the ad alive to the readers by hitting their hot buttons in a unique and believable way. Inquiries and sales immediately increased by over 60 percent. But the story doesn't end there. This headline became his "control." He then tested some other concepts against the low-price one. One concept was based on the observation that people usually know that wholesale diamonds are less expensive, but they are leery of buying from a dealer that doesn't have a big, fancy showroom. Basically, the customers' confidence in wholesale dealers was low. Remember, the advertiser's job is to raise confidence and lower risk. In this case there was high risk and low confidence.

His next newspaper ad attacked this concern head-on. He pushed the hot button. The headline read: *"Most people's greatest fear about buying their diamond engagement ring from a wholesale jeweler is that they'll be fooled into paying too much for an inferior diamond."*

It acknowledged their fears. The ad then explained how this wholesaler never considered any sale binding until the customer had the diamond appraised by a certified gemologist of their choice. It also described in detail the "better than money-back guarantee" that ensured total customer satisfaction. See how that lowers the risk and allows the customer to take specific steps to raise the confidence level?

The huge increase in response this ad brought drove home the importance of testing to this client. No advertiser can tell the market what it will respond to. Experience can show you what things tend to work best, but only testing can prove what works best in any particular situation.

Yes, it takes time to test, but testing every facet will make your marketing more effective. It will also make you more money and help your business grow more rapidly.

Start testing every ad you run against another one with a different headline or price or layout. You can even use your sales force to test. Send two relatively well-matched salesmen out with different pitches and see which one works best after a week. Test new and different ways to articulate each point of your case until you find one that works best. When you find approaches that make you money, keep testing to find out, "How high is high?" You never know how high is high, how fast is fast, how far is far until you've tried several different things.

An *A/B split* means running two different ads at the same time. Let's say you're sending a mail piece. Instead of sending one piece to the entire list, try sending one piece to half the list—piece A—and a test piece to the other half—piece B. The A/B split works great with emails and telemarketing as well. Some newspapers and magazines can print every other copy with a different ad. This allows you to see which ad pulls more effectively.

Test, test, test. Become a test-aholic. Don't fly by the seat of your pants. You'll find testing to be very rewarding in the long run.

When generating leads, you need to evaluate where your time, energies, and efforts are best spent. I recommend you spend most of your time perfecting your craft and innovating your company so that it's competitive. For most people, marketing and advertising is a new field, one requiring study and deep understanding. I have tried to give you a working knowledge of strategic marketing and lead generation. But I urge you to consult with professionals to implement what you know.

Chapter 14:

Marketing Tools

If you're serous about marketing, you'll learn how to use tools to facilitate your prospect's decision to purchase your products.

So far we've talked about creating a strategic marketing plan and discussed a strategy to generate leads if your company has a non-defined target market. Now I want to address one of the most critical cogs: marketing tools. Marketing tools educate your prospects without relying strictly on salespeople. You want your marketing program to do the heavy lifting in the sales process. You want the marketing to facilitate the decision-making process and lead prospects to the conclusion that they'd have to be fools to do business with anyone else, regardless of price. You want the salesperson to arrive on the scene to wrap up the details and answer specific questions—after the marketing has paved the way.

The problem with relying on salespeople to manage leads and close sales is that many prospects are resistant to the sales process. The last thing on earth they want to do is talk to your salesperson. The only exceptions would be lonely people who will talk to anybody, and people who already are on the far right hand side of the *educational spectrum*. These people are ready to buy. Their urgent need is to gather information and complete the sale right now. So, the first problem with salespeople as decision-making facilitators is that people don't want to talk to them most of the time, regardless how wonderful they are.

The second reason why salespeople aren't the ideal way to follow up with leads and educate your prospects is that most salespeople just aren't very good. In most businesses, 20 percent of the salespeople are superstars, and the other 80 percent are average to below average. The *Monopolize Your Marketplace* system will make average salespeople better and good salespeople great. It all depends on you setting up your sales system the right way. And marketing tools are a major part of this.

Marketing tools include anything that will educate the prospect. They include brochures, audios, videos, web sites, on-hold messages, signs, scripts, and reports. Depending on how your company is set up, it may be appropriate to send the marketing tool via mail or the Internet to a prospect who has inquired through your lead generating efforts. Sometimes it may be appropriate to have a salesperson deliver the marketing tool. The salesperson, in that case, can then use the marketing tool as a crutch. We operate from the "even a blind dog with a broken leg can deliver a report, video, or CD" mentality. The key is to say something that is compelling, that builds your case, and that is a product of your strategic marketing plan. The first part of this book was about finding the hot buttons, creating the case, and articulating the case in such a way that your prospects draw the conclusion: "I would have to be an absolute fool to do business with anyone else but you, regardless of price."

Let's talk about some of the marketing tools you can create to facilitate your prospects' decision-making processes and move them along through your sales system.

Reports. From a strategic standpoint, the report is the third component of the *marketing equation*—it's your case. You should already have an outline for your report in your *Master Letter*. The case should educate the prospect on what he needs to know when it comes to doing business in your industry and how you perform compared to the alternatives. You can get a general idea of what to put in the report from the industry category strategy. The service industry strategy is called S*tandard Bearer*. The report should describe those standards. For professional service providers, like CPAs, accountants and doctors, the industry strategy is called *Cliff's Notes,* which creates a short version of what the professional knows and does in the report. A mass retailer creates a *Consumer Reports* type of report that educates prospects about buying within certain categories. Remember, we said that a fitness equipment store could run a lead-generating ad with a headline that reads: "Compare and Price the Top 11 Treadmill Models Without Talking to a Salesperson and Without Setting Foot in a Store."

See how that headline captures people from the entire *Educational Spectrum*, especially those most reluctant to talk to a salesperson for fear of sales pressure? That headline also defines the content of that report. What would you put in that report? You would compare the top 11 treadmill models. That would facilitate the decision-making process of the prospect.

If a manufacturer created a report as a marketing tool, what would it contain? If a manufacturer is selling to distribution, it would push the hot button of making the distributor more money (see industry category strategies). The report, in that case, would quantify how much money distributors could make and compare it to other alternatives. If the manufacturer sells directly to end-users, or if the manufacturer wanted to help the distributor sell to end-users, then there would need to be a report about the product itself. If the product had several attributes, then the report would teach the prospect the standards to demand when purchasing a product in that category and then show how their products are superior.

That's the report from the strategic side—the "what you say and how you say it" side. What about the tactical side? What format should the report take? Should it be in an audio CD, CD Rom, printed report, online report, e-mailed report, video, or DVD?

The decision is not that difficult. You need to study and survey your customers to find out the most appropriate format. Generally, you can't go wrong with a printed report. As long as it's laid out in a clean, easy-to-read format, most people who are on the *Educational Spectrum* will at least skim through it. A printed report must contain headlines that hit the prospects' hot buttons to keep them interested. Other formats like audios, videos and web sites depend on your target market.

We created a video brochure for a large roofing contractor. Since the roofing company is a service provider, we needed to use the *Standard Bearer* strategy. We shot the video and talked about 21 points every buyer should consider when evaluating a roofing company. These standards included things like a lean release waiver from the materials suppliers, a letter from the roofing company's banker, a list of appearance and behavior standards for workers, and 1,000 current references. The video did a wonderful job of educating the prospect and helping them draw the "I would have to be a fool to use anyone else" conclusion.

We chose a video instead of a printed report because of the sales process for this product. When a salesperson meets a homeowner to give them a quote, he has to get up on the roof to measure it. There's no way around that. It normally takes about 10 minutes for the salesperson to do this. We created a video that was 11 minutes long to give the prospects something to do while a stranger was up on their roof. While the salesman was on the roof, the marketing tool was educating the prospect and facilitating the decision-making process. And because the video was professional and powerful, by the time the roofing salesperson got off the roof, he wasn't a stranger any more. He was the beacon of hope and the anchor of confidence in the sea of roofing uncertainty. All the salesperson had to do was not mess it up at that point.

To further *Franchise the Sales System*, we created an ***evidence packet*** for the salesperson. This showed the prospect exactly how this roofing company performed against the industry standards. We put the bankers' letters, lean release waiver letters, and appearance and behavior standards, along with everything else in a binder to show the prospect. Then the salesman would hand the prospect a huge 370-page printout of over 30,000 customers they had serviced.

We put all this together to add systemization to the sales process. Never leave the success of an organization in the hands of salespeople. Never. Can you count on your sales staff to create your strategy? Answer: Not in a million years.

Here's how well this systematized sales tool worked for one of their salesmen. The salesman noticed that one of his neighbors had a sign in his yard for another roofing contractor to re-roof his house. The salesman walked over to the neighbor's house, knocked on the door, said, "I live down the street, and I work for a roofing company. Here's a video that will help you make sure that the contractor you're using will do a good job on your roof." Then he shook his hand and went home. No more, no less.

The salesman got a call from the neighbor the next morning at 7:30. He said, "Hey, I watched this video. I want you guys to do my roof." By 8:15, the homeowner had already pulled the other company's sign out of the ground. The job was worth $15,000. Not a bad sale for handing a guy a video.

Remember: Even a blind dog with a broken leg can hand a guy a video. That's what we mean by *Franchising the Sales System.*

You'll need to figure out the appropriate format for your report. Maybe a combination of a video and a printed report would work best. In addition, some sort of online information is usually appropriate for most companies. You'll need to consider your prospects' situation and find out what works best. If you're not sure, contact one of our consultants for help.

Let's talk about four other powerful marketing tools that can make a huge difference in your conversion ratio: sales scripts, on hold messages, in store signage, and follow-up letters.

Sales scripts. The way you answer your phones or deal with customers in person has a massive impact on your sales. You need to script exactly what you want your people to say when they talk to a prospect for the first time. Your employees must follow the script with no exceptions. Remember, this is *Franchising Your Sales System.* McDonald's doesn't let employees determine what temperature to cook French fries because they're likely to screw it up! Remember: "Victory goes to the one with superior forces at the point of contact." What point of contact could be more important in the sales process than when the prospect calls your business? You don't want to leave this important interaction to an employee's discretion. You want to predetermine the message and make sure it's always the same and always powerful.

Imagine this scenario. A plumber runs the ad with a headline that reads: "The Three Biggest Problems You'll Have With Most Plumbers And How Johnson's Plumbing Overcomes Them All."

The ad educates the prospect about those problems and how Mr. Johnson overcomes them. The ad itself is a mini-report. The prospect is impressed and calls because his toilet is overflowing.

"Hello, Johnson's Plumbing. Can I help you?"

"Yes, my toilet is overflowing, I need a plumber."

"One moment please." (on hold for 30 seconds)

"This is Randy, how can I help you."

"My toilet is overflowing. What do you charge?"

"We charge $95 for the trip, plus parts, plus labor."

"When can you get here?"

"How fast do you need us?"

"I'm up to my eyeballs in you-know-what!"

"Let me see if I can get someone out there in a couple of hours. What's your address?"

"Hang on, my wife is calling." (hangs up).

This scenario is all too typical. Now listen to the difference when you put a script in place:

"Hello, Johnson's Plumbing, Wanda speaking. How can I help you?"

"My toilet is overflowing. I need a plumber."

"What is your name, sir?"

"Rich Harshaw"

"Thank you for calling, Mr. Harshaw. Have you ever called Johnson's plumbing before?

"No I haven't."

"I'm going to transfer you to Randy Adkins who handles emergencies; but quickly, before I do that, I want to let you know that there are three main reasons our customers like to do business with us. First, we always come when we say we will. We give you a guaranteed appointment time—and we stick to it or else your repair is free. Second, we always provide a guaranteed quote over the phone, so there are no surprise charges after the repair is completed. And third, we guarantee all our repairs for one full year to make sure you don't get stuck paying for the same repair twice. That's our three-point guarantee. Unless you have any questions for me, I'll transfer you now to Randy Adkins...."

"That would be fine, thanks."

On hold for 20 seconds.....

"Hello, Mr. Harshaw, this is Randy. Wanda has informed me that your toilet is overflowing. We can get somebody on that right away. Did Wanda tell you about our three-point guarantee?"

"Yes, she did."

"Did you have any questions about that?

"No, I think I get it."

"Okay, great, tell me your address, and I'll give you a guaranteed time window and guaranteed price for that repair."

Do you see how much more compelling that is? Providing more information facilitated the buying decision. Did you notice how the receptionist provided the information even though it was an emergency situation? Would you be surprised if I told you that this company's conversation ratio—that is, the number of callers who actually booked a job—went from 55 percent to 88 percent after they implemented this script? Imagine what impact that increase had on their bottom line. This is leverage in its purest form! You are already spending the money to generate the leads; now you just convert more of them. You're getting more results from the same raw materials!

We have used sales scripts with great success in almost every industry. We took a small Sprint PCS business from brand new to the No. 1 dealer in the entire Dallas-Fort Worth region in 60 days by utilizing a sales script like this. And this company achieved these stellar results using a lead-generating system and two salespeople. And these guys weren't superstars. One staff member was a 17-year-old who had no sales experience and not much of a personality, and the other salesperson was a 21-year-old who had been stocking grocery shelves in the middle of the night before coming on board.

See, it's all about the system. These two kids, by themselves, outsold the next biggest seller, a company that had been in business for years and had a huge sales staff of professional salespeople. Again, it's all about the system. Franchise the sales system, and outstanding results are not just likely—they are absolutely inevitable.

We've used sales scripts for financial planners, dentists, air conditioning companies, banks, IT companies, furniture stores, manufacturers, accountants, consultants, and office equipment companies—to name a few. And it works like a charm every time. It's all about the system.

On-hold messages. According to statistics provided by AT&T, 75 percent of callers to the average business are put on hold for 45 seconds or longer. Think about calls you make to businesses and how much you get put on hold. Now think of the opportunity you have to educate your prospects and customers while they're waiting on hold. In our plumbing example, the receptionist placed the prospect on hold while she located Randy. What do you think the on-hold message should say? If it were like most businesses, it went something like this: "Thank you for calling. We appreciate your patience. We'll be right back on the line." Music. "We'll be right with you in a minute." More music.

I think that message stinks! But you know what, that's about what you'll hear from most companies that even bother to have an on-hold message.

What about this one: Music intro. "Hello, and thank you for calling Johnson Plumbing. We've been serving the Dallas area for 50 years, repairing residential, commercial and industrial customers. We appreciate your call. We have emergency service 24 hours a day, seven days a week to help you anytime, day or night. Ask about our leak repairs and sewer and drain cleaning, and don't forget, we take Visa, MasterCard, and Discover for your convenience."

Can you believe the platitudes! Unreal! Now, compare those two with this one:

Male Voice; should sound like he's in his 40s....

Hi, this is Al Johnson, founder of Johnson Plumbing. I want to thank you for calling us. I know nobody likes to have plumbing problems, but when you do, you can rest assured calling Johnson Pluming is the right thing to do. While I've got you for a minute, I'd like to tell you why our customers love doing business with us so much—it's simple: We've eliminated the three biggest frustrations they normally have when doing business with a plumber.

Let me explain.

The first problem most people have is waiting around for the plumber to get there. Have you ever heard this before? We'll be there sometime between 9 and 5!?? Like you don't have anything better to do with your day than sit around and wait for a plumber! When you call Johnson Plumbing, we will give you a guaranteed appointment window of 2 hours or less. In other words, we'll narrow the time that we'll be there to less than 120 minutes. And if we miss the appointed time, the labor for your repair is absolutely free, no matter how long it takes us. But don't get your hopes up for free labor—we've only missed on our promise 4 times since 1993. With Johnson Plumbing, we guarantee you won't wait.

The second major frustration you might face with most other plumbers is that they always seem to quote the job low and then come in later with a higher bill—after the work is completed... At Johnson Plumbing, you'll never pay more than the original quote.....

Cut off there is fine, should be plenty long enough....

An on-hold message should be a part of your tactical marketing plan. It's a marketing tool that can educate your prospects and facilitate their decision-making processes while they're a captive audience. Go to www.mymbook.com for more information and resources about on hold messages and to hear samples of good and bad messages.

Again, we're trying to *Franchise the Sales System* by systematizing the selling processes so that the salesperson isn't the weak link. We're trying to get the marketing to do the heavy lifting and let the salesperson come in when the prospect already has a good idea that he'd have to be an absolute fool to do business with anyone else. Then, the salesperson simply has to answer any questions and wrap up the details.

In-store signage. Most businesses use in-store signage incorrectly, if they use it at all. They use in-store signage for sale announcements, directions, or worst of all, rules. What about using in-store signage to *educate?* In a retail or showroom environment, the salesperson has to sell. That's not only uncomfortable for the buyer, it's also dangerous since there's a good chance the salesperson is at best incompetent, and at worst, a total idiot.

We've all had horrible service experiences. Once I went to a major electronics store to buy a computer. I found what I wanted and was ready to pay, when the salesperson tried to convince me to buy a surge protector. He asked me if I had a surge protector. I said. "Yes, thank you very much."

He said, "How old is it?"

Now honestly, would I know how old my surge protector is? I might know how old my car is, but my surge protector? I said, "I don't know, I've had it for a while."

He said, "Have you had it more that a year?"

I said, "Yes. I'm sure it's more than a year."

He said, "Well then, you'll need a new one."

I assured him that my surge protector was fine.

He then explained, "Computers are higher powered and faster now. The computer you are buying requires a more up-to-date surge protector." He showed me one for only $49.99.

I thought that sounded like hogwash, so I said, "No thanks. I'll just take the computer."

But this guy said I was jeopardizing my $1,500 investment. He told me he wasn't on commissions and it didn't matter to him if I bought it, but it was important for my system.

I still doubted him, so I said, "Look, I just want the computer."

But this moron wouldn't back down. He went into analogy mode: "Look, it would be like if you bought a car that came with standard tires, but you were going to race it at high speeds. You'd be stupid to not get better tires on it."

So I said to him, "Now you're calling me stupid?"

He said, "No, I'm just saying it would be smart to buy the better tires."

I said, "Tell you what. You can keep your surge protector, and you can keep the computer too. I'll keep my $1,550 and be out of here." And I walked out. I couldn't believe it.

Here's my point: If there are real, legitimate issues that you need to educate the customer about, why not put up a sign in the store? If it were true that I needed a better, newer surge protector, why not put up a sign that talks about the dangers of old surge protectors? Why not reprint a relevant article from *Consumer Digest* magazine? Why not write a report to show customers how to tell if they need a new surge protector, and if so, how to chose the proper one? If your salespeople really aren't on commission, why not put signs in the store that say "Our salespeople aren't on commission. They are here to educate and help you make the best decision possible!"

Here's a rule of thumb: people tend to believe what they see, not what they hear. That doesn't mean that people automatically assume that everything they hear is a lie, but they do know that people can and will say whatever it takes to make a sale. But when it's in writing, it's hard to get away with a lie. There's too much at stake for the liar. So people tend to assume that things they see and read are true.

Here's an example of how to use in-store signage effectively. Once we consulted with a piano store owner who sold both new and used pianos. Baldwin was his primary brand. Remember the industry category strategies. This is a mass retail situation, since this store sells merchandise that is basically the same as what's available at other piano stores. They also sell products with many product attributes. So, we combined two different strategies. First, we created a report that educated prospective piano buyers about what they needed to know about pianos. The report contained a section on new pianos and another on used pianos. It walked prospects step by step through the process of buying a piano and showed them exactly what they needed to know. It was the *Consumer Reports* strategy.

Mass retailers also need to create additional value-added services to offer to their customers. These are services that are economical to fulfill but have a high perceived value. So, that's exactly what we did. We talked to the store owner and found out what they could give away for free that normally cost extra money—things most people never bought anyway because they didn't want to spend more.

What were those things? If you want to know why prospects buy pianos, you've got to see the world through their eyes. How many people who buy a piano already know how to play it? Not very many! Why not add free lessons as a standard part of the package? Even if the primary buyer already knows how to play, maybe somebody else in the family could take free lessons. We offered 12 weeks of free piano lessons. At $10 per half hour lesson, that's a $120 value. How can the piano store afford that? It's easy. Find a piano teacher who is looking for more students and offer to pay him or her $5 per half hour lesson. Give the students 12 vouchers. Put a time restriction on them so that they expire within about six months of the piano purchase (that way you don't have any long-term liability).

The piano teacher will go for this because if he or she does a good job, the student will continue when the three months are up. And since you're only paying the teacher for redeemed vouchers, your cost per voucher given out is closer to $1 to $2 each because many people won't use the vouchers. So, the actual cost is just about $20 per piano.

The second free "bonus" we added was a free lesson on compact disc. What else could we add for little or no cost? How about tuning, voicing, and regulation? Most people know that a piano needs to be tuned, but most people don't even know what voicing and regulation are! Voicing is making sure the hammers are in good shape so they produce the optimal sound when they strike the chord. Regulation is keeping each of the key's components in good condition so they don't stick, the pedals aren't sluggish, and you don't hear any rattles or weird sounds while playing. A piano should be tuned after one year, and at least twice a year after that, and voicing and regulation should always be done after it's tuned.

Hardly anyone does any of this. Inevitably, most pianos sound crummy. So why not include those services for free when buying a piano? You could make the quantity of those services contingent upon the grade of piano purchased. You could extend the duration of free service for the more expensive pianos that have a larger profit margin. It would be easy to afford if you had a technician on staff who could service all your customers' pianos in a systematic format. What if that technician cost you $50,000 a year, and you sold 500 pianos a year? That's $100 in additional cost per piano. But that technician would also surely have paying jobs in addition to the free jobs and not all of your customers would take you up on the free services. So that might lower your real cost to closer to $50 per piano sold.

But you could promote those services as being worth $175 a year, which is true. You could give five years worth of services for your premium lines of pianos, four years for lesser models, two for your most basic models and just one year for used pianos. You could also include for free a subscription to a sheet music magazine with a face value of $30 that you could get for free and $200 worth of sheet music, with a hard cost to you of just $15.

All told, you would be giving the prospect anywhere from $1,300 to $2,000 worth of freebies that would cost you anywhere from $30 to $300. See how we've innovated the service offering to make the product offering more appealing? All I've done is use the industry strategy for a mass retailer and innovate the service offering.

Ludwig Family Music

Preferred Customer Packages

Receive Between $1,305 and $2,005 of FREE
Services & Merchandise When You Purchase Any
Upright, Baby Grand, or Grand Piano

Packages For:	Ludwig 5 Years	Chickering 4 Years	Wurlitzer 3 Years	Special Use 2 Years	Used 1 Year
FREE Lessons	$120	$120	$120	$120	$120
Lesson Disc	$780	$780	$780	$780	$780
FREE Tuning	$375	$300	$225	$150	$75
FREE Voicing	$250	$150	$100	$75	$50
Regulation	$250	$150	$100	$75	$50
5 M Mag	$30	$30	$30	$30	$30
FREE Music	$200	$200	$200	$200	$200
Total Value	$2,005	$1,730	$1,555	$1,430	$1,305

At Ludwig Family Music You Receive the Most for Your Piano Investment.

So what about the in-store signage? You could put signs in the store that talk about your *Preferred Customer Packages* that list all the free services, what they were worth, and let the customer know exactly what they would get when buying the various grades of pianos. The example to the right is a simple sign because there's no need to be fancy. Just tell the customer what the deal is. Show him the advantages of doing business with you, and do it in a format that makes the sales job easier.

What other signs could you put in the store? How about a sign that reads, "Free Piano Buyer's Guide: How to Compare All Major Brands and Grades Of Pianos to Make Sure You're Getting What's Right For You." That sign could have a holder for the actual reports. Then your customers could do something more than walk mindlessly through the store pounding the keys on an instrument they knew nothing about. Instead, they could *educate themselves* as they shopped, and your salespeople could answer specific questions and close sales.

Any retail or showroom selling environment should include in-store signage that facilitates the decision-making process and helps close more business. Other kinds of businesses can use signs as well. Plumbers could put up yard signs. Chiropractors and doctors could put signs in their waiting areas. Think about your business. How could better signage help your situation?

Follow-up letters. We've already covered reports, sales scripts, on-hold messages and in-store signage. Now let's talk about follow-up letters. These tools help close more sales in cases where there is an initial contact by a salesperson and then an ensuing sales cycle. Just like the martial arts master, you've got to figure out all the prospect's situations before you start the sales process.

Years ago we owned an office supply company, and we had certain sales advantages over our four main competitors. But the advantages were different, depending on the competitor. If we generated a lead and the prospect said he was currently using Miller Business Systems, the salesperson would go to the secretary, who would pull up the follow-up letter on the computer that listed the

The Piano Buyer's Handbook

8 Things You Should Know Before You Buy Any New Or Used Piano

FREE

TAKE

ONE

Compliments of
Ludwig Family Music

specific advantages we held over Miller Business Systems. She'd print it out, with some customization if necessary, and give it to the salesperson for a signature, and she would mail it out. If we were competing against Office Depot or Office Max, the case we would build would be different, and so there would be different sales advantages. Those letters talked specifically about some of the problems customers were likely to encounter with those competitors and then detail how we overcame those problems. The tone of the letters was very matter-of-fact, but they didn't come across like mud slinging. They just honestly discussed the issues.

How Much Should You Pay For A Good Piano?

Read Our FREE Report To Find Out

What do you think would happen if we left it up to the salesperson to: 1) figure out what to say in that letter; 2) take the time to type the letter; and 3) mail out the letter. The chance is approximately zero. That's what I mean by *Franchise the Sales System*. It's like the French fry machine at McDonald's. It's either turned on or turned off. In my sales system, the salesperson has the same opportunity to send the same well-written, perfectly articulated follow-up letter, regardless of his sales skills. We elevate the performance of everyone because everyone gets the same results using the same tools. Of course there are variables that affect the performance of individual members of your sales staff. But systematizing lifts everyone's performance.

EVERYTHING
You've Ever Learned
About Marketing Is
WRONG.

Which Result Do YOU Prefer?

	Ad 1	Ad 2
Ad Cost	$3,000	$3,000
Calls Received	70	955
Conversion Ratio	17%	68%
Sales	$13,817	$451,987

All figures per month

Which ad do YOU THINK caused readers to say...
*"I would have to be an ABSOLUTE FOOL to do business
with anyone else but you ... regardless of price"?*

■ Strategic Marketing vs. Tactical Marketing

Strategic Marketing

Strategic Marketing has to do with what you say, how you say it, and who you say it to. In other words, it's the content of your marketing message.

Tactical Marketing

Tactical Marketing is the execution of your strategic marketing plan as far as generating leads, placing media, creating marketing tools, and implementing a follow up system. In other words, it's the medium your message is delivered in.

The distinction between Strategic and Tactical Marketing is huge. Most people mistakenly assume that when you talk about marketing that you're automatically talking about Tactical Marketing--placing ads, generating leads, sending out mailers, attending trade shows, creating brochures, implementing a follow-up system, and so forth. They fail to realize that the strategic side of the coin--<u>what you say</u>, how you say it, and who you say it to--is almost always MORE important than the marketing medium WHERE you say it.

This program will help you become proficient in BOTH.

Available Online:www.mymbook.com   ❶

■ What Marketing Is Supposed To Do:

1. Capture the attention of the target market.
2. Facilitate the prospect's information gathering and decision-making processes.
3. Lower the risk of taking the next step in the sales cycle.

Human nature **demands** that we always make the best decision possible.

Buyers want to have the **unshakable confidence** that they've made the the right choice.

Your job is to **help** them do that.

Do These Ads Do That?

Do smiling, happy people help you learn what you need to know about buying a home?

Do pictures of beautiful living rooms with furniture that's way nicer than yours help to facilitate your decision making process?

Do maps, addresses, and phone numbers lower the risk of taking the next step?

NO.

These Ads ALL FAIL.

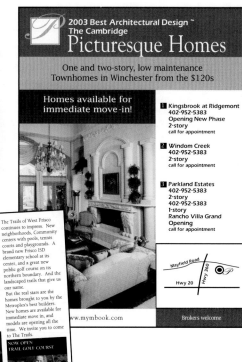

■ Inside Reality & Outside Perception

Inside Reality

Your Inside Reality is the actual value you bring to the marketplace. This is based on your products or services, your quality, your people, your systems, your service, etc.

A good Inside Reality can be developed by anticipating customer wants and needs and developing your business to meet them. To create an outstanding Inside Reality, you've got to live by the credo,

"If you want to know why John Smith buys what John Smith buys, you've got to see the world through John Smith's eyes."

"To be effective, you've got to make the product interesting, not just make the ad different."

-Rosser Reeves, Advertising Pioneer

Outside Perception

Your Outside Perception is the way your company is viewed by prospective customers. This is based on any communication you have with them. Advertising, marketing, and sales efforts all form your Outside Perception.

"Victory goes to the one with superior forces at the point of contact."
-Chinese Proverb

■ Why Inside Reality & Outside Perception Don't Match Up

History of Advertising

In the early days (late 1800's to 1950's) advertisements were thought of as "an army of tiny salesmen... all armed with the perfect presentation, and not afraid of the word <u>NO</u>."

- Headlines identified problems.

- Copy educated the buyer and built a case.

- Offers gave prospects a low-risk way to learn more.

The "Era Of The Brand Builders"

Starting in 1948, television changed marketing and advertising forever...

- Ads shrank from 1 to 2 minutes down to 30 seconds.

- Ad prices went up dramatically.

- Only the largest companies could compete.

- Slogans became the most cost-effective way to communicate.

- Creativity & Repetition (C&R) became the de facto advertising standard.

PROBLEM: Most companies' Inside Reality & Outside Perception don't match up.

In the "Era of the Brand Builders," Inside Reality and Outside Perception didn't have to match ... because relatively few companies could afford to play the game-- and they won by FORFEIT.

Available Online:www.mymbook.com

■ Institutional Ads

"Here's our best attempt at being creative and here's the biggest budget we could muster to support this crap."

- Utilized by most big companies and some small ones.

- Supported by huge ad budgets: (2002, Source: Advertising Age).

GM - $3.6 billion
Procter & Gamble - $2.7 billion
Disney - $1.8 billion
Sears - $1.6 billion
McDonald's - $1.3 billion
Pepsi - $1.1 billion

One dot com minute.

Fess up. Your office needs beefier Internet access. So call Berge. We bundle router, line, service in one package, at frisky rates. We include router, saving you hundreds. And we back it with 7-day a week tech support. Could it be any easier? Call Berge. We'll come running.

HOW BIG IS YOUR BUDGET?

BERGE telecom
www.mymvbook.com
408-959-1585

Platitudes Now Rule The Roost...

Platitudes are words or phrases that are drearily commonplace and predictable, that lack power to evoke interest through overuse and repetition... that are nevertheless stated as though they were original or significant.

Words & Phrases like:

Lowest Prices
Best Service
Highest Quality
Most Professional
Largest Selection

Biggest In State
Family Owned
Most Reliable
In Business Since 1431 B.C.

■ Menu-Board-Style

Just like a restaurant menu...
"Here's our name and here's a list of stuff we have for sale."

- Utilized by many small businesses.

- Commonly found in yellow pages, newspaper, magazines... even radio & TV.

- Basic offer: "Come buy from us for no justifiable, rational reason besides we have it."

Even A Dead Fish Can Float Down Stream

Just because your ads are done wrong and violate the Marketing Equation (page 7) doesn't mean they absolutely won't work. In fact, often times they work just fine. Why? Because none of your competitors are doing any better at marketing than you are!

MAY I TAKE YOUR ORDER PLEASE?

After all, people need to buy what you sell, and they're going to buy from <u>somebody</u>. If you have <u>any</u> ad you're going to get <u>some</u> business. We call this "situational results," meaning the momentum of the marketplace will bring you some customers. Here's a better idea: implement the Marketing Equation into your business and **Monopolize Your Marketplace**.

■ Platitude Evaluations

Evaluate & See For Yourself

Grab an advertisement or marketing piece from your company and run it through these three "Platitude Evaluations:"

1. **Well I Would Hope So!** Does your prospect expect you to say what you've said? If so, it's a platitude.

2. **Who Else Can Say That?** Could your competitors say the same things you've said? Not do what you do, but SAY what you say?

3. **Cross-Out/Write-In Test:** Cross your name off your ad and write in the name of your competitor. If the ad is still valid, you fail the test!

How do these ads stack up against the platitude evaluations?
What about YOUR ads!?

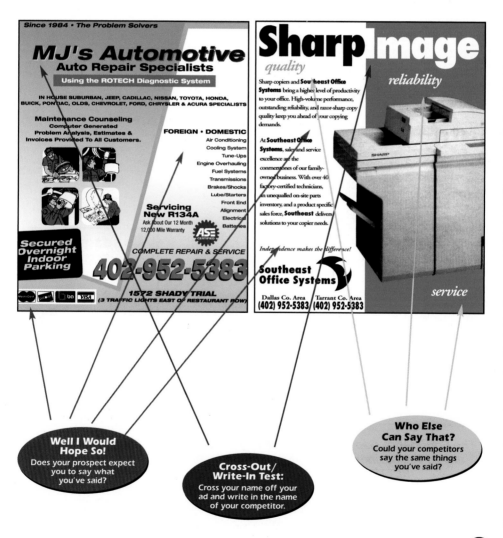

DAYS OF SIMPLE SELLING

Up Until The 1980's

The straight line represents the seller's ability to get in the door and make a presentation, use some closes, and walk out with a check.

- Fewer Competitors
- Fewer Choices
- Low Technology
- Low Education

- Low Information
- Low Resistance
- Easier to make a buying decision

The Seller Had The Power

THE CONFIDENCE GAP

1990's On...

The Gap in the line represents how hard it is to even get in the door to get a <u>chance</u> to sell.

Because of...	THE CONFIDENCE GAP	Leads to...
• Increased Technology		• Increased Resistance
• Increased Competition		• Longer Buying Cycles
• More Choices		• Price Competition
• Increased Information		• Products are Commodities
• "Entrepreneurial Boom"		• Identical Mktg. Messages

NOW - The Buyer Has The Power
(and the seller is at his mercy)

"The Confidence Gap represents the buyer's inability to distinguish whether any of the businesses, any of the products, or any of the services are any BETTER, any DIFFERENT, or any WORSE than any of the others."

RESULT: Buyers Stall and Shop PRICE.

■ The Marketing Equation

Recap Of Why Everything You Know About Marketing Is Wrong

These Problems...

- History of Advertising
- Era of the Brand Builders
- Platitudes
- Days of Simple Selling
- Confidence Gap

Resulted In...

Most Companies'
Inside Reality and
Outside Perception
**DON'T
MATCH**

SOLUTION: THE MARKETING EQUATION

Human nature demands that buyers always want to make the best decision possible. Marketing and advertising should get the attention of the target market, facilitate their decision-making process, and lower the risk of taking the next step in the selling process.

The process for accomplishing this is exactly the same every single time for every kind of business. Just like 2 + 2 always equals 4, the marketing equation always produces the right answer.

Interrupt + Engage + Educate + Offer = RESULTS

Interrupt:

Get qualified prospects to pay attention to your marketing. Accomplished by identifying and hitting your prospects' hot buttons.

Engage:

Give prospects the promise that information is forthcoming that will facilitate their decision-making process.

Educate:

Identify the important and relevant issues prospects need to be aware of, then demonstrate how you stack up against those issues. Build a case for your business.

Offer:

Give prospects a low-risk way to take the next step in the buying process... put more information in their hands and allow them to feel in total control of the decision.

RESULT:

The Right Answer Every Single Time.

■ Marketing Equation Components 1&2: Interrupt & Engage

"How John Smith's Brain Works" — 3 Major Concepts:

ALPHA MODE

Alpha Mode is when you automatically run patterns that allow your brain to habitually perform tasks without any conscious effort. Have you ever driven to work and realized when you got there you hadn't consciously seen a thing along the way? That's Alpha Mode. You can talk on the cell phone, listen to the radio, shave, put on makeup, whatever. But meanwhile, your brain can drive you to work without any conscious thought. Think of Alpha Mode as "Sleep Mode."

BETA MODE

Beta Mode is the brain's state of active engagement. It's like when you drive to work in a heavy thunderstorm and your hands are firmly gripped at 10 and 2 o'clock. Your eyes are wide open and you're sensitive to everything. You're in Beta Mode when you're watching a movie and the music is building to a crescendo in anticipation of something scary happening. The music puts you on the edge of your seat. Think of Beta Mode as "Alert Mode."

RETICULAR ACTIVATOR

The Reticular Activator is the part of the brain that is on the lookout 24 hours a day, 7 days a week for things that are 1) familiar, 2) unusual, or 3) problematic. When your brain detects any of these things on a subconscious level, it sends a message to the conscious side of the brain that says, "Hey, wake up! There's something you need to pay attention to!" Have you ever bought a new car only to realize afterward that everyone in town seems to have the exact make, model, and color?

ALPHA MODE

This is what
you see.

This is what
your conscious
brain sees.

■ Activators & Hot Buttons

ACTIVATORS

An Activator is anything that snaps a person out of Alpha Mode and into Beta. Any time something familiar, unusual, or problematic enters the Reticular Activator, the brain becomes "activated," hence the name.

Traditional "C&R" advertising likes to use unusual and familiar activators to interrupt people.

Can you match the the activator with the product?

Beware! Just because an Activator has interrupt value <u>does</u> <u>not</u> mean it has engage value. Activators that are not relevant or important to people must be constantly changed to keep people stimulated and therefore require huge advertising budgets to support.

HOT BUTTONS

What Your Brain Does When It Finds An Activator:

- Immediately and subconsciously searches for additional, clarifying info.

- Gauges importance/relevance.

- **If important/relevant:** Conscious bandwidth will be allocated and the brain will become Engaged. This means the Activator is also a Hot Button.

- **If NOT important/relevant:** Brain will immediately revert to Alpha Mode and NOT be Engaged. This means the Activator is NOT a Hot Button--it's a False Beta.

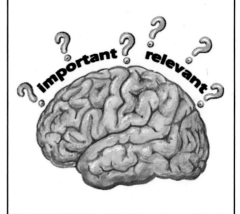

BETA MODE

This is what you <u>want</u> your prospects to see.

Celebrities are used in advertising because they are familiar and therefore register in many people's reticular activators. But since the celebrity often does not connect with the product...

Result: False Beta.

Activators that are strange, shocking, creative, or unusual will interrupt the prospect. But when the brain cannot immediately find additional, clarifying information, it quickly reverts to Alpha Mode.

Result: False Beta

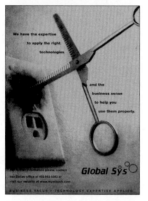

False Betas

If the prospect is interrupted but not engaged, that's a False Beta. For example, in a crowded airport, you hear a voice from behind you call out your name. You turn and realize that the person calling your name was actually calling to someone else who apparently has your same name. What do you do? Do you still engage that person in conversation? Do you ask them what they want? Of course not. In this case you are interrupted but not engaged--a False Beta.

Menu-Board-Style False Betas

This Menu-Board-Style ad will interrupt people who are thinking about buying a camera because the pictures of cameras will register in their Reticular Activator as something familiar, and flip them out of Alpha "Sleep" Mode and into Beta "Alert" Mode. But when the brain tries to find additional information, nothing is found, and all but the most urgent buyers will revert to Alpha Mode.

Finally, An Ad That Works!

Interrupt
Based on Hot Buttons of uncertainty and confusion

Engage
"5 Things You Need To Know..." promises to educate the reader

Educate
Allows reader to control information; identifies important and relevant issues

Offer
"Free Digital Camera Buyer's Guide" Allows reader a low-risk way to take the next step

You'll see this symbol throughout the rest of this book to help rate various marketing pieces. Each of the letters; I, E, E, and O stand for a component of the Marketing Equation--Interrupt, Engage, Educate, and Offer. The corresponding letter will be green if properly implemented, otherwise it will be red. Only when all four components are green will the marketing piece get results.

Headlines

Headlines must be full of hot buttons that will interrupt the prospect. Use hot buttons based on problems, annoyances or fears your prospects have. This triggers an emotional response and prepares them to become engaged.

Company names are NOT hot buttons, and therefore, not appropriate headlines.

Headlines should be used in all marketing pieces, not just advertisements. Even your brochures, websites, signs, and follow-up pieces should contain hot-button-loaded headlines.

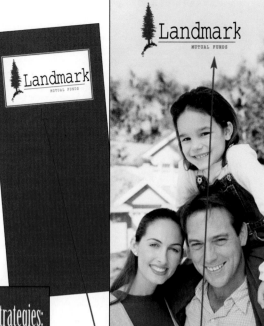

Building Your Future On Solid Ground.

HOT BUTTONS?

Mutual Fund Investment Strategies:

Which Ones Actually Work...

And Which Ones Are Guaranteed To

HOT BUTTON → **Drain** Your Savings,

HOT BUTTON → **Jeopardize** Your Retirement,

And **Squash** Your Quest For Financial Independence.

HOT BUTTON

Landmark
MUTUAL FUNDS

Nobody cares what your company name is until they know what you can do for them.

Will people actually read all those words? Yes, they will **IF** you have the right hot buttons... in which case the reticular activator is helpless. It has **no choice** but to "wake up" your conscious brain and pay attention.

This Brochure Is Just Begging To Be Read.

■ The Marketing Equation Component 3: Educate

Now that the prospect has been successfully interrupted and engaged, your job as marketer is to become the facilitator of information--the fountain from whence all knowledge flows when it comes to figuring out how to buy what you sell.

You've got to give them enough information--quantified, specific, delineated information--that they feel like they understand the important and relevant issues. They need to feel like they're in CONTROL of the decision.

You've got to give them enough information to give them the unshakable confidence that they're making the best decision possible.

The more you educate the prospect on what he needs to know and look for and look out for, the more you're going to sell. The information has to be delivered in a way that's easy to quickly scan and digest. We simply call this component of the marketing equation **Educate**... and the information that is given to educate them is called "CONTROL" information, because it puts them in control of the decision.

Build A Case

Your product or Service IS ON TRIAL

THE CUSTOMER is the Jury

YOU are the attorney

You must **EDUCATE** as to all of the relevant & important issues

Prove that you offer superior value

Present evidence of expert testimony to support your case

Remember, it's a life or death sentence!

How TO Buy SBC's $1,000 A Month 1.544M T1 For Only $399 A Month.

Now You Can Benefit From New Laws That Have Forced SBC To Make Their "Pipes" Available To Other Carriers For A Fraction Of The Cost...

It's True: SBC Has No Choice But To Sell Their Lines For Less Than They Can Charge You.
You know that the Baby Bells have enjoyed monopolies on phone service, but did you know that in 1996, a law was passed forcing the Baby Bells to make their lines available to other carries in an effort to promote competition?

What To Look For... And What To Look OUT For!
Comparing T1's is often like comparing apples to oranges. To make sense of a company's offering, you've got to understand what the important and relevant issues are, including:

1. What is the length of the contract? Most companies charge more money for shorter contracts. We charge on low flat rate, period.

2. **Is the router included or not?** If not, then the telco manages it for you, which will cost you more. We include the router so your cost is LOWER.

3. **How much is the "Loop" charge?** This is how much it costs to get the line from the ISP box to your office. With some companies, your Loop Charge can be as much as 25% of the monthly fee.

4. **Is monitoring included?** Most companies charge more money to monitor your ISP to make sure it's up all the time. We include monitoring even at $399 a month.

How Much SHOULD You Pay For A Good T1?
The bottom line is that if you know how to compare apples to apples, you can get the best value possible. T1's don't have to be expensive, especially if you are educated when you go to purchase one.

Call For Your FREE "T1 Cost Comparison Guide"

Name: _____

Company: _____

Address: _____

City, State, Zip: _____

BERGE telecom Phone: _____ Fax: _____
Please Fax This To (402) 952-5383 or Call (402) 952-5383

I+**E**+**E**+**O** = **RESULTS**

You would think that attorneys would be great marketers since they are experts at building cases. In fact, most attorneys are horrible marketers. If you're in trouble and you needed an attorney, would you call the platitude ad (above) or the marketing equation ad?

■ Marketing Equation Component 4: The Offer

The Educational Spectrum

Most marketing pieces only appeal to NOW buyers. Problem is, those who are ready to buy NOW only account for 1% to 5% of all prospects. By putting a low-risk offer in your ad that allows the prospect to get more information--become more educated--you can capture a much larger portion of prospective buyers.

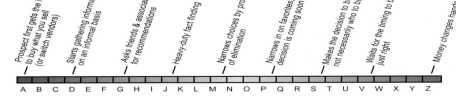

Prospect first gets the idea to buy what you sell (or switch vendors) / Starts gathering information on an informal basis / Asks friends & associates for recommendations / Heavy-duty fact finding / Narrows choices by process of elimination / Narrows in on favorites; decision is coming soon / Makes the decision to buy but not necessarily who to buy from / Waits for the timing to be just right / Money changes hands

A B C D E F G H I J K L M N O P Q R S T U V W X Y Z

Prospects from all points of the Educational Spectrum will respond to your offer, instantly increasing your ad's "pull" by 2 to 100 times. And the best part is that you can now control those prospects by pro-actively nurturing them along via a follow-up system... and capture more more long-term sales.

▶

This ad not only interrupts and engages with hot button-filled headlines, it also educates and extends an offer for a free report.

This Ad Is A Winner.

Compare this ad to those on page 2.

The Only New Home Community In Frisco, Plano Or McKinney With Homes From The $180's To $400's That Was Designed Specifically For Professional People With Children.

- 6 Playgrounds
- 5 Swimming Pools
- 4 Community Centers

- 3 Basketball Courts
- 2 Sets Of Hiking Trails

All Surrounding A Brand New Frisco ISD Elementary School...

Make The Trails of Eastland The Most Kid-Friendly Community In The Entire DFW Area.

The Trails of Eastland

Mayfield Road
Hwy 121
Mainstreet
Trails

Call To Get A Copy Of Our FREE Report -
Ranking Kid-Friendly Communities In DFW--
How They Stack Up & What To Look For

402-952-5383

I + E + O = RESULTS

14

■ Which Do You Think Works Better?
These 2 ads... or the one below?

Do you really want starving students touching your stuff?

If "look for the squirrel" is a hot button for you, then you've got issues!

Do you see how these ads force these companies to compete only on PRICE? None of the important and relevant issues when it comes to moving are discussed. Platitudes prevail.

■ The Marketing Equation: All Together Now

When all of the components come together, not only is it a thing of beauty, but you also make a lot more money!

Remember, human nature demands that people always want to make the best decision possible. Marketing's job is to facilitate that decision-making process. As long as you have each of the 4 components of the marketing equation in place, your ads will work every time.

Will people really read all that text?

They will if they are human beings whose nature demands that they always make the best decision possible. Use the Marketing Equation to facilitate giving them the information they need in an easy-to-understand format.

What can you systematize in your sales cycle? Just about everything. You can systematize the follow-up letters and procedures, the phone scripts, the element of "surprising" your customers, the thank-you letters, how you handle problems, lead generation, everything. You can even systematize your passion and thereby get your people to deliver the passion that *you* have for the business.

If you use marketing tools in your tactical marketing program to create a systematized sales process, you'll reap seven big benefits:

- You'll spend less time trying to create marketing materials and more time implementing and doing. You'll be closing business and making money.

- You'll take the decision-making process out of the hands of your people and put that burden on *your* shoulders as the owner or manager. You gain more control over the sales process by creating consistent performance.

- You can empower your people by giving them small victories consistently. If salespeople can show just enough faith to use your system, they will be successful. They'll boost their self-image and their ability to sell with each small success. It's an upward spiral—not the usual downward spiral of demoralized salespeople who quit all the time.

- Your salespeople can work more prospects at the same time. This allows you to have fewer salespeople and more prospects.

- You can train your people on what's really important: people skills, personal development skills and closing skills. Remember, we're not just trying to affect people's jobs; we're trying to affect their lives. If you can help that person in his personal development, you'll have a better salesperson to run your system. Unfortunately, most companies find no time for such training because they're trying to figure out how to generate enough leads to keep the people they have busy.

- You can duplicate yourself in terms of time, passion, and energy. You can perpetuate yourself beyond your physical limitations.

- You will attract more superstars to work for you. They'll see how easy you make their job, how they can work more prospects in the same time, and how much more money they'll make working for you rather than their competitors. There will be a line waiting to work for you. That's another clever way to swing your 80/20 rule around. Make your place *the* place to work.

Chapter 15:

Hopper Systems

You need to consistently contact your prospects with effective
marketing pieces to nurture them along the educational spectrum.

So far we've discussed your strategic marketing plan—figuring out what to say, how to say it and who to say it to. We introduced the *marketing equation* and explained how to make it the foundation for your strategic marketing plan. Then we examined your tactical marketing plan. We introduced *Franchising the Sales System* and described how to systematize many elements using lead generation and marketing tools.

Now you've identified your target market, and, in the case of a non-defined target market, you've generated leads through various media. Then you've created marketing tools such as reports, sales scripts, on-hold messages, in-store signage and follow-up letters. Those tools are all designed to increase the conversion ratio of all those leads you've generated. They also make your salespeople more effective, which will help you sell more products and services.

Because you've implemented the *marketing equation* and put offers in all of your marketing pieces—offers designed to get prospects from all points of the *educational spectrum* to respond so they can receive more information and education, you'll get two types of leads. The offer will attract prospects who will convert immediately and become customers. You sell to them right away.

However, your offer will also attract prospects who DON'T convert right away—even if you have good marketing pieces and the proper decision-facilitating information at their disposal. They are just not far enough to the right on the *educational spectrum.*

You need a **hopper system** for these people. You need to consistently contact your target market—whether that is a defined target market or a database of prospects generated by advertising—with compelling marketing pieces to nurture them to the point where they're finally ready to buy.

In effect, the hopper system trains your prospects to buy from you when *they* are ready. You'll be surprised how easy and cost effective this is to do.

Let me give you an example. Some years ago, I planted a plum tree in my backyard. Every year, this tree produced hundreds of plums. One year, when my oldest daughter was three, she was fascinated by the prospect of eating some fruit from a tree in our backyard. All spring, as the green plums grew bigger and bigger, she wanted to know if we could pick them. Of course, I explained that they had to turn red before they would be ready to eat. There must have been over 500 plums on the tree.

One day my daughter ran into the house, all excited. "Dad! There are red ones on the tree!" I went out there, and, sure enough, there were about six red, ripe plums hanging among the hundreds of green ones. We got a bag. I lifted her up and we picked those six ripe plums. She was excited.

But then for a few days, not another plum turned red. Of course, with sunshine and rain—and time—more plums became ripe. A week later we got a few more. Over the course of a month, every single plum turned red.

Think of that plum tree with all those green plums as your target market. At any given time, a few of them will be ready to buy (they'll be ripe and ready to harvest). All of the rest will not be ready for various reasons. Why would one of your prospects not buy from you right now? You spent all this money generating leads, and now they won't buy from you! Why not? There could be a hundred reasons, but we can break them down into six categories:

- They have a relationship with one of your competitors.
- They don't have the money to buy right now.
- They just bought one of what you're selling, and they don't need another one right now.
- Maybe they don't really realize that you're an option. Maybe they were in alpha mode when they saw your ad and don't even remember you.

- Maybe you haven't done a good job of building your outside perception and they just don't think you're the best deal.
- Maybe you're NOT the best deal, in which case you'd better go back to square one and innovate your inside reality.

The most likely scenario is that they're hanging out somewhere on the left hand side of the *educational spectrum*, gathering information, considering their options, and waiting for the right time to take action. But just because they're not buying right now, doesn't mean they won't buy!

I once heard a famous sales trainer say to a large group of salespeople, "If the prospect isn't ready, and you determine that he won't buy within 30 days, then he's not a prospect. Get rid of him." In other words, abandon the tree! That is the most inane advice I can imagine! It shows ignorance of the *educational spectrum*, not to mention a lack of common sense. But few companies put any effort into selling to their database of leads. They just cull the red plums from the tree and move on. Instead of waiting for the ripening ones, they look for another tree with those six ripe plums.

To *Monopolize Your Marketplace*, you have to wait patiently and encourage the green prospects. You accomplish this by setting up a system that nurtures your prospects. A plum tree needs water, sunshine, pesticide and pruning; your prospects need a system for receiving additional information that touches their hot buttons and is presented in an interesting and embraceable way to nudge them along the *educational spectrum* until they're ready to buy.

That suggests that you need a system for presenting them with interesting and embraceable information. Most businesses, if they do anything, use a highly ineffective method for nurturing their prospects. It's what I call the "annoying little voice on the other end of the phone." Every month or two, a salesperson will call the people on his list—his green plums—and say something totally non-compelling.

For example, the person calls and says, "Hello, may I please speak with Mr. Johnson? Hey, this is Bob over at American Widget Corp. Remember you called us last June on an ad you saw in the trade journal about some widgets? You don't remember? Well, did you get the letter and brochure that I mailed to you? Oh, don't worry about it. Anyway, I was just calling to see if you guys need any widgets yet? You don't? Okay, no problem. I'll keep you on my list and give you a call in a couple of months to see if you need any then."

Do you realize how stupid and annoying that sounds from the prospect's point of view? You probably do because you also *get* such calls from people who are trying to sell *you* something. They call and ask: "Are you ready to buy something yet? Can I have a meeting with you, please? Will you return my call? Why won't you answer my emails?"

I won't even talk to these people because I know they're only calling me because I popped up on a defined target market list for their company. Instead of trying to cram their personality down my throat via the telephone, why not nurture me with marketing?

Annoying phone calls from pesky salespeople add no value to your marketing efforts. It's like spraying poison on your plum tree instead of pesticide. Don't be fooled into thinking just because you're doing something—making annoying calls—that you're nurturing your prospects. Guess what? You're killing them!

What's worse, though, is not checking the tree at all! This is what most businesses do. It's like picking all your ripe plums, then just leaving the tree. No watering. No fertilizing. No spraying for bugs. No pruning. No anything. Then what happens? As the sunshine and rain do their work, the fruit becomes ripe, but you're not there to pick it. So, it falls to the ground and starts to rot.

In marketing terms, prospects get on the *educational spectrum*, gravitating toward the right-hand side of the spectrum over time. When they become ready to buy, they start trying to find somebody to buy from, and guess what!? You're AWOL! They can't find you!

This story then has one of two tragic endings: First, a competitor happens by, sees the ripe prospects, and says, "Look at that, ripe prospects who are ready to buy." You lose the sale. Or, when the prospects become ready to buy, they can't find anyone to service their need—so nothing happens. They just remain on the *educational spectrum* and never take action. What a tragedy!

Don't let that happen to you! Instead, put a hopper system in place to nurture your prospects. The optimal situation would be to hire one salesperson for each prospect—one person to baby-sit each and every green plum. Obviously, that's impractical; you'll to have to settle for something less. Most companies try "relationship selling," but relationship selling won't work to nurture your entire target market. And that is exactly what you have to do if you truly want to *Monopolize Your Marketplace.*

I'm not saying you shouldn't build relationships with your prospects or that you shouldn't have a couple dozen important accounts that you pay close attention to. In fact, in a minute, I'll discuss a relationship-sales strategy called the *"Knock-Down List."*

But we call our system *Monopolize Your Marketplace* for a reason. We're talking about achieving real-world market dominance. I understand that some people don't want to own the world, and they're satisfied with their little plot. That's fine. Just make sure that when you set your sights on a given geographic or demographic market—no matter how big or small—that you follow this system so you can dominate it.

Here's the mindset that I think is unacceptable: "We'll just take whatever business we can get." No! The attitude is, "Here's everyone who is a potential customer. Let's figure out how to get them all." I'm not naive enough to think that 100 percent of all the people in the world will buy from you. But I do believe you can knock down a high percentage of a given target market if you build your business the MYM way. You can dominate if you have a superior inside reality *and* outside perception. Then you have to put together a powerful marketing strategy and systematize the tactical execution of that program by *Franchising the Sales System*. Do all that and monopolizing your marketplace is a real possibility.

The entire marketplace won't buy from you right away. But there is a payoff for those with the patience and know-how to nurture. I want to set up a system that nurtures the entire orchard for me in one fell swoop instead of hiring 100 salespeople to work with every potential prospect individually. I want to create a system where a few people can do all the nurturing for me. I want to install a massive irrigation system that waters the entire orchard at the flip of a switch. I want to hire an airplane to drop pesticide on all the trees. I want to send in heavy equipment to prune and harvest when the time is right. I can thus work the entire marketplace with marketing.

This is how you educate your prospects and bridge the confidence gap. I send an army of tiny salesmen in the form of marketing tools to create a *hopper system*. Every two weeks we use marketing tools to build confidence, educate the prospects, overcome objections, and cause them to take action! Basically, we just nudge them along until they're ready to buy.

One tenet of traditional sales training is to ask the prospect a bunch of questions so that you can determine their needs and provide the exact solution—one that is unique to that prospect. That would be a neat way to do it if we had those 1,000 salesmen working for us. But that's a not valid approach since 80 percent of your prospects have identical needs and wants. You can validate this in the discovery portion of building your strategic marketing plan.

For example, think about the marketing strategy for manufacturers.

Manufacturers that sell through distribution use the *Make More Money* strategy. Most manufacturers typically have poor marketing that focuses on the products and how great they are. But, distributors only care about making money. So that should be the focus of the marketing program. All the great features of the products only entice the end-users. If more people need the product, the distributor will make more money! Why would you talk about anything else but making money? All the other features only support the fact that the distributor can make more money. So, build a case that shows how the distributor can make more money. Then send out marketing tools, piece by piece, bit by bit, until the prospect starts to believe it.

If 80 percent of your prospects have the same needs, then you can market to them on an on-going basis, solving their problems the whole time. From a strategic standpoint, it's easy to see what to say to your prospects when following up. What about the tactical side? What methods should you use to communicate regularly. Basically, there are three major message-delivery options you can use: mail, fax and email.

We like to follow up by sending large, oversized postcards 6 inches by 11 inches. There's lots of room to communicate your message and, since they are postcards, they don't have to be opened. This forces the prospect to read your message as they handle the piece of mail and decide what to do with it.

You might be saying to yourself, "They'll see this as junk mail and immediately throw it in the trash." That's true in many cases. However, postcards are perfect for the reticular activator, which is constantly on the lookout 24 hours a day, seven days a week for things that are familiar, unusual, or problematic. They allow you to tap into the prospect's reticular activator with hot buttons based on familiar problems. This interrupts the prospect and pulls him out of alpha mode into beta alert mode.

When the prospect receives your postcard, he looks at it for that split second and tries to figure out what to do with it. As long as the headline contains a valid, relevant, important hot button, you'll make a connection. Prospects might still throw the card away because maybe they are not far enough along the *educational spectrum* to take any action. But you've made the contact and sent a message. Then you must consistently follow up so that you can push them over the edge or be there ready to interrupt when events or circumstances push them over the edge. The goal is to *be there when they are looking for solutions.*

The same is true for faxes. The prospect has to look at the fax. This enables you to make an impression on the prospect's reticular activator—if you use a valid, relevant and important hot button in the headline of that fax. Again, I am talking about using faxes as a follow-up tool for businesses that have already contacted you in response to your offers. I don't recommend using fax broadcasting for lead generators.

And what about emails? Again, I know people get swamped with emails, both legitimate and "spam" solicitations. It's all about interrupting the prospect with the proper hot buttons, which you put into powerfully articulated headlines. In the case of emails, this is the subject line.

For examples of hopper systems, check online at www.mymbook.com.

A hopper system can cause a dramatic increase in sales. How can you implement a hopper system? Simply schedule your hopper system ahead six months to one year. Here's what you do.

1. Select the most important hot buttons, gleaned from the discovery section of your strategic marketing plan.
2. Rate the hot buttons according to importance.
3. Allocate your hopper system pieces accordingly.

You can write your schedule on a piece of paper or on a spreadsheet. Either way, make the column headings as follows: *Week, Date, Medium, Hot Button,* and *Headline.*

Under the heading of *Week* #, list every week in the six- or 12-month period you'll be scheduling; this is simply 1, 2, 3, and so on up to 26 or 52 weeks. Under the *Date,* list the actual date that the piece will launch.

Next, write the *medium,* whether that be mail, fax, or email. If you're on a tight budget and think mail is too expensive, you may decide to go with fax and email on alternate weeks. You just go down the sheet alternating fax and email until the end of the sheet.

The last two columns are ranked *Hot Buttons* and *Headlines.* Suppose you have three major hot buttons, and you determine that hot button #1 is the most important, hot button #2 is next, and #3 ranks third.

For example, we worked with a client that made soaps for car washes. This client had a defined target market: car wash operators. As we put together their strategic marketing plan, we identified three major hot buttons based on their inside reality. Hot button #1 was safety, #2 was price, and #3 was effectiveness.

Most car wash soaps are made from caustic, soda-based materials that are hazardous to just about everything they come in contact with (caustic soda is basically baking soda). Soaps are made from caustic sodas because they eat the dirt off cars. That's an effective way to get them clean; however, the side effects are near-disastrous. These materials are hazardous to car wash employees. They cause the car wash equipment to disintegrate over time, and, alarmingly, they destroy the clear coat and paint job on the cars.

Our client invented a different chemical solution for their soap that was completely safe for people, equipment, and cars. This made their car wash unique. Since they felt safety was their most important hot button, we felt they should spend most of their time, money, and energy promoting safety. The second hot button was the fact that their products actually worked better, because the soap got the cars cleaner. And third, their products cost less than the more-destructive, less-effective competitive soaps.

Here's how this works in a hopper system: We weighted the relative importance of each of those hot buttons. We decided that safety was 60 percent important, with effectiveness and cost ranked 20 percent each. Then we allocated the follow-up messages accordingly: 60 percent of the messages hit the *safety* hot button, 20 percent discussed the *cost* hot button, and the 20 percent addressed the *effective* hot button. We decided that that we would send hopper system pieces once per week, and send a postcard week 1, a fax week 2, and an email week 3. Then we repeated that cycle. So, on the schedule, under the column labeled medium, we listed postcard, fax, email; postcard, fax, email; postcard, fax, email.

In the column labeled *Hot Button*, we divided the hot buttons according to their relative importance. Six out of 10 postcards talked about *safety*, two out of 10 addressed *price*, and two out of 10 discussed *effectiveness*. Same for faxes and emails.

The last thing to complete on the schedule is to write in the headline for each piece. Of course, you have to write the pieces to know what the headlines are, but with this schedule, at least you know what to focus each piece on.

Write all the pieces before you implement the program. Our experience shows that no matter how good your intentions are, if you don't have it finished before you start, you'll get behind and quit. This is one of the key principles in making systems work: *finish planning before you start executing*.

Hopper System One Year Plan

Week Number	Date	Medium	Hot Button	Headline
1				
2				
3				
4				
5				
6				
7				
8				
9				
10				
11				
12				
13				
14				
15				
16				
17				
18				
19				
20				
21				
22				
23				
24				
25				
26				
27				
28				
29				
30				
31				
32				
33				
34				
35				
36				
37				
38				
39				
40				
41				
42				
43				
44				
45				
46				
47				
48				
49				
50				
51				
52				

So, start putting your *hopper system* together. Even if you can't write the pieces, you can fill out the sheet and know what to send and when to send it. Here's a copy of the blank sheet.

Once you've scheduled your *hopper system* and written the pieces, pull the trigger and let it fly. Again, if you are trying to manage more than 200 prospects, I recommend you outsource the execution of the system. It's easy to intend to do this and then never do it. You may need help with layout, design, and mailing of the postcards. You may need help managing email distributions. I recommend calling or emailing us to get help with this.

Chapter 16:

Knock-Down Lists

A certain number of your prime prospects should be selected, assigned to salespeople, and given some preferential treatment.

In the last chapter, I insisted you need a *hopper system* to nurture prospects along the *educational spectrum* because you can't "relationship sell" an entire target market. However, *knock-down lists* allow you to systematize relationship selling. A *knock-down list* is a smaller subset of your entire target market—those select prospects you'd like as clients (the ones you want to close or "knock down").

Here's how it works: Depending on the nature of what you sell and the time restraints of your salespeople, you'll want to assign between 10 and 25 prospects to each of your salespeople's *knock-down list*. Decide who to put on the list by carefully studying the leads list you've generated through the media in the case of a non-defined market or from your entire target market that you've pinpointed, identified, and collected in the case of a defined target market. Either way, choose about 10 to 25 prospects per salesperson based on companies that fit the profile of your ideal customer. You know who these people are. But what do you do with them?

1. *Manage your prime prospects along with other prospects in your hopper system*. Your *knock-down list* will operate side-by-side with your hopper system, not instead of your hopper system.

2. *Set a budget.* How much money will you spend on each prospect on

your *knock-down list* monthly? You'll need that budget to buy them stuff and send them things. Say you've got five salespeople and you assign 20 prospects per salesperson, for a total of 100 prospects on your *knock-down list*. If you spend $10 per prospect per month, that will cost you $1,000 per month to fulfill. If you budget $50 per month per prospect, that will cost you $5,000 to execute. Since these are prospects you'd really like to land, allot a decent budget to chase them. Calculate their future profitability (use the ROI worksheet if you need to).

3. ***Decide how and when to spend the budget.*** Make deposits in their "emotional bank accounts" regularly to build the relationship. I'm not talking about taking prospects to lunch or playing golf. Those things are okay, but I am talking about buying them stuff that will interrupt them—get them out of alpha mode and into beta mode and give them a good feeling about your company to nurture the relationship.

One of my friends, Glen, runs a successful manufacturing business in the Dallas-Fort Worth area. We helped Glen put together a defined target list of 2,000 prospects to launch his *hopper system.* In addition, we identified 25 prospects for each of his four salespeople to put on their *knock-down lists.* First, we sent each person a sincere letter to let them know that they were on the list; we put them "on notice" that they were now on our radar and that we were serious.

Next, we thought of some good stuff to give these people. A big part of Glen's philosophy is that business should be fun; so we looked for some fun ideas. Glen budgeted $50 per month per prospect. We bought some advertising specialties (promotional products with the company's name printed on them.) We started out with pens, mugs, slinkies and foam light bulbs. But instead of just giving his prospects a pen, he made little boxes, put about 50 pens in them, and placed them on the prospect's desk.

Glen had fun sending this stuff to his prospects, but after a while, he wanted to do something with more interrupt value. After all, the point of the *knock-down list* is to get prospects out of alpha mode and into beta mode—and give them a good feeling about your company and its products and services.

So, after a couple of months, we shifted strategies. We searched for items that had better interrupt value. One thing we sent was the "World's Largest Hershey Bar," a Hershey Bar that weighs five pounds and measures 18 inches long (50 times bigger than a regular Hershey bar)! Instead of sending it to the person, Glen or his salesperson would hand deliver it to the receptionist of the intended recipient and ask him or her to make sure it got to the right person.

Glen believes that there's added value in not always giving stuff that has your corporate name or logo on it. This allows the recipient to feel like it's an actual gift. There's also value in giving the gift without being there. It allows you to add deposits to that person's emotional bank account because there's no immediate expectation of reciprocation, as there would be in a face-to-face gift-giving situation.

Then Glen got really creative. He found a source for shocking cigarette lighters. He went to the receptionist and said, "I've got this gift for so and so. It's a cool lighter. You should see how high the flame goes on this thing. Here, try it." He'd hand the lighter to the receptionist, who would respond by trying the lighter and then receiving the electric shock. This was followed immediately by laughter. The point of the *knock-down list* gift is first to interrupt, and second, to give the person a good feeling. Does shocking them with a cigarette lighter give them a good feeling? Ironically, it does, because then you give the recipient of the practical joke the chance to become the prankster and the center of attention on the next "victim." It taps into people's core emotional need to feel important.

Then Glen found a remote-controlled flatulence machine. You hide the sound-emanating device under somebody's chair and then push the key-fob control button from inside your pocket. Glen would go into meetings and ask his host for a drink of water. He would then plant the device. Four minutes into the discussion, the fun began. Again, this allowed the victim of the joke to turn around and become the prankster, the center of attention. And Glen always got the credit of being the one who supplied the fun.

Glen next rigged his Internet contests. Contests on his web site included drawings for prizes, often $100 gift certificates to popular restaurants like the Outback Steakhouse. He'd put a pass code on all his *hopper-system* pieces that discussed the drawing. Glen then phoned his *knock-down list* prospects and told them in passing that they could rig the results of the contest by hitting the back button on their web browsers to enter again for another chance to win. They could do this as many times as they wanted.

Some of his prospects entered the contest as many as 300 times. Since the contest was rigged anyway—it wasn't actually a drawing—he'd just look for the people who took the time and effort to act on his "inside" information. Glen sent them the gift certificates after calling to congratulate them on their victory.

Glen's efforts made deposits in the "emotional bank accounts" of his prospects. I'm not saying you have to do these same things, but I am saying that you can get a lot of mileage from showering small but interesting—and inter-rupting—gifts on your prospects to build a relationship with them. These gifts lead to a reciprocity that comes in the form of orders.

On a more conservative level, you may want to use promotional products with your name or logo. If so, we suggest things that are either fun or useful—things like mouse pads, calendars, clocks, letter openers, rulers, coasters, highlighters, thermal mugs, or toy trucks. Mixing in some lunches or golf won't hurt either.

If you want to take the *knock-down list* to the next level, gather as much per-sonal information as possible about the prospect. Find out about birthdays, spouses, children, interests and hobbies. If you find out your prospect is a big NASCAR rac-ing fan, send them NASCAR-theme stuff or tickets to NASCAR races. You can send them toys or games they can give to their children. You can find a unique gift for their spouse if you are traveling overseas. Become genuinely interested in the per-son and show it to build a relationship. Make consistent deposits in the "emotional bank accounts" of your prospects—the ones you want to build a relationship with.

This kind of systematized effort works well in building any relationship. In fact, I use this in my marriage. When I got married 12 years ago, I looked at my wife and told her, "I love you." Being a man, I thought that ought to last for life. I mean, I said it—and I'm still here more than a decade later. I take out the trash. I empty the dish-washer. For a man, that's enough. But for most women, they want to hear those magic words and see that you really care. So, I've created a system to prevent things from falling through the cracks. That's what a *hopper system* is all about. Here's how this system works. The first of every month I fill out four different cards from Hallmark. Then, I send one card every week. She loves that. Every couple of months, I send her on a getaway just by herself or with a friend to get away from the kids. Every three months, I take her on a two-day getaway with just me, again away from the kids. Once a month – but on a different day of the month so it doesn't look like a system—I send her flowers. And she loves it. It's all systematic.

When you systemize things, you keep important things from falling through the cracks. That's what *Franchising the Sales System* is all about. For each sales-person, identify 10 to 25 prospects whom you can nurture into customers. The number of prospects might differ for each salesperson. A new salesperson who has few regular accounts and spends a lot of time prospecting could use more, and a veteran salesperson with a full client roster that requires more time and attention might use less. You decide. But implement this important tactical strat-egy. The money invested will reap a big reward for you and your company.

Chapter 17:

Your Tactical Marketing Plan and Budget

Your plan and budget should reflect your enlightened understanding of the importance and place of marketing in your organization.

We are often asked, "How much will it cost to implement a tactical marketing system?

To estimate the cost, we need to synthesize lead generation, marketing tools, *hopper systems,* and *knock-down lists.* We use the *Tactical Marketing Plan Overview/Cost Worksheet.* Each section on the worksheet has columns for the specific media, quantity, cost, start date, and duration.

Because every company's tactical plan and budget will be different, I'll talk in generalities. Let's start by answering the most basic question: How much money should I allocate to execute my marketing plan? I believe you should spend as much money as you can possibly afford on marketing. Of course, you don't want to spend any money on the *wrong* marketing program. You only want to spend your hard-earned cash on a marketing plan that's deeply rooted in the *marketing*

equation. You only want to invest in a plan you have tested in small-scale tests to ensure a return on your marketing investment when you roll it out on a larger scale.

Marketing offers you the ultimate leverage in your business. It allows you to create a "profit faucet." If you can figure out how to generate leads, why wouldn't you want to generate as many leads as you could handle? Assuming that those leads are profitable, why would you want to limit the number of leads—and the amount of money you can make—to some arbitrary number that your bean counters call "the budget?"

Please understand: ***Marketing is the most important activity in your business***. It offers you leverage. Its upside potential is unlimited. Every other function in a business is subservient to marketing—including your bean counters! Your production capacities, employee-retention strategies, and everything else are subservient to marketing. You should maximize your investment in marketing because that will make the biggest difference in your company's bottom line. Let your accountants figure out what to do with all the money you're making after you've made it; don't let them throw some arbitrary budget restraint at you.

How do you know how much you to spend? Look at the worksheet. Start with lead generators. Figure out which media will work best for you. Test your ideas. Remember, our consultants can guide you through this process if you need help.

List your lead generation methods on the worksheet. If you decide that a radio campaign on certain stations would work, write each station individually on the worksheet, along with the other information for each column as appropriate. If you decide that direct mail would also be an effective way to generate leads, put that down. List all components of the direct mail campaign, including the cost to rent the mailing list, the cost of the printing, the cost of the postage, the cost of processing, and so forth. Get it all down. At the bottom of the worksheet, add it up to gain an at-a-glance view of your tactical plan and the total costs.

Next, determine marketing tools to use. If you decide to implement an on-hold message, you have some production costs. Estimate the costs for web sites, signage, and reports. After you put together a written report, you can use the material for audios, videos, even DVDs, once you know the strategic message in the report is on the money. There's nothing worse than spending tens of thousands of dollars creating the best DVD only to realize that it's got the wrong message. You'll need to figure out how many reports to print, determine the print cost, as well as the design and layout expenses. Again, the point of this worksheet is to put all your costs in front of your face so you can evaluate them.

The *hopper system* is next. There are three major hopper system components: mail, fax, and email. Again, when it comes to mail, we like to use 6 x 11 oversized postcards. Estimate a cost of 50 cents each. This includes the printing, postage, and the mail house processing. Layout and design would be additional, and you'd need to adjust those prices to your country and current mail prices.

For example, if you decide to send a postcard every two weeks to a database of 5,000 prospects, that will cost you $65,000 (26 times per year x 5,000 prospects = 130,000 postcards x 50 cents each). Let's also say that you allocate about $3,000 for the design and layout of those postcards. That's a total cost of about $68,000 for the year.

Sending out follow-up faxes is more economical, but there's a trade-off: it's less effective. Faxes typically cost about 15 cents each to deploy. (You may need to adjust that for the same reasons as we discussed for mailings.) To reach those same 5,000 prospects with faxes twice a month would cost you just under $20,000. Layout and design costs would be nominal or non-existent, since there's not a whole lot to a fax. Emails are cheaper still—costing anywhere from free up to a couple cents apiece. One of your biggest challenges will be getting the email addresses. Let's allocate $5,000 for email address acquisition and sending, bringing the total cost of implementing this *hopper system* to about $93,000 a year.

You might think $93,000 is a lot, or perhaps not enough. But, you've got to figure out how much your average customer and sale is worth to you before determining the true value. First, that number translates to $7,750 per month. That's a reasonable marketing figure. Next, look up your ROI worksheet. We used it earlier to determine how much to spend on advertising. But we can also use it for evaluating the profitability of a *hopper system*. Now you can make an intelligent decision about your *hopper system*. Will the gross profit of your average sale justify this expense?

Here's an example of how this works. We consulted with an automotive battery distributor that that did annual sales of $22 million in a seven-state region. We determined they had a defined target market, meaning that we could identify, pinpoint, and obtain a list of their prospects who were automotive parts stores and mechanics. We determined they had about 12,000 prospects with 2,000 already in their database. That left 10,000 prospects.

We decided to send one postcard every two weeks and a fax the other week. We would have to spend about $130,000 for postcards. We determined that only half the prospects on the list had fax numbers, giving us 5,000 prospects x 26 weeks x 15 cents = $20,000. We further determined that only about 20 percent had available email addresses. They would cost us some manpower to call those prospects and get them, to the tune of about $5,000. Total implementation cost for this *hopper system* was $155,000.

Jim, the owner, practically fainted when he saw that number. Why? Because as a distributor, he had never spent *any* money on a marketing program before, let alone $155,000 in year. And that price didn't include another $18,000 for marketing tools or our fees for putting it all together. No wonder Jim was stunned.

We asked Jim how many communications each of those 12,000 prospects, excluding current customers, had from his company last year. The contact could have been via mailers, salespeople, advertising, anything. The answer was close to zero. We explained to Jim this was why he was unable to increase his sales much over the last 10 years. He wasn't contacting anybody about anything! His prospects didn't even know he was an option!

Then we explained what the $155,000 would buy him: all 10,000 prospects will receive a well articulated, powerfully stated, *marketing equation*-styled postcard from his company every two weeks that hits their hot buttons, identifies with their problems and puts his company's inside reality on shining display 26 times a year; and 5,000 of those prospects will also receive a fax every two weeks that will do the same thing. Those 5,000 prospects are now receiving 52 contacts a year from him. Each of the contacts will follow the *marketing equation* and will make offers for more educational information. Since his inside reality is solid, and since his company adds value to its customers by solving problems nobody else solves, is it likely that at least *some* of those prospects will take Jim up on those offers, move through his sales system and become customers during the next 12 months. Jim says, "Well, I guess it would make sense that at least some of them would respond and buy."

This is the next question for Jim: "What is your average sale?" After some arm twisting, we found out the average number of batteries ordered per year from the average customer is 240, and the average gross profit per battery is $21. That's an annual gross profit of $5,040 per customer. Let's round that off to $5,000 per customer. We had to determine how many average customers this *hopper system* would have to convert to at least break even on this tactical marketing plan. Here's the math:

Divide $155,000 by $5,000. Answer: about 31 new average customers. Just 31 out of 10,000!

Jim was still a little gun shy. So here's what we did. So, we cut out the 5,000 prospects who don't have a fax machine. It's a decent bet that if they don't have a fax machine, that means that they're a smaller player and they won't be one of his best customers anyway. We chopped those 5,000 right off the top, deciding not to send them anything. That reduced the postcard load by 130,000 for the year and cut $65,000 from the budget. That brought the cost down to $90,000, with the break-even at just 18 new customers.

This worksheet allows you to adjust your numbers to see what works. If Jim didn't want to spend that much money, but he also didn't want to cut out part of the database, we could have adjusted the frequency of the mailers. Instead of every two weeks, we'd send them every three. Since we'd only send so many times a year, we'd only have to spend $85,000 for postcards. Or, we could send postcards once per month and increase the frequency of faxes or emails to compensate. This tool allows you to play the "what if" game to run different scenarios.

Use this sheet to map out your plan and estimate your costs. Get all the costs on the table and then evaluate them before proceeding.

Before we move on to *Maximizing and Optimizing* your business, I want to make an important point: using this tool, you can also determine the lifetime value of your customers. The automotive battery distributor determined that his average customer buys 240 batteries a year at an average of $21 gross profit. That equals an annual gross profit of $5,040 per average customer. The next step is to determine, based on historical averages, how long your average customer stays with you. We asked the automotive battery distributor how long his average customer was likely to stick around; mystified, he said, "We lose a few customers per year. Sometimes a company goes out of business or gets sold. Occasionally they drop us for another brand. But, once we get a customer, we basically keep them forever." I asked him to define "forever." Jim responded, "Maybe 20 to 30 years? We've been in business 55 years, and we've had a consistent loyal client base ever since my dad started this business." I asked him if he was keeping new customers who just started buying batteries in recent years. Jim says, "Yeah. Not much of a problem."

Let's assume that the average new customer stays on board for just three years. That customer would be worth $15,000 in gross profits during that time. If the retention rate is 5 years, then they would be worth $25,000. Look what that does to the ROI equation. If you spend $150,000 on marketing, you'd only need 10 new customers to pay for the implementation! Granted, it would take five years to recoup the cash outlay. Using the lifetime value of your customers helps you evaluate the costs of your *hopper system* in a different light. Now, you can make rational decisions how to invest your marketing money.

Let's take this one step further. Say the battery distributor decided on a tactical plan that cost $150,000 per year. Let's say that program hauled in 25 new customers a year. Remember, we bombarded 5,000 prospects with as many as 62 marketing messages a year. And these messages were well articulated, powerfully stated, *marketing equation*-oriented powerhouses. Let's say that those numbers hold up for five consecutive years. In year one, the cash outlay would be $150,000, and the return would be $125,000 in gross profit, for a net loss of $25,000. I realize nobody wants to lose $25,000, but stick with me on this.

In the second year, the company spends the same $150,000 on the marketing plan, realizing an additional $125,000 in gross profit from these new customers. But in year two, you'd have to factor in the $125,000 in gross profits from the new customers who are still on the books. Add that to the current year's loss of $25,000, and that gives you a profit of $100,000 for year two.

In year three, there would be the usual $25,000 front-end loss on the new customers. But now you add the new customers from the past two years who are still on the books at $125,000 gross profit per year. Now year three profit equals $225,000. Year four yields a gross profit of $350,000, and year five yields a nice $475,000 profit. Assuming that each new customer only lasts five years, the profit for year six and beyond would remain at the $475,000 range. Remember, this is *additional* profit—above and beyond what the company was earning before we implemented a marketing program.

By year five, your profit statement looks like this: Expenditures on the tactical marketing program: $750,000. Gross profits resulting from the marketing program: $1,875,000. Net profit: $1,100,000.

Do you see why we call this a ***profit faucet***? It's easy to win business when you understand these numbers.

Now consider the what if's. What if you increased the marketing expenditures to $250,000 a year and brought in 50 customers instead of just 25 per year? In that scenario, you would double the expenses and the gross profits; you'd spend $1.5 million on marketing to generate $3.75 million in gross profits to produce a $2.2 million net profit. Wouldn't you spend twice as much on marketing if you felt reasonably confident that you could double or triple your profitability? Do you think you can make those kinds of returns in the stock market? Business is where the money is made, and marketing is the engine that fuels its profitability. Never forget that all other functions in business are subservient to marketing.

Now it's your turn. Calculate the lifetime value of your average customer. Multiply the average gross profit per customer by the average duration of the customer relationship. Once you know this number, you'll have a greater appreciation for how much money to spend on implementing your tactical marketing program. You'll be one step closer to creating your own profit faucet.

As we wrap up the *Franchising Your Sales System*. I strongly encourage you to go back and fill out the various worksheets and templates. You'll find them tremendously helpful.

SECTION V:

Maximizing and Optimizing Your Business

Get your customers to come back more often,
spend more when they do, and bring their friends, too!

Maximizing and optimizing has to do with taking the resources and assets you already have at your disposal and leveraging them for even more profitability. The biggest of these assets are your current customers. I'll teach you how to implement strategies to increase the average amount of money your customers spend with you. That's on a per-transaction basis or a frequency basis or both.

Think about it. What if it were possible to increase the automotive battery company's gross profit from $21 to $23? Or, what if you could nudge the average annual sales from 240 batteries to 250? What if you could do both? How about adding incremental sales and profits that weren't necessarily "batteries?"

This is what maximizing and optimizing is all about—getting a fatter paycheck from the existing assets you already have. Not by deceit or trickery, but by implementing strategies that add more value to your customers and, as a result, earn you more money.

Another asset that you have access to is other businesses. You can access their customer lists and springboard off the credibility they have with their customers to increase sales for both companies. You can even do this, surprisingly enough, with your competitors.

Monopolize Your Marketplace

We'll cover four ways to maximize and optimize your business: 1) perpetual sales strategies; 2) joint ventures; 3) upselling; and 4) referrals.

Chapter 18:

Perpetual Selling Strategies

Would it help, for starters, if you could entice your current
customers to come back again and again to buy more and more?

The idea behind *Perpetual Selling Strategies* is to get customers to come back for more, forever. Many companies are so busy harvesting the "red plums" off any tree they can find that they only see the ripe fruit in front of their faces. We already discussed how to set up a hopper system to capture more of the non-buyers and turn them into paying customers. But what about taking those customers who do buy from you and turning them into repeat customers who come back over and over again? Or, if they already come back, what if you could get them to come back more often?

Most companies leave the repeat sales totally up to chance. They cross their fingers and hope that the customer has a good enough experience to venture back. They hope the customers appreciate their inside reality so that coming back is a no-brainer. Sometimes this works; sometimes it doesn't. But it *never* maximizes the relationship with the customer. In addition, many businesses think that just because their customers DO come back, they are buying as much as they could be or should be. This is rarely true.

Everyone's heard that it costs more to capture new customers than it does to keep existing ones. The beauty of *Perpetual Selling Strategies* is that spending just a little bit of money on your current customers goes a long way. You don't have to spend a ton of money to keep customers on board; you just need to know how much money to spend and, more importantly, what to spend it on, strategically and tactically. These ideas show you a few low cost, easy-to-implement ways to **keep your customers coming back for more**.

My aim is not to give you specific ideas on what you can do in your business. Napoleon Hill states that the value of reading books lies more in the thoughts they produce in our minds than in the words themselves. My hope is to spark thoughts of how you can implement these strategies in your business. So, keep an open mind—and pen and paper handy—as we talk about four different *Perpetual Selling Strategies*: 1) follow-ups with specific offers; 2) frequency programs; 3) club memberships; and 4) free loss leaders.

1. Follow-ups with specific offers. Retail stores are notorious one-shot sellers. Car washes, dry cleaners, restaurants, hair salons, health food stores, and video rentals all use the "cross fingers and pray they'll come back" method. Again, it's not that customers WON'T come back. It's that retail stores generally don't make a proactive effort to GET them back.

There's a simple formula for implementing this strategy which you can apply to any business:

1. Capture the names, numbers, addresses, and emails of all your customers.
2. Contact all your customers and ask them for more business.
3. Make them a special offer or offer them a gift when you ask for more business.

Surprisingly, very few businesses do these three simple things. Suppose you own a new and relatively unknown municipal golf course in your town. You're just a few miles from the more well-known golf course, which seems to be getting a lot of the business. How could you make this formula work for you? In this example, I want to concentrate on how to get your customers to come back for more golf.

Most businesses, if they put any thought into getting perpetual sales, might send a lame brochure or postcard that wouldn't even get the prospects' attention, let alone coax them into a return visit.

Here's what you would need to do. First, print up some professional-looking cards with a space for each customer to write his name, address, telephone number, and email address. The top of the card should read "Grand Prize Eligibility Card" or something similar. After each golfer has paid his greens fees, but before he leaves the clubhouse for the course, have the cashier hand each person one of the cards to fill out. Don't leave a stack of them in a pile so it looks like anybody can fill it out as many times as they want. Have the cashier pull it out from behind the counter. The cashier would then tell the golfers that your golf course is giving away a complete round of golf for four—including free range balls, cart rental, unlimited drinks and snacks. The cashier should tell the golfers that the course has one drawing per week, and, with an average of only 100 to 200 cards per week, the chances of winning are good. Photos of the previous winners mounted on a bulletin board would be a nice touch and make the possibility of winning seem more real. Have the cashier limit registrations to one card per person in the golfing party. The cashier would then tell them that the course will notify the winner by email.

Assuming you can get most of the golfers to fill the card out, you now have nice customer list to work with. Don't underestimate how powerful this can be and how far ahead of the game you already are compared to most businesses. Now it's time to systematically contact all customers and ask them for more business, and to do so by making them a special offer or offering a gift.

First, pick a winning card every week and email the winner to inform the player of his good fortune. That's the obvious part. But the strategy does not end there. In fact, it's only just begun. Send an email to everyone else who entered that week with a subject line that says: "Congratulations! You've won the weekly drawing from River Bend Golf Course!" Immediately, this subject line will interrupt and engage. This email won't get lost in the shuffle of bogus spam emails. Golfers will immediately pick the words "River Bend Golf Course" and "Weekly Drawing" as familiar, and instantly recall they filled out the card.

Here's what the email should say:

Dear Larry,

My name is Bob Jones, owner of the River Bend Golf Course. I'd like to thank you for entering our drawing for a complete round of golf for four with all the goodies that go with it. Jack Stevens of Smithville won the prize last week, and as you can imagine, he's excited. I'm sorry you didn't win the first prize.

But here's the good news. You've won a valuable second prize. If you will print this email and bring it the next time you come, I will present you with two large buckets of range balls and your cart rental will be free for you and your guest.

Congratulations on your prize. We hope to see you soon.

Sincerely,

Bob Jones, Owner

P.S. Your prize is good any time in the next month. You don't need to call ahead, but please remember to bring a copy of this email with you. Thanks again.

What if you collected 500 entries in a month and sent out 500 emails with second prize offers? If only 10 percent of the people respond, still that's 50 people who are coming to the golf course for the second time.

Since they have to bring a copy of the email to claim their prize, the cashier can greet them by name and congratulate them. The range balls and free cart rental cost you basically nothing, and a certain percentage of these repeat customers will become regular customers. And since you now have a complete customer list, you can contact any or all of your customers at any time for any reason. You'll probably want to get contact management software like *Act* or *Goldmine* to keep track of your customers and remind you who you've made offers to and who's accepted them. The computer software can also help to send out the emails.

Even though this marketing program works wonders, most companies won't do it. "It's a hassle. It's too hard to administer, even with a software program." But if you feel like that, I have a serious question for you: Why did you get into business in the first place? The time it takes to cultivate perpetual sales compared to the ROI is ridiculous. It's a cash cow. There is no excuse for not putting this system into place.

Beyond getting current customers to come back more often, this same strategy can be used to acquire new customers. All you have to do is alter the formula a little bit. Instead of gathering the names of your current customers, buy or rent a list of prospective customers from a list brokerage company. Once you have your list, use the same formula: send a letter that asks for their business and offers a reward.

Here's a way to start: Let's say you decide to invite accountants to your golf course. You can rent a list of CPAs in your area for a few cents per name. There should be anywhere from 200 to 2,000—and there's a good chance that many of them play golf. Write them a letter that goes something like this:

Dear David,

I'm writing you this letter because you're a CPA.

My name is Bob Jones, owner of the River Bend Golf Course here in Silver Springs. Every day for the rest of this month, I'm going to give two large buckets of range balls and free cart rental to every CPA and their guests who play golf at my golf course.

My reason for being nice to CPAs is very interesting. Ask me about it when you come in. Make sure you bring this letter with you.

I hope to see you soon!

Sincerely,

Bob Jones, Owner

This isn't a classical marketing letter, but it does interrupt and engage. It has a specific offer, and it works. Your reason for being so nice to CPAs could be anything. Your accountant saved you a lot of money last year. Your best friend from college is a CPA. It could be anything. Who cares about the reason? Just get them in there! After the CPAs have taken you up on your offer, then write the same letter to lawyers, executives, and sales managers—any group that might play golf and be on a list to buy.

You must pro-actively entice your customers back using the *Perpetual Selling Strategies*. Most businesses let their customers dictate what their buying habits will be—how often they'll come back and how much they'll spend when they do buy. Most businesses are *reactive* when it comes to re-selling their customers. If you have already sunk the cost of generating and nurturing a customer once, get them to perpetually come back for more!

2. Frequency programs. The second *Perpetual Selling Strategy* is frequency programs. You're already familiar with this concept. It's the same thing as the airlines' frequent flyer programs, where customers accrue points or rewards based on the purchases they make.

Don't assume that frequency programs can only work for the airlines. If you use your imagination creatively, you can come up with a frequency program for your company that is both effective and easy-to-manage. Your program could be as simple as a punch card that gives your customers a free sandwich for every six they buy. Or the seventh haircut free. My local Marble Slab Creamery has an effective frequency program. You get one free ice cream for every five you buy. Since I have six kids, we always get one free on the spot!

If you want to get more sophisticated, you can allow your customers to accrue points for free products or services. However, my preference is free gifts that aren't related to what you sell. This frequency program is better suited for companies that sell a higher ticket item than haircuts, sandwiches, or ice cream.

We implemented a frequency program for a client that sold high-end flooring primarily through interior designers. While the designer's customers were the ultimate-end users, we geared our marketing to the designers. That included the frequency program. The challenge was to get the designers to use our client's showroom consistently instead of using multiple stores, as they tend to do in the absence of a good marketing program. The frequency program awards designers one point for each dollar that they or their clients spend in the store. They can redeem those points for different prizes—everything from spa treatments, dinners at upscale restaurants, big-screen televisions, even Caribbean cruises. How many other flooring stores have a frequency program available for designers? Zero. Talk about locking in perpetual sales. The designers must buy flooring from somebody. Why not from our client? This strategy works like a charm.

Here are a few suggestions to ponder when implementing your own frequency program.

First, make the rewards obtainable without too much effort. Even the most loyal sandwich eater will lose the card before he gets to 10 sandwiches. Maybe five sandwiches is more reasonable. Southwest Airlines trumped the frequent flyer industry when it came out with its simplified program where the flyer accrued one free flight for every seven purchased. Southwest also removed the restrictions for using the free flights by allowing the recipients to transfer them to other people without hassle. This program is effective because it makes customers feel that the airline actually wants them to earn and use the reward instead of setting a high bar that few can cross. Is it any wonder that Southwest keeps posting quarterly profits while all the other airlines are hemorrhaging cash and filing for bankruptcy? So, it's important to make the reward easy to obtain.

Second, keep it simple from the customers' point of view. If at all possible, don't make customers keep track of their own progress. Do it for them. Think about it. You spend $150,000 to open a shop, but you won't spend $1,000 on a computer that will capture customer information, keep track of repeat purchases, and send customers email offers that could make you a fortune? Why not have the customer database at the point of sale and ask customers for their name each time they come in, keeping track of their progress for them? Then you could pleasantly surprise your customers by informing them at the point of sale that their purchase—or a portion of it—would be on the house.

What about your company? Do you have a simple frequency program in place now? If not, hopefully you will start one soon. Remember, the point of the frequency program is to turn occasional customers into perpetual customers. The more you let the customers feel that they are getting a "win," the more they'll reciprocate and stay with you.

3. Club memberships. The third *Perpetual Selling Strategy* is club memberships. The idea is to heap benefits on your customers above and beyond what they would normally expect and do it regularly to keep them coming back. This is a take-off on the strategy for mass retailers, which was to add services for free or low cost that complement the purchase of the product. Remember the piano store that added free lessons, tunings, and the other services customers normally would have to pay for separately? With a club membership, you organize those services under the banner of a membership.

After the high-end flooring store that primarily sold through interior designers implemented a frequency program, we also added a club membership that made the designers feel that they'd be fools to buy their flooring from anyone else but our client. First, we looked at the world through their eyes and tried to determine what benefits would be useful. The first thing we realized is that most designers are solo business owners who are running their businesses out of their homes. They typically meet their clients at the showrooms of various vendors. But they always have the sense of being a visitor themselves in those showrooms.

We decided to change that. Our client's store had a loft that it was using for storage. They cleared out the junk, leaving enough space for three small offices with desks, phones, a fax machine and a copier. In addition, they added a small lounge complete with sofas, fridge, and microwave. We invited the designers who were members of the club to use this area, which we dubbed "The Designer's Loft." Club members could use the loft free of charge. Then we promoted the Designer's Club, playing up the advantages of the loft, in this letter:

Introducing the All-New Designer Club
with 11 FREE Benefits for You to Enjoy:

1. *Office Space for You to Use—Free:* We've created the "Designer's Loft" and made it available to all members of the Designer Club for free use. If you're in the area, you can swing by the office and make

phone calls, send faxes, make copies or just relax. We've got three desks that are available on a first-come, first-serve basis, as well as sofas and a television.

2. *FREE Use of Our Conference Room and Our 3,100 Sq. Ft. Showroom:* When you have clients that you need to impress, bring them to *your* showroom to browse around. Have private meetings with them in our extra-large conference room. Show them the 19,423 carpet samples available or 5,144 rugs in stock everyday. You'll make a tremendous impression on your clients—but only if you're a Designer Club member.

3. *Food, Cold Drinks, and Coffee:* When you stop by yourself or with a client, feel free to grab some snacks and cold drinks from the new dessert bar. We've installed a FREE, self-serve soft drink machine and a cappuccino machine—complete with snacks and finger foods for you to enjoy. As a member, you don't have to ask permission— just walk right in and grab a drink *just like you own the place.*

4. *50 Percent More Discount for Members Only:* Our normal professional courtesy discount to designers is 10 percent off, which is already very generous. But when you join the Designer Club, you will automatically receive a *15 percent discount* on all items ordered. You can either *pass the savings along* to your clients (and stay *ultra-competitive*), or *keep the difference* and increase your profitability immediately. Either way, this is a good deal.

5. *Free Carpet Cleaning for Your Customers:* When your customers buy carpet or rugs from us, they'll automatically be eligible for FREE carpet cleaning. This is an *excellent selling tool* for you to promote to your customers—you can tell them that their purchase includes FREE carpet cleaning and it costs YOU *nothing* extra. We'll also include a small supply of professional strength stain remover for small spills.

6. *Insurance Benefits at Group Rates:* Designer Club members will enjoy group rate discounts on complete insurance coverage—health, life, and dental—at low rates usually reserved *only* for huge companies. Please ask for details on this money-saving program.

7. *Credit Union Membership:* Credit unions mean lower interest rates

and fewer fees for all your banking needs. When you join the Designer Club, you'll automatically be eligible for all our credit union benefits. Ask for a brochure for details.

8. ***Financing for Residential or Business Clients:*** Another way you can stay competitive is by offering financing to your customers. Now we offer six-months, interest-free, and 90-days-same-as-cash programs. Customers can apply at our store.

9. ***Perks, Perks, Perks:*** We've arranged discounts on some of the *things you use all the time* in your business and personal life—things like cellular phones, pagers, rental cars, health club memberships, traveling, local courier services, overnight delivery, and formal wear. Some of these services are already in place for Designer Club members, and we're still working on others. Check the newsletter for updates and details.

10. ***Marketing Advice for FREE:*** We've hired a local marketing consulting agency, Y2Marketing, to work with any or all of the members of the Designer Club *at our expense*. They will schedule FREE consultations with you here in the office and will include a free subscription to their weekly email marketing newsletter. We've had tremendous success with this company.

11. ***Incentive Program You Wouldn't Believe:*** We'll give you a point for every dollar you spend with us. You can redeem your points at any time for exciting gifts and adventures: everything from restaurant gift certificates to VCRs and TVs to luxury cruises. All you have to do is buy your flooring products from us and you're automatically eligible.

All these benefits were available to designers if they just signed up. We sent this letter with an invitation to a formal kick-off event, complete with appetizers, desserts, drinks and light entertainment, followed by an introduction of the program. We mailed the invitation to 340 designers, including approximately 50 active customers, 50 inactive customers, and 240 non-customers. We offered a free charter membership to the first 50 who RSVPed and then came to the event; the membership fee was $100 a year for all others. We hoped at least 30 people would show up. We got 166 RSVPs, and 151 designers showed up. The place was packed. We gave free charter memberships to all 151 and promised we would extend the free offer to two additional designers per member, which generated another 56 members via referral. That's a total of 207 members.

This is a *Perpetual Selling Strategy!* The idea is to lock in repeat customers and make them feel that they'd be fools to take their business anywhere else. And you know what? It works.

To implement this strategy into your business, think about your customers and the additional products and services you could make available to them. Think about ways you can make them feel that they're part of something special, not just another customer. People are begging for acknowledgement. They want to belong. They want to be treated with respect. They want to get a good deal. All you have to do is acknowledge your customers, give them a way to belong, treat them with respect, and offer a genuine good deal. Then you will develop perpetual sales.

4. Free loss-leaders. The fourth perpetual selling strategy is called free loss-leaders. They are simple to understand and implement, but like the other strategies, they require a little creativity to have an impact. Find things to give your customers on an on-going basis that entice them to come back to get something for free. By doing so, you will either sell them something else while they're there, or at least give them good, solid reasons to keep coming back for more later at full price.

Suppose you own a hair salon that caters to men. You want your customers to come back again and again for haircuts (or hair styling). What can you give them to keep them coming back? Let's do a little "out of the box" thinking. The average length of time between haircuts is three to four weeks. What if we gave the customer a dated card that said "Free Neck and Sideburn Trim" and specified that the customer could use the card any weekday between 10 a.m. and 3 p.m.? You would then need to write a script (a marketing tool) that your stylists would use. It could go something like this:

"Thanks for coming in today, John. I really appreciate your business. Based on the feedback we've received from our customers, we find that one thing that almost all men hate is that their neck and sideburns need trimming before they need a full haircut. So they end up either looking ragged for a couple of weeks or try to trim them themselves, which doesn't always look good. To keep our customers looking good all the time—even between haircuts—we've put together a program to get let you get your neck and sideburns trimmed for free. Here's a card you'll need to use to get it done, and you'll notice that you have to get it done on a weekday between 10 to 3. Since those are our least-busy times, we figure that we might as well keep our stylists busy. I know this schedule won't work for everyone, so you're welcome to call ahead or check in at other times. As long as we don't have haircut appointments waiting, we'll try to accommodate your schedule."

Do you think that people would use the card for the free neck and sideburns trimming? Even those who didn't use the card would be favorably impressed. And this kind of gesture fosters a more loyal relationship with your customers. Never forget that customers are just people. No matter what you sell, customers want to be treated with respect. They all want to get a good deal. All you have to do is show them you'll go out of your way to take care of them—and they'll reciprocate by staying loyal. This is just as true for business to business as it is when selling to consumers.

Embassy Suites hotel chain has staked its position in the marketplace by giving you more for money, which if you think about it, is a position just about every company should strive for! Every room in the hotel is a two-room suite—not the little semi-suite that some hotels call suites, but a full two-room suite with a living room in the front and a bedroom in the back with a door in between. When you check in, they have a reception for their guests with free drinks and snacks, and every morning, they offer a full, cooked-to-order breakfast free. All this is available for roughly the same price you'd pay for a regular hotel room. So, how could the Embassy Suites take it to the next level?

How about free loss-leaders to get customers back with even more frequency. Because even as great as Embassy Suites is, I've never received any offer coaxing me back. Like every other business, the hotel uses the "cross your fingers and hope the customers' experience was good enough to motivate them to come back" method. That's insanity! You need to proactively recruit them back!

I encourage you to apply ideas from other industries to yours. In the hairstyle example, the salon gave away a service—neck and sideburns trimming—that customers had no good way to deal with outside the free service we innovated. What problems or frustrations could Embassy Suites solve for their guests by giving them a little certificate? How about a coupon for a free pay-per-view movie? Those normally cost $11 each. What about a coupon for free unlimited local calls on their next visit? Or high-speed internet access for business travelers? Or appetizers or drinks at the restaurant?

The idea is to selectively give your customers free stuff that they'd normally have to pay for or just do without. This way, you don't ruin your profit model by always making those services free for *everybody*. You can't *always* give away free pay per view movies. That would be a major loss of revenue. You can't always give away free local calls or room service desserts. But you can selectively give those away to keep your best customers coming back. It would be easy to either give those items away at checkout or attach them to the bill they slide under your door, or send them in the mail to select customers.

Think of some ways to implement this strategy into your business. Here are a few more ideas. Restaurants love to give away vouchers for free kid meals inside report cards to kids who get good grades. This comes across as an award to the child—one that almost demands to be redeemed. You can't just throw Johnny or Suzy's major award in the trash! You *must* use it! Of course, kids have to come in with their parents who are practically obligated to buy full price meals. If you had a restaurant, could you use the same strategy for your current customers? Could you send out free coupons for the kids' birthdays? How about free dessert coupons? You could send these for any occasion. But make sure they offer a real value. Sending your customers a coupon for "buy one, get one free" or for "30 percent off" looks bad and leaves a bad taste in your customers' mouths, no pun intended.

Blockbuster Video used this concept well. The store printed a coupon book for 10 free video rentals good only for kids' movies as a Valentine's gift. Parents could buy the coupon book for only $2. That made the net cost for each video only 20 cents. With all my kids, I was all over that, and guess what I found out? Every time I used the free coupon, I inevitably rented at least three movies and two video games at full price.

How could you use this strategy? Say you own a clothing store. Send your customers a letter with a voucher for a certain tie or shirt. If the tie retails for $35, but it only costs you $17, couldn't you afford to send that offer to customers who spend $300 with you? Even if they only came in and got the free tie, you'd be fostering a relationship that would pay off in spades in the future. But chances are, you'd also make sales on the spot that would more than pay for the tie!

If you have a chiropractic clinic, invite your customers for a free massage at designated times. If you run the local dry cleaners, give them a "three items for FREE" day once a quarter. If you have a hardware store, invite your customers in for a free "make as many back-up keys as you need" day, or bring in your old paint cans of paint for new ones. Show your customers that you really care about them, and let them have a "win" sometimes. Let them feel like they got the upper hand for a change. Let them feel that they can walk in and get something for free, even if they don't buy anything else.

Do all this in small-scale tests so you can track the extent of your customers' willingness to reciprocate your kindness. I promise you this. The golden rule is alive and well in business: Do unto others as you would like others to do unto you. How's that for a marketing strategy? Powerful.

By way of review, we covered four *Perpetual Sales Strategies*: 1) follow ups with specific offers, 2) frequency programs, 3) club memberships, and 4) free loss-leaders. Use these strategies and examples to stimulate your thinking—and then test and implement one or two of your best ideas.

Chapter 19:

Joint Ventures

You can leverage millions of dollars of good will
for very little money with the right alliances.

The next part of Maximization and Optimization is *Joint Ventures*. One of the best ways to leverage your time and marketing dollars is to enter into joint ventures with other businesses. The previous section made a strong case for reselling to your own customers—that's the first place you should look to maximize profits. But if you see that your customers are one of your businesses' most valuable assets, imagine the potential profits available if another business made *its* customers available to you. They become available through a joint venture with your company.

There are many different kinds of joint ventures, but they all work in one of two basic ways:

- You let other companies market to your customer base and then take a percentage of each sale.
- You market to the customers of other companies and pay them a portion of each sale.

Here's why this works: A business will spend some finite amount of time, money, resources, and sweat developing a relationship with its customers. Their customers will have some confidence in that company, which translates into their willingness to respond to their offers. For instance, a company might spend $250,000 a year in advertising, $180,000 a year on commissioned salespeople, and $15,000 a month for prime retail space. These three factors alone—not to mention dozens of other expenses—account for well over $500,000 a year spent to develop customer relationships. If you work a joint venture with the owner of that company, you can leverage that entire expenditure for the cost of a letter.

The key is to find other businesses that have customer bases with good prospects for what you sell. Here are three *Joint Venture Starter Questions* to help you identify potential partners:

- What companies are kindred to yours but not competitive?
- What other businesses do your customers patronize in connection with your business?
- What other products or services do your customers purchase or need to purchase that you don't sell?

Think about an automobile dealership. They sell you a car, but what other things do people need when they buy a car? What products or services are kindred but not competitive with new car sales? What other products or services do new car buyers purchase or need to purchase after they get the car? Here's a quick list: car insurance, tires, auto parts, car washes, gasoline, custom stereos, cell phone hands-free kits, air fresheners, window tinting, car alarms, custom wheels, roadside service, oil changes, collision repair, engine repair, preventative maintenance, batteries, oil and fuel additives, XM Radio service, coffee and donuts, maps and accessories. These are things your customers will buy anyway. And you can steer the relationships because you already have their trust and confidence. As the new car seller, you can make money by putting together joint ventures with these companies.

Let's say you own a company selling a product on that list. Why not coordinate relationships with the car dealer to get them to refer business to you? Here's how this works:

Years ago we engineered a joint venture for Chris, the owner of a small, neighborhood True Value Hardware store. Chris had spent an enormous amount of money on inventory, advertising, and leased space in the nine years he'd been in business. During that time, he developed a customer list of 1,600 people—people who knew him by name. One day while I was in the store talking to Chris, a customer asked him if he knew anyone who could install a sprinkler system. Chris gave him a name and even looked up the phone number. Not 10 minutes later, another guy came in and asked Chris if he knew a good fence man. After Chris gave him the information, I asked Chris how often he got these requests. He replied, "Maybe four or five times a day, I guess." Do you see the opportunity?

The joint venture involved over 30 companies that offered all types of home improvement and repair products and services that went hand-in-hand with what Chris' store was all about. All the businesses became members of the True Value Service Center—a place where customers could find answers to any question about anything around the house. We carefully screened and evaluated each business that wanted to participate to make sure they offered True Value's customers outstanding service and value. We allowed only one business from each industry to participate. Each business paid a $50 fee to join, which we used to build the service counter in the store and to send promotional materials to the customers.

At $50 apiece, Chris immediately raised $1,500—more than enough to build the service counter in the store. But the $1,500 was only the tip of the iceberg. Chris negotiated deals with each of the businesses for a percentage of each of the sales that resulted from his customers' use of the service center. The percentage ranged anywhere from 5 percent to 30 percent, depending on the sale's margins.

Next, we promoted the service center. First, Chris concentrated on his current customers. We staged a huge grand opening sale. About half of the member businesses set up booths in the store to show their stuff—it became the first annual True Value Home Show. We mailed an invitation to each of the 1,600 referred customers. They could enjoy a 20 percent discount on any merchandise in the store that day as well as special bonuses for large purchases. Also, each of the Home Show participants donated prizes. That meant every one of the preferred customers was guaranteed to be a winner just for showing up.

That day turned out to be cold and rainy. But True Value still had its highest sales day ever. In fact, it was 48 percent higher than the next highest day that year. The best part was that everyone who came found out about the service center. We tendered over 30 service requests that first day; dozens more came in the weeks that followed. The service center was an instant success.

The next step was to advertise to the rest of the people in that city. Chris advertised in the service directory of the classifieds in the local paper. His ad told readers that instead of picking and choosing through all of the service ads and calling an unfamiliar company, they could make one call to solve all their problems. This headline summed up the service center: ***"Before You Look in the Yellow Pages for Anything Around the House, Call Us First."***

Then every two weeks, Chris sent a four-page newsletter to everyone on his growing customer list. Each issue contained a feature article about one of his joint-venture partners. The best part was that the spotlighted business paid for the mailing—and Chris still got his percentage from each sale.

Chris had leveraged the entire operations of some 30 businesses. In essence, he became a landscaper, drywall technician, carpet cleaner, and fence builder without having to make an investment in those areas. His customers wanted those products and services, and they trusted Chris' judgment. If Chris said these were the companies to do business with, they believed him. The participating companies leveraged Chris' entire customer list by entering into the joint venture. Basically, they paid $50 plus a percentage to gain over 1,600 customers who would use them in good faith. Now *that's* leverage!

Three Ways to Joint Venture

All you're trying to do with a joint venture is identify other companies who have customer databases that could use what you sell. Let me describe three other ways to put joint ventures together: 1) consignments, 2) gifts, and 3) endorsements.

Consignments. *Consignment* simply means you let another business sell your product to their existing customer base. You supply the inventory, but don't charge them until the product is sold. In retail, this is a useful way to test the viability of a new product before the store commits to purchasing inventory. The key to making this work is to find a retail store that sells items along the lines of what you sell. Approach them and say, "If you give me shelf space, I won't charge you for inventory until the merchandise sells."

A *consignment* is when Company A actually completes the transaction with one of its customers and then pays Company B who provides the product or service. That's different than a *referral,* which is when Company A simply refers its clients to Company B who then transacts the business. We also call this an *endorsement.*

As you think about how to put together a consignment deal in your business, don't limit your thinking to strictly retail situations or tangible merchandise. Take a service company like a lawn service. I have a company that takes care of my lawn, and they charge me $400 a month. I have used them for a couple of years now, after having gone through four other companies. So now, after a couple of years of good service, I trust this company and am open to their suggestions about other related services. How could this lawn company sell other companies' products or services to me on consignment?

Consider the *Joint Venture Starter Questions*:

- What kinds of companies are kindred but not competitive?
- What other businesses do your customers patronize in connection with your business?
- What other products or services do your customers purchase or need to purchase that you don't sell?

For the lawn company, the answers form a long list: pest control, landscaping, outdoor lighting, tree trimming, pool service, fencing, paving, and more. Now, the strategy is to form alliances with those companies to sell these services seamlessly by the company with the original customer list. My lot is two acres and has about 80 mature trees. What if my landscaper came to me and said: "Rich, I know you've got all these trees, and our lawn maintenance contract does not cover tree trimming. But because there's so much shade on your lawn, and because it just makes your yard look cleaner, you need to get them trimmed periodically. We would like to handle that service for you. We'll offer you an annual service to trim your trees once a quarter. For your lot, that would run $500 per trimming or $2,000 a year. If you prefer, we can divide that number into monthly payments and just add it to your bill. It will be an extra $160 a month."

Come and take a look at my yard. You'll agree that I need my trees trimmed! They're a mess. They grow out of control! But you just never think about spending money on tree trimming, unless they are just so bad you can't stand it. Now my lawn maintenance supervisor, whom I trust, is offering me this service. Let's say that he offers this service to 10 customers. How many do you think would take them up on it?

Let's take a look at how that would affect my lawn company. First, they have to make a deal with the tree-trimming company. They could negotiate a deal where they bought the tree trimming at wholesale for 70 cents on the retail dollar. The tree trimmer would go for this because it locks in perpetual sales without incurring any advertising expense. Now the lawn maintenance company could call the tree trimmer, giving them a window of time to complete the trimming. The trimmer could work it into his schedule giving his full paying customers priority, but still getting the job done in a timely manner. Over one year, the lawn maintenance company would bill its customer $2,000 and only be liable to the tree trimmer for $1,400. That's $600 annual profit per customer—$600 for essentially doing nothing. That's also $600 that will continue to come in forever because the customer's relationship is still with the lawn maintenance company, not with the tree trimmer directly.

Now let's say the lawn maintenance crew gets two out of 10 of its higher-end customers with bigger lawns on that program. They have 100 of these customers. This program adds 20 tree trimming customers at an incremental profit of $12,000 a year.

You might think $12,000 isn't that big a deal, not worth the effort for a larger company. I beg to differ. First of all, that's $12,000 for FREE, for making a few phone calls at the most. Second, that doesn't take into account the smaller customers. Third, we still haven't talked about forming relationships with pest control, landscaping, outdoor lighting, pool service, fencing or paving. Your customers need that stuff anyway. Why not give them the chance to buy it from you so you can make the money?

If you need help coming up with ideas, speak to one of our consultants.

Gifts. *Gifts* are one of my favorite kinds of joint ventures. It's very simple. Invite a business to give a sample of your product or service to their customer base as a way to introduce you. I've already given you a couple of examples earlier in the book. The piano store gave free piano lessons to everyone who bought a new piano. Remember how that worked? The store found a piano teacher looking for more students and offered to pay him or her $5 per half-hour lesson. They gave each new piano purchaser 12 vouchers, each one good for a lesson. They put a time restriction on them so that they expire in six months of the piano purchase so they wouldn't have any long-term liability. We said the piano teacher would go for this because many students would want to continue after the three months are up because they like the lessons. And since the piano store was only paying the teacher for redeemed vouchers, their cost per voucher was closer to $2 each or $24 for each piano sold because most people won't actually use the vouchers despite their good intentions. See how brilliant that is from the piano teacher's standpoint? He can leverage the goodwill the piano store has accrued with its customers and even get paid for the privilege of getting new customers!

In another example earlier in the book, an upscale flooring store offered free carpet cleaning so its designers could offer this to their customers as a value-added selling point. Think about that from the carpet cleaner's standpoint. It's the same setup as the piano teacher, isn't it? How much money does it take the carpet cleaner to find a new customer? Traditionally they will take out ads in the local newspaper, spend money in the *Yellow Pages,* and put coupons in the money mailers and Val Packs. It could cost as much as $60 to $100 to find customers who only spend $200. Think about how much more cost-effective it would be to acquire a new customer if they just approached flooring stores and said: "Think how much easier it would be for you to sell carpet if you offered two years of free carpet cleaning. Normally carpets need to be cleaned once during the first year, and every eight months after that. I will provide this service for your customers if they buy at least 150 square yards with a retail value of $400. I'll provide it to you for only $50 per cleaning, and you don't even have to pay for it until we take the voucher from the customer."

This is a real win-win for everyone involved. The flooring store adds additional value for its customers, which supports the case they'd be fools to buy carpet from anyone else. And the carpet cleaner gets a steady stream of new customers at a relatively low cost. It's similar to *consignment*, but with a couple of twists. Now generate your own ideas.

Here's one more gift example. We had two clients at the same time located in the same area. One was a Lexus dealership, the other one a high-end spa. You can see how to put this one together! In this case, we made the gift go both ways. No, we didn't give spa customers a free Lexus. But we did offer to let them drive one for a full 24 hours to test it out, which turned out to be huge in getting people to buy the cars. And we gave all Lexus test drivers a voucher for a free facial at the spa.

Notice we gave them a *voucher*—not a coupon or a certificate. What's the difference between a coupon and a voucher? A voucher *sounds* better. We used the voucher in a couple of ways. First, in-store signage promoted the fact that we were giving vouchers to anyone who test-drove the car. Second, we sent mailers to prospective customers, letting them know they would receive this free gift when they came into the showroom. We also used the voucher for existing customers to lure them back to the dealership for oil changes and routine maintenance, which are major profit centers for dealerships.

Remember the first *Joint Venture Starter Question*: What kinds of companies are kindred but not competitive to your business? The word *kindred* means related, and the products or services that you look for can be related in different ways. They could be similar in nature, like lawn services and tree-trimming services. Or financial planning and real estate investing. Or marketing consulting and web site development. Or auto dealerships and tire stores. But *kindred* does not *only* mean that products or services must be similar. You could also find other products or services that are not necessarily similar, but that lend themselves well to the demographics of your customer base. If you have a Lexus dealership, you could find other products or services that cater to the affluent crowd, like spa treatments, golf equipment, jewelry and higher-end retail stores. Same thing goes for other demographics as well. Think about your particular business and you'll come up with dozens of appropriate ideas.

Endorsements. One powerful joint venture strategy is an *endorsement* where one company proactively recommends another company's products or services to its customers. An endorsement is different from a testimonial. A testimonial is a statement from a customer who likes your product or service. The endorsement, on the other hand, does not come from a customer—it comes from a company. And it's not just a statement of "We like these guys." It's a *proactive* attempt to sell the other company's products or services.

There are dozens of ways to do this. But in almost all cases both companies participate in the profitability of the endorsement. The hardware store was an example of an endorsement. Chris rounded up several companies that offered products and services that were kindred but not competitive and then recommended them to his customers.

But you can also do a *direct endorsement* where one company encourages its customers to buy from one specific company. We do this all the time in our business with associations and chambers of commerce. We want them to recommend us to their members, usually with the idea to invite them to our seminars. Since the Chambers of Commerce already has a credible relationship with its members, it's usually not too hard to get them to recommend us once they are sold on our program.

Here's how an endorsement letter from the President of a Chamber of Commerce would read:

From the Desk of Gene Randall, President

Dear Mr. Smith,

I want to personally urge you to take immediate action on a life-changing, business growth opportunity that just became available—if it is appropriate and if you qualify. Plano Chamber members tend to be very entrepreneurial and bottom-line oriented—and this program I have arranged is uniquely suited to you, our valued members.

Last February, we invited Rich Harshaw from a consulting company called Y2Marketing to speak at our quarterly profit forum seminar. To be perfectly honest, I wasn't sure what to expect. Rich told the group he would teach them how to **separate themselves from their competition, then eliminate them**. And you know what? He wasn't kidding.

In one short hour, I listened to the most fascinating discussion of the topic of innovation, marketing and **making money at business** that I've ever heard. Usually, I sit quietly and listen politely to the speakers. But this time, I found myself scrambling to take notes. By the time the hour was over, **I had taken three full pages of notes** and had **swarms of ideas** in my head on how to improve the Chamber!

What struck me the most was Rich's ability to **explain in simple terms** what it really takes to make more money at business. Rich has consulted with all types of businesses—everything from retail stores and service businesses to manufacturing concerns, charities and real estate companies.

Rich contends that your ability to find and retain customers depends on your ability **to innovate your business** to become "the best deal," and then to **communicate those reasons** to your potential and current customers. Rich teaches you how to consistently innovate and stay in front of the field. Once you have staked your position in the marketplace, Rich shows you how to implement what he calls the "marketing equation" to effectively grow your business.

The concepts he teaches cover every aspect of building your business—everything from advertising to sales training to innovation and customer service. Whatever it takes to make more money at business is on his agenda. He'll show you how to spend less money on marketing and get more results.

I'm not the only one sold on Rich's system. Thousands of business owners nationwide regularly flock to his Monopolize Your Marketplace seminars to learn his methods. Just ask any of his clients who have profited 100 times over the fees they paid. Ask Octavio Sanchez, the vice president of Merrill Carpets down in Dallas' high-end designer district. MYM not only revitalized his business. They also helped him identify a completely new profit center that will net his company a minimum of $250,000 in pure profit this year with just $746 in extra advertising costs per month. Or ask Steve Williams, marketing director of Butler's Plumbing in Dallas, how he feels about going from $20,000 in monthly sales just 18 months ago to a record-breaking $132,453 in sales in January. These are real examples.

Maybe you need to see results even closer to home. Why don't you ask Jerry Kensington, owner of MJ's Auto Shop in Plano, what MYM did for him? Or talk to Roy Pinkston, owner of a brand new sign shop on Avenue J. He hired Rich a month before his store opened, and by using their system, he had orders totaling nearly $100,000 before he even opened his doors. Jacob Gonzales, co-founder of Automatic Software in Richardson credits the MYM System with his three highest sales months ever just from the FREE advice he got from them in a free follow-up consultation after a seminar he attended. He's since hired them to help him take his business to the **next** level.

Feel free to talk to John Collins, owner of Suntime Cruise Center on Pleasant Run Rd. Just one tiny suggestion increased the effectiveness of his newspaper advertising by over 10 times! Or talk to V.K. Glover of Homestead Real Estate on Custer Rd. Or Tommy Akers, owner of a $20 million insurance brokerage firm on LBJ in Dallas. You might want to talk to Dr. Dorothy Potter—she's the director of PR for Piper Chiropractic College. She attended a Monopolize Your Marketplace seminar—at my personal suggestion—and has since arranged for them to conduct seminars for the students there. She is confident that the business-building skills they teach are just as important to her students as the chiropractic skills they learn at the college. These are the same business-building skills that I have arranged for Rich to teach you on May 23.

I do NOT lend my name to anyone lightly. For me to go way out on a limb and not only invite—but urge, implore and outright cajole you to participate in this program should tell you something.

The full-day seminar, scheduled for May 23, is not your usual seminar. Rich will include all your materials in your registration fee. This includes a detailed, step-by-step workbook crammed with real life examples and go-home-and-use-it-the-next-day information. Rich holds back nothing.

Plus, I've arranged with Rich to give Plano Chamber Members the following FREE bonuses:

1) Free one-year newsletter subscription (26 issues)

2) Free bonus reports "Quick Fix Marketing" and "Five Ways To Increase Bottom Line Profits Without Spending An Extra Dime,"

3) A FREE one hour follow-up consultation for each business that attends.
All in all, you just can't lose by showing up for this seminar.

Please take the time **right now** to set time aside on May 23 to attend
this unique seminar. If you need more information, call our office and we'll
send you out a FREE audio CD program Rich has put together that explains
some of their concepts in detail. This is the last time we'll offer this program
at this special price with all the free bonuses.

Warmly,

Gene Randall
President

P.S. If history is any indication, this one-day seminar will sell out rapidly.
There is only room for 100 businesses to attend, and at the special, reduced
price I have arranged, seats will go fast. Fill out the enclosed registration
form to guarantee your participation.

This letter builds a compelling case explaining why the reader should take
action. This letter has worked like a charm dozens of times for our company and
our consultants.

Now I can hear some of you murmuring, "Yeah. That works great for you.
But that's your company, not mine. We don't sell seminars—we sell widgets and
digits." There always seems to be a disconnect in the minds of some people that
prevents them from taking an idea and translating it into their situation!
Remember, one of the most valuable skills you can develop is that of lateral
thinking—learning how to apply strategies and ideas from one industry, situation,
or scenario into your own.

Here's how you can translate this letter into an endorsement letter for your
company. Hopefully this will help you to see how to apply these ideas to your situation. Here's the same letter written for a CPA to endorse a high-end home
builder to his client list.

From the Desk of Steve Parker, CPA

Dear Mr. Smith,

**If you've even considered building a custom home, please read this let-
ter immediately.**

I want to personally urge you to take immediate action on a time-sensitive
opportunity that just became available if it is at all appropriate and if you **qualify**. I

feel like part of my responsibility to you is to identify superb values and pass them along to you, my valued clients.

As some of you may know, last February I began the daunting process of building a new home. I really did my due diligence on the entire building process, learning everything I could about what makes a builder great (instead of just good), how long a home in this size range (5,000 to 7,000 square feet) should take to build and how much a home should cost to build using the highest standards. Based on my research, I identified 13 builders that seemed to be a good fit for the home I wanted to build according to the standards I had found. I then conducted a personal interview with the owner of each of these builders.

My 11th interview was with Robert Muller of Stonewood Custom Homes. It was perfectly clear within 45 minutes of meeting Robert that I had found my builder. For over two hours, I listened to the most fascinating discussion of the topic of innovation, quality, and **building the best home imaginable** that I've ever heard. For most of the builders, I sat quietly and listened politely to their canned presentations. But with Robert, I found myself scrambling to take notes. By the time the two hours were over, I was convinced I was going to get the absolute best quality home for less money than any other builder.

What struck me the most was Robert's ability to **explain in simple terms** what it really takes to build a high quality home and what you OUGHT to get for your money. He revealed to me all of the formulas that builders use to calculate their prices and showed me exactly where they inflated their margins, which means ripping off their customers. I learned how they overcharge for land, overcharge for materials and overcharge for finish out on high-end homes—finish out that can account for as much as $100,000 of builder profit on a $750,000 home!

Robert contends that most builders prey on your unfamiliarity with the building process and can easily cut quality corners and still overcharge you without your ever knowing. Even appraisers can't detect most of the cut corners and overcharges because they're structurally built into the home. And most problems never show up until the second or third year of ownership. He went on to show me exactly what his company does versus "most" builders and how their processes are better. He armed me with a checklist of 23 questions to ask any prospective builder—questions about quality, reputation, workmanship and builder stability—and showed me how these questions would cause even the most "honest" builder to cringe.

After our initial meeting, I was excited but still wanted to prove what I had learned. Armed with the checklist and corresponding educational report Robert gave me, I went back to each of the 10 other builders I had already interviewed and went over the list. I could see the absolute terror in each of the builder's eyes as they realized that I had found out their secrets. To the credit of two of the other builders, they held up pretty well under the pressure. It appeared that they too could build the quality of home I was looking for at a price that was appropriate. The last two of the 13 builders I had initially staked out also ended up "failing" Robert's test.

Based on my research and Robert's evaluations, I decided to go with his company, Stonewood Custom Homes. All through the building process, from designing the plans, to planning the home, to construction and move in—everything was wonderful. My construction coordinator, Larry Jones, worked with me personally every step of the way to keep me up-to-the-minute on what was happening. The estimated build time was 8.5 to 9 months. They were finished in just over eight. All those horror stories you hear about getting "waxed" by a builder just never happened.

Best of all, I know that I got a great deal on the home. I ended up paying $662,000 for 5,840 square feet. As you know, the price of a home of this caliber is highly dependent on the type of finish out and the land. I am 100 percent convinced this same home would have cost me at least $800,000 from most other builders. The appraiser seemed to agree with my conclusion: the home appraised for $779,000. Between my 20 percent down payment and the spread in the sales price and the appraisal price, I already have a quarter million dollars in equity in my new home. Do you see why I'm sending you this letter?!

I'm not the only one sold on Robert's homes. He's built homes for dozens of the area's most successful people, including several professional athletes.

Just ask any of Robert's highly enthused clients what they think. Ask Bill Cummins, a magazine publisher in Arlington, how he feels now that he built his dream home for less money than the home he was living in before (certainly not his dream home!). Ask Octavio Sanchez, the vice president of Downtown Flooring store. Stonewood not only built his home; they also built a home for his sister, his brother and two of his colleagues from work. Or ask Steve Williams, marketing director of a major plumbing company, how he feels about paying $425,000 for the home he thought he'd have to wait five more years to build because he thought it would cost $550,000 to $600,000. These are **real** examples. Many of these people have been in their homes for more than five years and are still thrilled at the quality. Trust me, I interviewed each of them personally prior to committing.

You might want to talk to Dr. Dorothy Potter—she's the director of PR for Piper Chiropractic College. She's already begun building her new home with Stonewood at my **personal** suggestion—and has since turned the dean of the college on to Stonewood.

I do not lend my name to anyone lightly. For me to go way out on a limb and not only invite but urge, implore and outright cajole you to consider Stonewood Custom Homes should tell you something.

I know you may not be in the market for a new home right now. But if you're even thinking about it, you really need to check into this. I've mailed this letter to our firm's top 250 net worth clients, the only ones who can truly take advantage of this phenomenal value. The fact is, Stonewood absolutely WILL NOT build homes less than $400,000 and prefers to build them in the $750,000 to $1.5 million range. To make their profit model work (a model that Robert will show you, by the way), they have to build higher-end homes.

Stonewood only has the capacity to build 18 to 22 homes a year. Last year, despite their unbelievable abilities, they only built 16. When I asked Robert why, he said that they don't really do any advertising or marketing, and that almost all of their business comes from word of mouth. Last year happened to be a little slow. This year they are already on track to do 20 homes, which means that they can really only take on two more projects. I asked him if he would mind if I touted him to my clients, and of course he consented. In fact, he said that if I would do this, he would even be willing to offer my clients a special video report that they put together that explains their processes.

Watch the video and see for yourself. Robert will send you one if you just shoot him a quick email at rmuller@xyzmail.com, or call him at 555-1212. If you like what you see, you may want to set an appointment with Robert. Or if you prefer, you can **come tour my personal home**. I'd be proud to show you how everything on the video is actually implemented into my home.

Why this letter and this invitation? It's simple. Your home is a big deal, and Stonewood is so good, that if I had built a home with another builder, and then found out what I had missed, I would be downright mad. I'd feel ripped off. This letter is my way of letting you in on what I consider to be one of the best pieces of financial advice I could give you. And since Stonewood can only contract two more homes this year, I wanted to give you a heads up if you are close to being in the market. Please call me personally if you have any questions.

Warmly,

Steve Parker

President

P.S. If you are even just thinking about building, I recommend you get the video. If you just built a home, however, don't get it. You'll just get upset!

Well, what do you think? Powerful, isn't it? How can you retrofit this letter to meet your needs? And what about this: If you received that letter from your CPA, and you were in the market for a home of that caliber, do you think you might at least respond for the free video?

Guess what? That's a real letter. This CPA mailed this letter to 250 of his high-net-worth clients: 33 responded for the video presentation. Of those, 12 met with Robert and five built homes with him. The total contract price of the five homes was $4 million—from a mailer that took us two hours to adapt and $150 to mail. Would you spend $150 for $4 million in sales?

Of course, there were other costs involved. The home builder paid us consulting fees to put this strategy together as well as a percentage of the gross profitability of the homes sold. They also had to pay for the development of the video. And they also had to pay a percentage to the CPA firm who sent the letter. All things considered, still not a bad deal.

Don't think an endorsement has to come in the form of a long letter like this one. The endorsement of the True Value Service Center came in a Xeroxed flyer on red paper. It wasn't long or fancy. It just followed the *Marketing Equation*: interrupt, engage, educate and offer. That's the important thing. And don't think you can only use endorsements for fancy things like custom homes or business seminars. As long as somebody has a relationship with somebody else, you can leverage that relationship.

Here's a simple example. I have a friend that started a garage sale business to make extra money on the weekends. Here's a letter I wrote that my friend sent out to my neighbors in an envelope with my name and return address on it.

Dear Neighbor,

My name is Rich Harshaw; I live on 1231 Whispering Oaks (the red roof Victorian house down the hill). Please pardon the intrusion, but I agreed to send this letter to my neighbors in an effort to help out a friend. You might find this letter helpful also.

A couple of weeks ago, I was gathering up a bunch of stuff to haul down to Goodwill when a friend stopped by. He asked me what I was doing, and when I told him, he asked me why don't I have a garage sale and make some money.

I told him I didn't want to have a garage sale and that there wasn't enough stuff to matter anyway—probably just a couple hundred dollar's worth at most. Being a young guy with a young family (one kid and one on the way), he asked me if it would be okay if he took the stuff, sold it at a garage sale at his house in Mansfield, and gave me half the money—he would keep the other half.

Since he's a young kid who works hard and who is struggling to make ends meet, I said, "Sure, why not." So, he loaded my stuff in his car and hauled it off. He came by the next day with a truck and got an old bed and a chair, and two weeks later he had the garage sale and sold most of the stuff.

I was right: the sum total he generated was just $244 and he gave me $122 in cash. He then kept the same amount for himself and took whatever was leftover to the dump or Goodwill. The money didn't mean much to me, but it was a big deal to him to make an extra hundred bucks on a Saturday for a couple hours of work.

I told him that there were probably other people in my neighborhood who had the same **junk accumulation** problem I do, and that they might be willing to give their stuff to him also. To help him out, I agreed to send you a letter to see if you had any stuff you wanted to get rid of.

If you're interested, here's what you can do: My friend's name is **Dave Johnson**; if you have any stuff, he can pick it up anytime on a Saturday. He'll sell it at a garage sale at his house and give you half the money. If you don't want the money, he'd be happy to donate it in your name to your favorite church or charity and provide a receipt.

He's a good kid trying to support his young family. If you have any stuff, don't hesitate to give him a call.

Thanks,

Rich Harshaw

P.S. Dave also sold a Sony digital camera and walkman for me on Ebay. If you have some more valuable stuff like that, maybe he can help you out there, too.

Then I gave Dave's contact information. He sent this letter to 64 homes in my neighborhood on two occasions at a total cost of $55. Three out of 64 responded, and he ended up taking enough stuff to make over $330 for himself so far. One of those customers also had a truck they let him sell for a $250 fee. Dave's earned a total of $570 so far on a $55 investment. That's the power of the endorsement.

Whether your endorsement nets you $4 million or $570 in sales, the principles work. Just use the *Marketing Equation*, tell a story, and be sincere. Endorsements are extremely powerful and effective.

Identify prospective endorsement partners for your business. Use the *Joint Venture Starter Questions* to give you ideas of what companies might be appropriate. Then approach those businesses and show them how they can leverage their customer bases or how they can leverage yours. You may have to take your idea to several companies to get someone to bite off on the idea, but stick with it. You'll be glad you did.

To wrap up our discussion on joint ventures, let's go back to our original example of an auto dealership and see how they could use the three joint ventures we just covered—*consignments*, *gifts* and *endorsements*. We used the *Joint Venture Starter Questions* to come up with a list of companies that might be a good fit to partner with the dealership. What about consignments? Can the dealership sell another company's products and services, collect the payments from their customers and then pay the joint venture partner on the back-end? What about custom stereos? Did you notice when you buy a new car, you have to take it to a custom stereo shop if you want a different stereo than the one that comes with the car?

How stupid is that? What if they had a brochure at the dealership that in essence said: "We know the factory installed stereo is just fine for most people. But 30 percent of our customers want something a little (or a lot!) more beefy. If that's the case, here's what we can do. We have partnered with ABC Custom Audio Auto to install stereo for our customers prior to taking delivery of the car. The benefit is that you can take the incremental difference in the price of the stereo and work it into the price of your car and finance it right into your loan. You'll pay the exact same prices as if you went there yourself after you bought the car, but now you can roll the cost in with your financing."

Custom Audio Shop agrees to pay the dealership a 15 percent commission on every stereo sale. If the average price is $1,200, that's $180 to the dealership. And if they sell 300 cars a month, and just 10 percent take them up on the offer, that's 30 stereos times $180 which equals $5,400 a month or $64,800 a year.

You could do the same thing for cell phone hands-free kits, custom wheels, window tinting, XM radio service and car alarms. Dealers do offer these things, but at rip-off prices. And everybody knows dealerships don't specialize in this stuff. That's why customers go elsewhere. Both parties benefit when the dealership establishes relationships with these specialists. Both make money when the dealership steers its customers to them right off the bat in the form of a seamless consignment.

What if the customer didn't take the dealership up on these offers at the time of purchase? Is the chance to leverage the relationship over? Of course not! Then the dealership could move into endorsement mode, sending letters to their customers recommending the various services on an on-going basis. Here's a good endorsement letter for the dealership:

> Dear Rich:
>
> I wanted to thank you once more for purchasing your Hummer H2 from Frank Kent Hummer. Now that you've had your vehicle for three months, I'm sure you're in love with it and wonder how you ever lived without it. I wanted to let you know about a product that many H2 owners have found to be just as hard to live without as the H2 itself. This product will be of interest to you if you are a music lover, and if you are somewhat computer savvy.
>
> It's the Kenwood Music Keg. Maybe you've seen articles about it in *GQ* magazine or *The Robb Report*. It's a digital music server for your car that allows you to store up to 5,000 songs on a tiny cartridge, then browse your collection and select any song you want in an instant. Everyone that has one absolutely loves it, and the only problem with them up to this point has been the price. At $899 plus installation, the price tag has been a little more that most want to spend. We've cut a special deal with Car Toys and Kenwood where we now have them for just $489 and installation is free. In fact, we'll even arrange to have your H2 picked up at your home or office, install the Music Keg, and return your Hummer within four hours.

This is a good example of how to think up ways to add more money to your bottom line. Mail this letter to H2 owners and you'll make money. It's just that simple. Identify stuff that people are going to buy anyway, or would buy if they knew about it, and offer it.

Here's how to use the gift strategy as a joint venture for the dealership. The dealership approaches a tire store chain and says:

"You spend a bazillion dollars of advertising every year in this market, hoping and praying that when a guy gets a flat or when he needs new tires he'll remember you. We sell 300 cars a month at our dealership, and, based on our new, improved marketing program using the MYM System, we anticipate that we'll sell 500 a month by the end of the year. But to do that, you are going to play a part. We are setting up a bonus benefit club for our customers to attract them to buy their cars from us. We are creating exclusive relationships with certain companies that sell batteries, tires, stereos, and other auto products. We extend special offers to our customers when they need what you sell, in your case, tires.

Here's how it works. See this nice leather portfolio? This will go in the glove box of each car we sell. In it will be the offers from the various partners. We'll print your name and phone number and let our customers know that anytime they have any issues, they need to call you.

For our tire partner, it works like this. We offer our customers free flat-tire replacement anytime, anywhere, under any circumstance. We also offer them free towing any time they can't get the car into your store. Based on my research, these are all things you do for your customers anyway, and that's why I'm contacting you. Your "inside reality" is already outstanding, and even though you don't know what that means, it's evident that your own advertising could really use some work, because you outside perception is that you're just like everyone else. (I'm kidding). Nevertheless, that's why I've identified you as our best bet as a tire partner, because you already offer an outstanding value."

If you said that to the owner of the tire store chain, you would get a favorable reaction. The next thing is to figure out how much advertising money the tire store spends to get customers in the door, then charge them a monthly fee that would go on their P & L as advertising expense. Let's say that is $250 a month. Is it worth the effort? First, you've added another $3,000 a year in income, which is not a lot of money. But stop looking only at the obvious. What are you trying to accomplish with these joint ventures? Yes, you're trying to make more money from the relationships you have. But you're also trying to add more value for your customers so they will be more likely to buy from you in the first place. When we talked about industry strategies, we said that for a mass retailer, like a dealership, the key is to add **value-added** products and services on top of the normal sale.

So, what else could you put in that little leather portfolio that goes in the glove box? Think in terms of the *gift* joint venture strategy. What about gasoline, batteries, oil changes, insurance, and collision repair? You could even put certificates in there for coffee and donuts. Also, depending on the kind of car, you could have vouchers in there for free golf or a discount on jewelry or a barbeque grill. These joint venture can make you the dealership that looks out for its customers. It makes the car-buying decision more than just price comparison, which is *almost always* the only thing people bring to the negotiating table at car dealerships. How silly is that?

Here's the principle that you need to take to heart: If you take your customer's needs seriously, earnestly endeavor to serve those needs and take care of them across the board, it will come back to you financially in spades. The problem is most business people are far to busy trying to just get through the day that they never think to step aside, identify opportunity and take advantage of it.

We've talked about *Perpetual Selling Strategies* and *Joint Ventures* and I'm sure you've been energized at their simplicity and power. Let these ideas energize you. Let them inspire you. But please, don't fall prey to what I call the *Law of Diminishing Intent*, which means that you hear an idea, you're inspired by an idea, you intend to act on an idea. But then, due to time pressures and the need to get by day-to-day, you push the idea out one more day, then a week, then a month. *The Law of Diminishing Intent* dictates that as that time rolls on, your desire to act on the idea diminishes. After a month the ideas are faint and dim, and after a year, they're gone. So commit yourself now to taking definite action to maximize and optimize your business. Implement some *Perpetual Selling Strategies*. Put together a couple of *Joint Ventures*. Then you'll be ready to consider our next topic—*upselling*.

Chapter 20:

Upselling Strategies

When upselling, you give your customers
a gentle nudge to purchase additional items
or spend more money on items they buy anyway.

Upselling finds ways to get your customers to spend more money with you at the point of purchase than they normally would if left to their own devices. Upselling gives your customers a gentle nudge to purchase additional items or spend more money on items they are buying anyway. As we go through the upselling strategies, you will notice similarities to the *Perpetual Selling Strategies* and *Joint Ventures*.

• The first upselling strategy is called *Packaging*. I'm not referring here to the actual wrapper that your product comes in. I'm referring to the way you package various products and services together to make a more attractive deal for your customers. Take something that would normally cost money to the customer and include it for free as part of a package. The computer manufacturers got really good at this back in the late 1980s and early 1990s. They gave away of free software if you bought the computer.

How might you create a package deal? Think about a golf course. Look at the components necessary to play golf: green fees, cart rental and range balls. What if the course packaged all those things together? By doing so, the course could get more money from the golfer. Let's say that green fees are $38, cart rental $15 for a half cart, and range balls $5 for a large bucket. That's $55 for all three. And let's say that sales statistics show that 100 percent of golfers pay green fees, 50 percent pay cart fees (meaning the other 50 percent chose to walk), and only 25 percent buy range balls. That means out of 100 customers, the total revenue would be $4,375. That's $3,500 for green fees, $750 for cart fees and $125 for range balls.

Now let's say you put together a special package deal: you get all three components for $47.50. You know 50 percent are going to buy cart rentals anyway; those people are paying $50 before your package deal. So you know you'll get buy-in from them. In fact, you'll actually be losing $2.50 revenue per person. So, the key is to get more of the people who normally don't buy range balls or cart rentals to do so because of the package deal. Let's say that 85 percent purchase your special offer, and the other 15 percent just want only green fees. That would be revenue of $4,037.50 from package deals and $525 from greens-fee-only golfers, for a total of $4,562.50. That's a net increase of $187 per 100 golfers. Big deal, right? Well, it depends on how you look at it. Do you think that the package deal would have any bearing on some of those golfers' decision to come back? I think it would.

Now, suppose you also sell sandwiches and Gatorade on the golf course. Gatorade and sandwiches are both low-cost, high-margin items. You normally sell Gatorade for $2 a bottle and sandwiches for $4 each. You also know, based on sales history, that only 20 percent of your golfers buy a sandwich and 40 percent buy Gatorade. That means that your snack revenue from these two items per 100 golfers is $120. Since both items only cost you 50 cents hard cost, that's a total hard cost of $30 and a gross profit of $90.

Let's add a free sandwich and bottle of Gatorade to the package deal. Each golfer gets green fees, cart rental, range balls a sandwich and a bottle of Gatorade, totaling $61. Instead of asking $47.50 for the package, we offer it all for $50, or $11 off the price when purchased separately. The sandwich and Gatorade are only going to cost us an extra $1 per golfer, but now we're getting an extra $2.50 for a profit of $1.50.

Play with your numbers and your offering to see what works. Chances are excellent you will find ways to accomplish upselling's stated purpose: to get customers to spend more money than they normally would. In addition, we'll probably also get them back to come back more often. So in essence, in this case, the package deal serves as both an *Upselling Strategy* and a *Perpetual Selling Strategy*.

If you pay attention, you'll see package deals all over the place. Computers are commonly sold in bundles, including the CPU, monitor and printer. Infomercials tell you if you act now, they'll give you two sets of knives instead of one. You've seen the cell phone companies give away the phone free to those who sign a service agreement. But don't think that because you are familiar with these offers that the strategy is easy. You need to be constantly thinking in all directions, borrowing good ideas from everywhere! There's not a business in the world that can't implement the *Package Deal Upselling Strategy* immediately.

• Another upselling strategy is **selling compatible item(s) at the point of sale,** possibly—but not necessarily—at a discount. This is different from the package deal because you're offering the compatible item separately, as an add-on instead of part of the package.

Say you buy a trash compactor from Sears. When you're paying for it, the clerk says, "Sir, you'll need compactor bags to put in your new compactor. We have our own premium line of bags over here. They are paper bags with a special plastic liner that keeps them strong and durable even with wet trash, but because they are paper, they are fit snugly into the compactor. This makes them easier to handle than comparable plastic bags. They come 10 bags to a package. How many packages can I get for you today?" That's an upsell.

The problem with this kind of upselling is it requires your salespeople to execute, and you already know how I feel about salespeople making these decisions, since my goal is to *franchise the sales system*. You'll need to train you salespeople on this. At the same time, this is a perfect time to use marketing tools—specifically in-store signage and brochures—that can also do the selling for you.

How about offering a service warranty as a complementary item at the point of sale? The service warranty is particularly big at electronics stores like Best Buy, Circuit City, and Ultimate Electronics. Salespeople push these so hard because they are extraordinarily profitable for the store. If you buy a television for $699, the store will try to sell you an extended warranty for between $79 to $150. The problem, again, is that the salespeople can't sell them effectively because they just tack it to the end of the sale and can't articulate the benefits very well. They push hard for the sale, though, because of the fat commissions. So, most consumers just end up being annoyed and frustrated by the sales pitch. Instead, the company should put up signs and flyers talking about the extended service plans and build a case for how often equipment breaks down and the alternatives to not having the service plan. It could be very compelling in prodding the customer to spend more money at the point of sale.

Think about your business. Think of complementary items you could sell at the point of purchase. This case is different than a joint venture, where you identify products or services that you DON'T sell that are kindred to what you do sell. For upselling, the idea is to find other things that you DO sell that you could also sell at the point of purchase to increase your profits. Come up with your own list for your company.

• Another upselling strategy is *selling in bulk quantities at a discount.* For example, in the case of the trash compactor, you could offer the prospect to buy one package of bags for the normal price of $8.99 or five packages at only $6.99 each. Again, don't lose sight of the objective: to get more dollars in your pocket right now. If each package of compactor bags cost you $3, if you sold one package for $8.99, that's a profit of $5.99. If you sold five packages at $6.99, that's a profit of $3.99 per package, for a total of almost $20. What would you rather make? A profit of $6 or $20?

It's as easy as asking. Sometimes people resist this idea because it lowers their profit margins or looks bad on some accounting report. Let me remind you why you're in business: *to make money.* You're not in business to maintain an arbitrary profit margin. You're in business to maximize the total number of dollars you make in profit every day. As long as the customer pays in a timely fashion, you should be more concerned about total dollars than profit percentages.

The final strategy offers a premium as an incentive for the customer to spend more money. In a hypothetical retail situation, your customer is deciding among several televisions. One is priced at $600, one at $800, and another at $1000. Each product has a profit margin of 30 percent. So the $600 sale is worth $180 in gross profit, the $800 TV produces $240 in gross profit and the $1,000 unit generates $300 gross profit. Which TV would you rather sell to this customer? Obviously, the most expensive one, because it will generate the most profit.

What FREE item could you offer customers on the most expensive TV ONLY to induce them to want to buy the expensive model? It's simple math at this point. As long as the premium you offer is less than $60 in hard costs, you make more money selling the $1,000 TV than the $800 model. What costs less than $60 that would make the customer want to buy? It could be anything! What about a DVD collector's set that retails for $60 but only costs you $30? How about a gift card to a restaurant or your store?

You need to know your numbers before you can effectively test this strategy. You need to know what percentage would buy the expensive TV versus the cheaper TV in the first place. And you don't want to give your customers incentives for buying something they're already going to buy anyway. It all comes back to testing. Roll out offers on a limited basis and track their results. Why do most companies never do any of this stuff, even though it relatively easy to execute? Because it's even easier *not* to execute and just get through the day.

But that's not you. You've now got the faith and the strength to redouble your efforts to maximize every situation in your business. All it takes is a little focus and concentration. Imagine how powerful implementing these strategies would be for your business? There's no telling how your business would soar after you've built a marketing program based on the *Marketing Equation* and our *Franchised Sales System*. Things will change radically once you have a powerful strategic marketing message. Finally, you are saying the right things in the right way to the right people. You are tactically executing your plan in terms of lead generating, marketing tools, hopper systems, and knock-down lists. Your strategic and tactical plan are adding more new customers to your business than ever before. Your conversion ratio is going through the roof. You are *maximizing and optimizing* your business—bolstering the lifetime value of your customers, getting more sales out of each customer, and extending the life-cycle of each customer. The results are a truly optimized business that is poised to *Monopolize the Marketplace*. All of this is within your reach. All you have to do is extend yourself and apply what you're learning.

Chapter 21:

Referral Systems

*Word of mouth is the best form of advertising, but only if you
have the right mouths saying the right things to the right people.*

Referrals can be one of the greatest sources of new business for any company. Like joint ventures, referrals work because of *confidence*. People referred by excited clients already have confidence in you. The problem is, you have practically no control over the process using traditional methods of generating referrals. Referrals come in sporadically, if at all, and only if your customer happens to get into a situation conducive to talking about your product or service with a friend or colleague. Most owners and managers expect their salespeople (or chance) to generate referrals, which is why it so rarely happens.

Even for companies who generate a substantial business via referrals, it's still usually by chance, not on purpose. Without a ***proactive*** system for gathering referrals, you miss a major opportunity to get new clients, because it's highly likely that your customers have many friends and associates who are qualified prospects. Like other components of maximizing and optimizing, referral generation isn't hard, expensive or time-consuming to do; you just need to force yourself to think about it, plan it and do it.

The object of the proactive referral process is to get customers excited so they'll let you access their database of friends and associates. They are so excited they allow you to use their name when introducing your company to their friends who fit your target market. If you can get between two and 10 referrals per client (even first-time call-in prospects), you can increase your prospect—and customer—base.

You do this using a simple three-step process: 1) identify a premium; 2) send an offer to your customers; and 3) send the premium to the referrals.

First, find a premium to fuel your referral program. Years ago, I read a great little book called *GMP* by Michael Leboeuf. GMP stands for the *Greatest Management Principle* in the world. In Chapter 1, LeBoeuf reveals the principle: **Things that get rewarded get done**. I think we could all take a step back, take a look at our businesses, and find ways to integrate this intuitive principle. And the place I want you to start using the GMP principle is in your referral program.

Your customers will be more likely to give you referrals when there's something in it for them. It's not that you have to bribe them to say nice things about you or to give you referrals. Remember our discussion earlier about alpha mode, beta mode and the reticular activator? Your prospects are busy with their own lives and businesses. The last thing on their minds is figuring out ways to help you—even if they feel like they'd be absolute fools to buy from anyone else, regardless of price. So when it comes to helping you, they're in alpha mode all the way. You've got to do something that will land in their reticular activators and flip them into beta mode, which is the only way to get them to take action.

Offering something for FREE will accomplish this. This premium is the free gift you can send to your customers in exchange for their referrals. Select a premium that has a high perceived value but low cost. The premium could be what you sell, in the form of free stuff or a gift certificate. Or, use the *Gifting Strategy* from the *Joint Venture* section. You could send to your customers something provided by another company that would serve as an incentive for them to act, and, at the same time, expose them to another company's products or services. Either way, decide on a premium that your customers perceive as a true gift that would get them to take action.

Next, decide on a premium to send to the referrals that you get from your customers. This allows you to be very specific with your customers. Tell them that if they will give you referrals, they will get something free and so will their referrals. This premium also needs to be of high perceived value. It could be a free sample of your products or services, or it could be an offer for a marketing tool to educate and inform the prospect. The marketing tool could be a report, video or an audio, whatever seems appropriate. Just make sure the premium seems like a real value to the prospect.

Now, create a letter informing your customers you're sending them this free gift as a token of your appreciation. Take time to reinforce all your most important selling points; let them know how you have innovated your business, and why the value is so superior. Tell them that because of the tremendous value you offer the marketplace, that you would be willing to send the free gift to any of their friends or associates who might benefit from your superior value as well. Then create a form that your customers can use to fill out and mail, fax or email back to you with the names and contact information for the referrals. Let your customer know that you would be happy to send this gift in their name, unless they don't want you to use their name for some reason. When the gift arrives for the referral and it's in the name of their friend, it makes the friend look good.

When executing this plan, send the premium along with the letter. Don't offer to send your customer a gift in exchange for the referrals. Just send the gift. Yes, this means that you'll be sending gifts to some of your customers who won't respond, and you'll be out the gift. But, are you so cheap that you can't give your customer a gift? Don't you sincerely appreciate them anyway? Second, the net number of referrals you receive far outweighs the cost of the gifts for those who don't send referrals. Don't look at this on a customer-by-customer basis; instead, look at it on the program level. Finally, you should conservatively test everything before rolling it out on a large scale. Don't get excited about this idea and send a gift worth $25 to 1,000 customers before you know your ratios and your numbers. Test the program on much smaller numbers first. Test different premiums—both for your customer and for the referrals—to see if one gift out-pulls another. It's almost certain that you'll find some winners and losers.

If you understand human motivation on a deeper level, you understand why you have to send the gift up front. In another outstanding book called *Influence, the Psychology of Persuasion,* Robert Cialdini describes six major human motivators. The first and most important motivator, according to Cialdini, is called the *Law of Reciprocity.* That means if you do something for people, they will feel obligated to do something for you. It's human nature. It's immutable. If you send a letter offering a gift for referrals, your prospects might feel inclined to help you out, but inevitably, even your most stalwart, loyal fans will fall prey to the *Law of Diminishing Intent.* If you send the gift up front, you've now captured them via the *Law of Reciprocity.* They are now obligated to give you referrals. Plus, you are offering their friends a gift too. You've made it simple for them to comply by giving them the form. This process is sure to work for just about any company.

That's the process. Here are two examples of how works.

First, let's return to the golf course. You might send your customers two certificates for large buckets of range balls, free cart rentals, or free green fees. You have to test to learn what works best. Make sure the certificates look nice and fit the image your company is trying to portray. Certificates photocopied on bright yellow paper don't look as good as ones professionally designed and printed.

Then you would tell your customers you'd send the free premium to their friends and associates for simply filling out the form and faxing it or mailing it back to you. Remember, you're sending the gift in your customer's name. Let's say in this case you decide to send the referred friends free green fees and free range balls. The letter might read something like this:

Dear Rich,

As you've probably noticed, I've sent you two certificates for large buckets of range balls and a certificate for free green fees for you and a guest at River Bend Golf Course. To be honest, I've sent you these free gifts for two reasons. The first reason is to thank you for being a loyal customer at River Bend. Only customers who have golfed at least five rounds in the last two months received these special gifts.

The second reason I'm sending these gifts is to thank you ahead of time for helping us get the word out about River Bend. I'm hoping your experience with us has been so good that you'd feel comfortable recommending us to some of your friends and associates. I'm sure you've decided to golf with us regularly because of our guaranteed tee times for frequent golfers, our exclusive "play well or play again for free" policy, not to mention our course, which is ranked number two in the state for public courses and number eight overall. I'm sure that some of your friends would be interested in taking advantage of all these benefit and more.

So, if you don't mind, do me a favor and fill out the enclosed referral form. There's space for up to five of your friends and associates. When I receive your form, I will immediately send them the same certificates I sent you with this letter so they can try us out and see for themselves. These certificates will be sent in your name so they know that you're responsible for their good fortune. My only request is that you refer friends that have not golfed at our course before.

Thanks again for your patronage!

Sincerely,
Bob Jones, Owner
PS. You do not have to participate in this referral program to redeem the certificates I've sent you. Those are yours to use anytime as a sincere token of my appreciation for your business. Thanks again.

What do you think? It's sincere, concise and honest. And it asks customers to take a specific action. It will be hard for your customers not to comply, because the offer is so good and because you've bestowed a major benefit on them. Do you really think your customers can come into your clubhouse and redeem the certificate you've sent them in good conscience if they haven't forked over the requested referrals? Of course not. You need to mark these certificates to know if they are being redeemed as a result of the referral program. That way when people come in, you can know if they have participated in the referral program. If not, you could hand them another referral sheet on the spot if they express any desire to do so. If they don't want to participate, then don't worry about it and move on.

Here's how a professional could use this strategy. How about an investment advisor? What kind of gifts can investment advisor give to his customers? In this case, maybe some kind of a joint venture free gift. Let's say that the investment professional caters to business owners and executives who don't have time to manage their money, so they turn it over to this firm to handle. Here's a powerful letter:

Dear Dave,

As you've probably noticed, I've sent you an audio book on CD entitled Monopolize Your Marketplace. Separate Your Business From The Competition, Then Eliminate Them. *To be honest, I've sent you this free gift for two reasons. The first reason is to thank you for being a loyal customer of First Capital Investments. Only customers who have been with our firm at least five years received this special gift.*

I first found this unique audio book through one of my clients, Rich Harshaw, who is the author of the audio book. When I first listened, I was immediately captivated by the simple but powerful truths about marketing that I knew were right on the money the instant I heard them. On the CDs, Rich claims that everything you've ever learned about marketing is wrong, and then proceeds to tell you exactly how to maximize every marketing dollar you'll ever spend. I have since hired one of his consultants, Steve Jones, to implement these powerful strategies into my business. So I thought since you're a business owner, you might find some useful insights as well. Let me know what you think.

The second reason I'm sending this gift is to thank you ahead of time for helping us get the word out about First Capital Investments. I'm hoping that your experience with us has been so good that you feel comfortable recommending us to some of your friends and associates. I'm sure you've decided to invest with us because of our guaranteed, no-surprise fee schedules, our exclusive "invest well or you pay no fees" policy, not to mention our "Low-Risk, High-Reward" investment which caters specifically to people of your caliber. I'm sure that some of your friends would be interested in taking advantage of all these benefit and more.

So if you don't mind, do me a favor and fill out the enclosed referral form. There's space for up to five of your friends and associates. When I receive your form, I will immediately send your friends our exclusive investing report entitled "Investment Strategies: Which Ones Actually Work And Which Ones Are Guaranteed to Drain Your Savings, Jeopardize Your Retirement And Squash Your Quest For Financial Independence." As one of our clients, you've already read this report and benefited from it. The report details our methodologies and shows readers exactly how we achieve our outstanding and consistent results. We will send this free report in your name so they know you're responsible for their good fortune.

Thanks again for your ongoing loyalty!

Sincerely,

Cornelius Ogelthorpe, Owner

PS. Participation in this referral program to is strictly optional. The free marketing program I've sent you is yours to keep regardless as a sincere token of my appreciation for you business.

This letter is sincere, concise and honest. And it asks for a specific action. I encourage you to use this plan in your business. Decide on a premium for both your customer and the referee. Then send a simple letter to your customers. Test different offers and ideas and see what works best. When you calculate the lifetime value of your customers, I think you'll find this easy profit builder to be well worth your time and energy.

Chapter 22:

60-Second Elevator Pitches

If you only have a minute with a prospect, what might
you say to present your business in the best possible way?

I want to leave you with a little nugget that can make a huge, immediate impact on your business. I have saved this for last to reward those who diligently read to the end. Let me teach you this quick, simple way to immediately implement what you've learned. It's called the *60-Second Elevator Pitch*.

Technically the *60-Second Elevator Pitch* is a marketing tool. You can guess from its name what a *60-Second Elevator Pitch* is. Maybe you've even put one together before. The reason we call it the *60-Second Elevator Pitch* is because it's what you'd say to somebody if you were on an elevator and you didn't have much time to describe what you do, and you wanted to get the most bang for your buck. And no, the *60-Second Elevator Pitch* does not have to be 60 seconds long. It can be shorter or longer. Most tend to run a little long.

Simply put, the *60-Second Elevator Pitch* is a quick synopsis of who you are and what you do. It should follow the *Marketing Equation* to the T. It should interrupt, engage, educate and offer.

Here's the cool thing about the *60-Second Elevator Pitch*: Once you've done the discovery work, it's easy to piece yours together from the answers to the discovery questions.

Here is an outline for your *60-Second Elevator Pitch*:
- We provide… (state the nature of your product or service).
- For… (state who your target customer is).
- Who… (answer the *Qualification Question).*
- And are looking for… (list the answer to the (*Customer Values Question).*
- Most people who buy… (list your product/service)
- Aren't even aware that… (list your most important answers from the *Need To Know Question)*
- We always offer… (list information from your *Case Building Question).*
- To help our target customers make the best decision possible.
- We offer a FREE (list your offer).
- Which contains… (list the information you listed in the *Evidence Question).*

You might also look at the *Master Letter* we wrote for the fence company. The *60-Second Elevator Pitch* is a shorter, verbal version of the *Master Letter.*

Here's a *60-Second Elevator Speech* for the fence company. First you just simply state what you provide and who you provide it for. In this case, we would say:
- *"We build wooden fences for homeowners…. Who…"*

Next, take the information from the *Qualification Question* to wake up the prospect with something familiar and problematic. In other words, list the hot buttons:
- *"Who have old, worn-out fences that sag or lean, and who are concerned about the safety of their children, the looks of their yard and the resale value of their homes.*

Use as many of the hot buttons as appropriate given your audience and the time constraints.

The next thing is to list some of the customer value points to let the prospect know you've got answers for the problems that are plaguing them:
- *And are looking for a fence that will look good, last a long time, have no hidden charges or fees, and is built by certified, uniformed fencing specialists.*

You just stood there on that elevator and interrupted and engaged. But we aren't done yet. You still have to touch on the "need to know" information to engage more:
- *Most people who buy fences aren't aware that the materials used are critical to the fence's longevity, and that almost all fencing companies compromise on the quality in order to offer a lower price and get jobs from customers who don't know any better.*

That's pretty good, but I'd feel better if we gave one quick example:

- *For instance, it's critical that the posts and rails be pressure-treated or else they'll sag or lean within six months. It's also important to use 2 x 4's on the rails instead of 2 x 3's. The difference can double the lifespan of the fence.*

Now it's time to educate. Since it's a quick pitch, we don't have to give massive details. Just a quick glance at the answer to the *Case Building Question* should be sufficient. We've already implied, based on what we've just said, that other companies can't compete on our level. Here goes:

- *We always offer only high-quality materials; we also implement several other quality controls that most fence companies don't use. We also carefully screen our workers and certify them before they ever pick up a hammer.*

Now into the offer, which includes a quick description of some of the evidence the prospect can expect to find in that educational report:

- *To help homeowners make the best decision possible, we offer a FREE Fencing Standards Checklist, which contains all the questions they'll need to ask any fencing company to make sure that they're getting the best fence possible for the money. We also have over 1,100 references and a 13-minute quality assurance video showing comparison pictures of fences done the right way and the wrong way 6, 12, 24 and 36 months after the job.*

At this point, if you were giving the pitch, you would verbally offer to give the prospect the checklist either on the spot or send it later, if you didn't have one with you. So, here it is:

> *We build wooden fences for homeowners who have old, worn out fences that sag or lean, and who are concerned about the safety of their children, the looks of their yard, and the resale value of their homes. These homeowners are looking for a fence that will look good, last a long time, have no hidden charges or fees, and is built by certified, uniformed fencing specialists.*

> *Most people who buy fences aren't even aware that the materials used are critical to the fence's longevity, and that almost all fencing companies compromise on the quality in order to offer a lower price and get jobs from customers who don't know any better. For instance, it's critical that the posts and rails be pressure-treated or else they'll sag or lean within six months. It's also important to use 2 x 4's on the rails instead of 2 x 3's. The difference can double the lifespan.*

> *We always offer only high-quality materials; we also implement several other quality controls that most fence companies don't use. We also carefully screen our workers and certify them before they ever pick up a hammer.*

To help homeowners make the best decision possible, we offer a FREE Fencing Standards Checklist, which contains all the questions they'll need to ask any fencing company to make sure that they're getting the best fence possible for the money. We also have over 1,100 references and a 13-minute quality assurance video showing comparison pictures of fences done the right way and the wrong way 6, 12, 24, and 36 months after the job.

Let me show you how to implement this strategy for your company so you can start benefiting from this immediately. First, go back to the outline of the *60-Second Elevator Pitch* and fill in the blanks. Develop your *60-Second Elevator Pitch*, then write it on paper. Next, record it and burn it onto CDs. Next, distribute the written and audio version to all of your employees—yes, *all* employees! I'm talking everyone from salespeople to stock clerks to accounting to human resources to the receptionist. Everybody needs to memorize the *60-Second Elevator Pitch*; in fact, you need to make its memorization a condition of employment. Conduct frequent "spot check" pop quizzes to make sure everyone knows it, and reward those employees who learn it and know it well.

Why do you think it's so important for everyone to know it? Because *everyone* in your company has to be completely dialed in to what you do. Everyone has to know exactly why your customers buy from you. They need to know the reasons why people would be absolute fools to buy from anyone else but you, regardless of price. Do you think that would make a difference in your company? Do you think it would start to wear off on them and show up when they're in front of customers?

Let's say you worked for a bank that caters to businesses. Let's say that your bank has a *60-Second Elevator Pitch* that goes like this:

We serve the banking needs of businesses and business owners who are sick of banks that charge fee after annoying fee for anything and everything under the sun. Customers who hate being treated like a computer number instead of a person and who hate the haughty-toitty contemptible attitude that most bankers have toward their customers.

Our customers are looking for a bank that will treat them well, not make them wait in long lines for the simplest transaction, eliminate all hidden charges and fees and not make them feel like they should be thankful that a bank actually houses their money for them.

Most businesspeople aren't even aware that most banks' policies absolutely prohibit their employees from using their own common sense, and that almost all banks lie to their customers and tell them that it's the computer's fault anytime they get irate over fees, inconveniences or rude and arrogant employees who should know better.

We always treat our customers like actual human beings; we empower every employee to be able to make customer- sensitive decisions and override "the computer" anytime it's necessary. We carefully screen all employees and train and certify them before we ever let them loose in front of a customer.

To help businesspeople make the best banking decision possible, we offer a FREE Banking Standards Checklist which contains all the questions they'll need to ask any bank to make sure that they're getting the absolute best customer service possible. We also have over 1,100 references and a 13-minute customer service assurance video showing comparisons of different situations and how various banks handle them.

If a bank had a *60-Second Elevator Pitch* like that, do you think it would affect the thinking and actions of every employee? Do you think the customers would notice the attitudes and actions of the employees who worked hard to live up to that *60-Second Elevator Pitch?*

If Bank of America had that *60-Second Elevator Pitch*, I wouldn't have walked out in disgust and ordered my CFO to cancel every account we had with them. I want to be treated with respect by employees who know what their bank stands for. I want to do business with people who know how to treat their customers. I can guarantee you that if Bank of America had this *60-Second Elevator Pitch* and every employee was required to memorize it as a condition of employment, I wouldn't have been treated like a sack of dirt by employee after worthless employee. They wouldn't have treated me like I should have been bowing down and kissing their feet for finding the goodness in their hearts to take my money. Elevator pitches give employees a standard to live up to, an expectation to meet, and a benchmark to strive for. Think that sounds like an out-there example? Go ask Bank of America now that they don't have any of my deposits how they feel about it.

Do this: Strive for excellence in your company. Innovate and offer superior value and service. Give customers a reason to feel like they'd be absolute fools to do business with anyone else but you. Create a business strategy that clearly makes you the best. Then execute that strategy tactically in a way that makes you the instantly obvious choice. That's what the elevator pitch can do for you: the pitch makes it obvious at a glance that you offer unsurpassed value.

Chapter 23:

How It All Ties Together

It helps to see an extended case study to see how all of this can come together and result in you monopolizing your marketplace.

Now I want to show you how everything you've learned works together. Using case studies is a tricky proposition since, no matter what case I select, some people won't see the relevance to their companies. I only hope that by this point, I've used enough different examples that you're at least beginning to say, "Maybe there is something here for me."

I use stories and examples to illustrate principles. This entire program is principle-oriented. I know some people prefer a laundry list of techniques. But techniques are hard to apply to many different situations. Here's an illustrative example to show you what I mean.

My oldest son's name is Sam. When he was just a toddler, he went through that "I won't eat anything but French fries from McDonald's" phase. Being a new parent, I was dumb enough to fall for it. Sometimes the French fries would come out too hot to eat for Sam, who was only three then. He'd ask me to cool them down for him. How do you cool down a hot French fry when you're in the car? We invented a technique: we held the hot French fry up to the air conditioner vent for a few seconds.

One time I saw Sam holding a French fry up to the a/c vent, all by himself, without any prompting. I was thinking, "Wow, he's smart. Look at the kid. He's figured out how to cool down the French fry." Then I did a double take and realized that there were two problems: First, the French fry he was holding up wasn't hot, and second, the air conditioner wasn't even turned on! Sam was executing the *technique* to perfection—it's just that the situation was wrong. Sam didn't understand what *conditions* had to exist for the technique to work. In other words, he didn't understand the principle, just the technique.

And that's how it is with sales, marketing and advertising techniques. Take direct mail. Back in the 1970s and 1980s, guys started coming out of the woodwork teaching techniques for tricking people into reading their junk mail. Remember the technique of sending your sales letter in a plain white, standard-sized, hand-labeled envelope with a regular stamp and no return address? People would look at it and go, "Wow! A letter from someone I know who forgot to write their return address! I wonder who it is?!" Then they'd open it. What do you do with a white, standard-sized, hand-labeled envelope with a regular stamp and no return address now? You *pitch it* without even opening it! You know it's junk. You know it's a waste of your time. But people are still using that technique—just like a three-year old holding a cold French fry up to an a/c vent that's not even turned on! That's why the MYM program emphasizes principles, not techniques.

Case Study

I want to give you one final case study to illustrate several of the points we've made throughout the program. This client was suffering from a classic case of "churning out horrible marketing because they simply didn't know any better." They were suffering a severe downturn in their industry, and, even though they had a fantastic inside reality, their inability to communicate their advantage was killing the business.

At the time, this client was running neck and neck with one major competitor for the title of the leading manufacturer of coin-operated pool tables, air hockeys and foosballs. Ten years earlier, both companies sold all the products they could stand by sheer momentum. Why? Because back then, if you owned a pool hall, bowling alley or bar and wanted a pool table, air hockey table, or a foosball table, there were ONLY two choices: Our client's company and their main competitor.

Five years before we began working with them, they ran into a little problem. Two or three little companies sprang up that made pool tables and sold them for up to 40 percent less. And then a bunch of foreign companies—mostly from Korea and China—started trying to edge in on their business. One Korean company had the nerve to import a table that they sold for *50 percent less* than our client's table. In a span of five years, our client's market share went from just under half to less than 30 percent. That percentage drop represented almost $20 million a year in lost sales.

That's a big problem. Unfortunately, the days of simple selling were *over* in their industry. Just having the product—*even an innovative and superior product—didn't* ensure sales any more.

So, this company did what most companies do when they come face to face with the Confidence Gap. They complained, whined and griped about what a bunch of jerks the competitors were and how lousy those tables were and how their own tables were far higher quality and well worth the extra price.

Guess where that strategy got them? Nowhere! And here's the sad part—they were right! Their tables *were* substantially higher in quality. The internal parts *were* engineered better and lasted longer and required less maintenance. Their tables *were* worth the extra 30 to 50 percent.

Here's the crux of the problem: There are so many choices available; there are so many competitors saying so many different things, there's so much information available to buyers, there are so many stories in the media about people getting ripped off that the buyer can't tell who offers a better deal. It's the condition called NOISE. Now, instead of the days of simple selling where a seller could make a beeline straight to the buyer, there's a huge GAP that keeps the seller as far away as possible until the buyer, who now has the power, initiates a sales situation.

The owners of this company showed up at one of our seminars frantically looking for a solution. They spent almost a $100,000 the previous year hiring a so-called marketing research firm to figure out what was happening and why. The marketing research firm gave them a big fat report that said that competitors were now making inferior tables and selling them for less money, destroying their market share. Hey thanks for the info, guys. Any change on that $100,000 bill?

By the time the seminar was over, the owner, the sales manager and the top salesperson insisted that we remain afterward to consult with them individually right there on the spot. They pulled out the research reports along with a huge green-bar printout of sales information that drew a very dismal picture of the future for them and their industry. They were desperate for a solution. Their stated goal at the time was to "not lose money again next month like we have for the last two years." In fact, when we went back to their office to discuss a client relationship with them, officials from their main competitor were touring the facilities entertaining the idea of buying the company and consolidating their operations. The owner had had enough and was looking for a way out.

First, we looked at their inside reality and examined their marketing and advertising. In a nutshell, we found they had a great inside reality for all of their products but a lousy outside perception that stemmed from only considering the tactical side of the marketing plan. Like just about every other company on the planet earth, they didn't understand the distinction between strategic and tactical marketing, incorrectly assuming they were one in the same. The results were the predictable smattering of institutional and menu-board advertising, reminiscent of the era of the brand builders.

Marketing didn't play a very big role in the grand scheme of their business. Like many manufacturers, they marketed their products through trade shows, industry magazines and an internal sales force.

The tradeshows were doing okay for them, but there were more and more tradeshows each year, and they were getting very expensive to attend, especially when the returns were questionable. Years ago, there were only two tradeshows, and everyone who was anybody attended them religiously. Now the number had mushroomed to 15, so the owners made a financial decision to only attend the six most important ones in the coming year.

They couldn't track the responses from their ads in trade journals. And, as far as anyone knew, the ads never did anything other than increase so-called *awareness*, the creative agency's measuring stick. They took their tradeshow ad slicks and adapted them for their print advertising; they were classic menu-board ads, featuring picture of a table and some cold facts about the product.

Almost all their sales were a result of their internal sales efforts. But even the sales efforts were reactive; they were primarily orders from long-time, repeat customers. They recruited very few new customers from any source.

Because of this, the entire company was demoralized, and pessimistic about the future. In fact, during that first consultation, we had a 10 minute debate as to whether there was even a project to work on. They insisted their entire industry was down with no relief in sight; they felt cheap competition was now a permanent fact of life. We challenged them. We felt that if they had lost hope, they ought to just close the door and quit. Why try if there's no possibility of winning?

Finally, they agreed that maybe marketing could make a difference. They decided to give it a shot.

What's the strategy here? A strategic marketing plan has to do with what you say, how you say it, and who you say it to. Let's start with who you say it to. First, we had to identify the prospect. This company had two levels of distribution in place. The first one consisted of 20 distributors around the country who sold all kinds of amusement equipment to operators, including multiple brands of pool tables, hockey tables and foosballs, plus stuff that our client didn't sell—things like juke boxes, dart games, games for kids and skee balls. The volume of business going through these distributors was minimal, so we decided to pass them up and focus all of our efforts on the operators themselves. An operator is a business that buys these kinds of games and equipment and then finds locations to install them; locations include bars, bowling alleys, family fun centers, restaurants and college campuses. Usually the operator has an agreement with the owner of the location—in addition to maintaining and servicing the machine, the operator splits the profits with the owner of the location in exchange for space to put the machine. This arrangement keeps all the risk in the hands of the operators and was a potential cash cow for the location owners.

What strategic marketing message would be appropriate? Think back to the *Industry Category* strategies for the answer. Our client was selling to resellers, in this case, the operators. The most important hot button for the resellers is to make more money. If you want to know why the prospect buys what he or she buys, you've got to see the world through the prospect's eyes. Think about an operator. They have all this risk and potential exposure when they put these games in a location. If people don't play them, they don't make money. If the tables break down or are vandalized, they don't make money. If the tables wear out fast, they've got to pay to replace them. For the operators, it's strictly a business, and so their hot buttons all revolve around making more money. It was clear to us that they bought pool tables, foosballs and air hockeys to make money, so we decided to build a case proving our client's tables made operators more money than any other brand.

This company had several product lines. When a company has multiple product lines that are distinct, you have to run the *Marketing Equation* and build a case for each one. We decided to focus first on their core business, which was pool. Then we would tackle hockey and foosball. We decided to work on video game cabinets, a relatively newer product line, last.

Monopolize Your Marketplace

When we started the discovery for pool, it was evident right away that their pool tables were built to far higher quality standards than any of the other manufacturers in the industry. The tables were engineered better and built out of better materials. They lasted longer and had less maintenance problems, which made them well worth the extra money compared to their competitors. The inside reality of their pool tables would support our case that the tables made operators more money without having to innovate the product itself. Of course, this was the source of their frustration. They knew they were better. They knew their quality was superior. They couldn't understand how anybody could want to buy the cheap stuff since it was such a poor investment.

At this point, they weren't even worried about going to battle against their main competitor, whom they had fought for years. They just wanted to reclaim the territory they'd lost to the cheap suppliers; this would go a long way toward solving their financial problem. We found the same thing to be true for each of their major product categories; high quality wasn't just lip service with our client—it was a way of life.

In putting together a tactical plan, the first thing we did was overhaul a newsletter they decided to put out just before our coming on board. It was an eight-page, full-color piece printed on oversized glossy paper that basically informed readers who won their recent corporate golf tournament and who attended the last trade show. They were excited because it was a marketing piece, and they had received a lot of positive response from the first mailing.

True enough, it was a marketing piece, tactically speaking. But it didn't have any strategic message. And when we drilled them to quantify how much response "a lot" was, we learned that five of the marketing director's best friends had called to tell him they'd received it and appreciated him including their picture from the golf tournament. When we tabulated the tangible results, like leads or sales, we saw that they amounted to ZERO. The marketing manager got upset when we pointed this out, much to the chagrin of the owner. For the next 18 months, we never saw the marketing manager. He was reassigned to international sales so he would be overseas and out of the way for weeks at a time.

We overhauled the newsletter using the *Marketing Equation* as our guide. We wrote articles about several of the products that interrupted, engaged, educated and made offers. We included articles about topics like how to decide what ratio of pool tables to air hockey tables a location should have. The determining factor was the percentage of female customers, because we found females liked hockey more than pool. We gave tips about how to reduce the noise level from air hockey pucks. We wrote case studies about operators who had increased their profits when switching from other brands of tables to our client's tables. All in all, there were five separate offers in the newsletter for various marketing tools that educated about the company's various products, and one offer for a free "Silencer" hockey puck—the noise-reducing puck we had talked about in the article.

We mailed the overhauled newsletter to the subscriber list of the major industry magazine, *Replay*. Literally everybody in the industry subscribed to *Replay*, so it was a good bet to send the newsletter to this group, which totaled about 5,000 operators in North America. The newsletter gave the reader two different ways to request any of the free offers: either by fax or mail. Within one week of mailing, we received nearly 200 responses via fax. Then the mail responses started coming in. We received over 350 total responses in three weeks, which is a 7 percent response. Wow!

While we were printing the newsletter, we started working on the marketing tools—the reports to further educate the prospects and build the case. The first marketing tool was a report for pool entitled "16 Pool Table Innovations Designed To Make You More Money." The report contained a summary of everything that supported the case that these tables made the most money. We put together similar reports for hockey and soccer as we watched the 350 requests roll in. We didn't have time for a professional graphic designer to lay out the reports or a printer to produce them in full color. Our client couldn't afford that anyway. So, we went the cheap route. We did a basic layout on our word processor and printed them on colored card stock at Kinko's. But the information was good, and that was what was important.

For instance, the Hockey Report was titled "Make More Money From Your Table Hockey Locations." Then it had a subheadline, "Dunahoe Hockey Outsells All Of Its Competitors By 12 to 1. Here's Why." The report interrupts based on the hot button "make more money," and then it engages by promising to educate the prospect by explaining how. We placed another set of subheadlines under the main headline and subheadline because we wanted the reader to quickly understand our case without having to labor through too much text. Here's what the next four lines said: Players love fast tables. Fast tables get played more often. Tables that get played more often make more money. And by the way, these tables are practically maintenance-free and cheat-proof.

The goal of these reports is to educate and facilitate the prospect's decision-making process. Under that was the first headline in the body of the report which read, "The Fastest Tables On Earth... Up To 81 MPH." Then that section of the report described how and why their tables are faster based on the blower, the holes in the playing surface (both the size and number of holes), and the playing surface's materials and durability ratings. You might think that "The Fastest Tables on Earth" is a platitude, and you're right. But we already addressed the issue of speed in a very powerful way in our opening headlines and subheadlines, and the phrase, "The fastest tables on earth" serves more as a topic heading than a headline. In other words, it allows the reader who sees the initial headline about making money because of faster tables to quickly scan the report and find the section on speed. And, even though we used a platitude, we qualified it by quantifying the speed—81 miles per hour.

The next major section, called "Maintenance-Free and Cheat-Proof," explained how our client's tables had no micro switches and instead used infrared optics to keep score. Most hockey tables have a mechanical switch that registers scores, and that switch is prone to getting the puck stuck as it passes through. Our client's tables had no mechanical switch, but instead used an infrared optic system that accurately recorded scores *and* posed no threat of jamming. In that same section we also explained how cheaters hated our tables because they were impossible to jam for free games—unlike our competitors' tables. This meant more revenue for operators—their number-one hot button.

Other sections of the report talked about awards the table had won to provide evidence of our tables' superiority. Another section gave the guidelines for deciding how many hockey tables to put in a location versus pool tables. Table hockey was our client's most dominant product in the marketplace. The 12-to-1 ratio mentioned earlier in the report was true. But the ratio was slipping daily, and the total number of table hockeys sold compared to pool tables was very small.

They wanted to stimulate more sales of this product, which incidentally, was more profitable on a per-table basis anyway. One section of the report talked about the new Silencer puck, explaining how our client had to develop a whole new puck to keep the noise down and reduce the risk of what we coined "puck flyage" since the tables were so fast.

Here's what we wrote about the Silencer puck that helps build the case and facilitate the prospect's decision-making process:

"After six years of experimentation, including 132 failed attempts, our chief engineer has finally solved the SPEED vs. NOISE problem. Our exclusive Silencer puck is made from a special nylon polymer that reduces the friction coefficient of the puck, even though it outweighs normal pucks by more than one-third. The nylon polymer material has a hardness rating of just 16 compared to a regular puck's 23. Even though the silencer is softer, players can't tell the difference because of its heavier weight. The result is a faster puck that is about 55 percent quieter than regular pucks."

Do you see how that builds the case? Do you see how it's a believable story? Do you honestly think anybody ever knew anything about hardness ratings or friction coefficients? But do you see how those things are easily understood within the context of the report? Do you see how creating and describing this new puck supports the larger case that the table is so freaking fast that it can't use ordinary pucks? After all, what do faster tables do for operators? That's right, they make them more money. That's brilliant using a simple, almost mathematical formula called the *Marketing Equation*. At the end of the section on the Silencer Puck we made the reader an offer for a free sample.

The final section of the table hockey report educated the operators about available upgrades that could make them potentially even more money. All in all, this little report was a powerhouse, despite its non-professional appearance. The pool and soccer reports were just as engaging and powerful. With the reports done, it was time to think about other parts of the tactical plan. We had already created one lead generator, the newsletter, and several marketing tools, the reports. As we pondered ways to generate more leads, we looked at their situation. Because they sold to a defined target market, the 5,000 operators, conventional wisdom says they could treat the entire target market like warm prospects, skip lead generation and just set up a hopper system to nurture all 5,000 operators at once.

But there was a major hitch in this plan. Even though they had been in business for over 25 years, they still didn't have a comprehensive list of those operators. In fact, they only had about 2,200 of those companies on file.

Here's what we decided to do. We placed ads in *Replay* magazine to generate leads and add the new leads to our existing database of 2,200 companies. Then, we rolled out a hopper system to that database on an on-going basis. We figured if we did it long enough, and if we gathered information at the trade shows they attended, we could eventually build that database to at least 4,000 operators.

The next thing we did was revamp their magazine ads. We found that three years prior to our arrival, they developed a product they felt like would turn the tide, if only temporarily. The product was an upscale pool table called *Top Brass*. They thought this table, because of its good looks, would get pool tables into locations that traditionally wouldn't consider pool. Top Brass featured a beautiful, dark-blue, felt surface with a black-laminate case and luxurious-looking brass pocket liners and trim, as opposed to the traditional green felt, brown wood and plain metal pocket liners. It really did look great, making it appropriate for more upscale places like restaurants and sports bars. And it was supposed to earn more money per play—one dollar per play compared to 50 or 75 cents per play.

They developed this great, innovative product that nobody else could compete with but then committed the fatal marketing error. They ran ads with a big picture of the table and this lame-brained, non-stimulating, hot button-devoid headline: TOP BRASS POOL. Even though several operators had good success with the table, overall sales were disappointing. After two years on the market, they were considering discontinuing Top Brass. It was a good example of a great product with a great inside reality selling poorly because of poor marketing and a poor outside perception.

All the marketing focused on the table's good looks, even though this table satisfied the operators' No.1 hot button—to make them more money. So we defined the ability of a pool table to make money on four factors, listed in order of importance:

1. How much money the table made each time it was played.
2. How many times the table got played in a week.

3. How frequently the table was out of service due to jamming, vandalism and breakdowns.
4. How many years the table would last.

Since Top Brass earned more money per play (Value No. 1 on the list), we decided to rewrite the Top Brass ad and lead with it. Remember, money was extremely tight with the client, and they couldn't run five or six ads in the magazine like they had done in years gone by.

Our ad still showed a picture of the table. But instead of the hot button-barren headline "TOP BRASS POOL," we chose a headline that conveyed the idea that this table made money. It simply said, "COMMAND $1 PLAY" with a sub-headline that said, "Double Your Money, Get 50 Percent More Plays Per Table, And Capture New Locations." Interrupt and engage, right? To appreciate how powerful the headline was to the reader, you have to realize that most operators were getting just 50 cents, maybe 75 cents a game for regular pool tables. One dollar per play was a big, big deal. It represented a 100 percent raise.

Of course, there was an offer at the bottom of the ad. The offer was a cut-out coupon that an operator could fax, mail or phone in to our client to receive an "Upscale Pool Industry Report." If an operator was even remotely interested or intrigued by our $1 play claim, he would ask us for this report, which was very low risk on his part. Hey, we weren't asking him to buy the table, just ask for a little report. And oh, did they ask. The first placement of the revamped Top Brass ad in *Replay* magazine drew 277 requests for the *Upscale Pool Industry Report* the first week. People wanted to know how they could get a buck a whack on their tables, too.

That was the lead generator. Our marketing tool, the *Industry Report,* contained evidence galore.

- A newspaper article from *The Dallas Morning News* that talked about how upscale pool was the fastest-growing segment of the pool industry. The article reported more people with lots of money were starting to play pool and how they loved fancy pool tables. This view, by the way, was directly opposite of our client's attitude at the time, which was, "The industry is down. Nobody's buying pool tables any more."

- A one-page interview with one of the most well-known operators in North America. Guess what he had to say? He was getting no less than one dollar per play and as high as $1.50 per play at some locations. And the tables were being played more frequently than regular pool tables. And they were able to place these tables into locations that they never dreamed would have a pool table.

- A worksheet with a table so the operator could figure out how much *more* money he would be making a month if his tables got an extra 25 cents, 50 cents or 75 cents per play, and if the tables were played an extra 10, 25 or 50 times per week.

- Operator route collection reports—before and after—from operators in different parts of the country to prove the increased earnings.

* A maintenance audit that proved these pool tables broke down less frequently and were easier and faster to fix when they did.
* A testimonial letter from an operator in Florida who said that when he got Top Brass, he increased his per play price by 25 cents. He said his biggest problem now is that he has to re-cover the tables more often because they get played so much.

We used the exact points from the *Customer Values Question* and built the case. We built evidence showing how the tables got more per play, were played more often, broke down less and lasted longer. In short, they make an operator more money.

After the Top Brass ad was done, we created other ads for their other products and ran them in subsequent issues of *Replay* magazine. The client was so enthused by the early responses that the company decided to pony up and run three ads for different products in later issues, which only accelerated the growth. We also put together additional marketing tools, things like sales scripts, on-hold messages, 60-second elevator pitches, and in-store signage for their trade shows. We literally transformed their tradeshows from a mere social appearance (the point they had degenerated to) to a powerhouse lead-generating and business-closing venue. The signs had the best headlines from the magazine ads, like "Command $1 Play." The investments in those shows quickly showed a profit; they stopped being a money hole.

After that, we put together a hopper system to deal with our original database, plus all the new leads we were generating. We discovered that over half of the contacts on the database had fax numbers and very few had email addresses. So we put together a hopper system that was primarily fax-based and supplemented it with emails where we could.

We began sending faxes one time per week. Each week we focused on a different product—pool, Top Brass pool, hockey, soccer, video game cabinets. Later on, we introduced two new products, a glow-in-the-dark pool table and a glow-in-the-dark hockey table. We slipped these new products into the hopper system mix with their corresponding offers for reports. We wrote every hopper system piece according to the *Marketing Equation,* and each one produced quantifiable, measurable results.

After four months, we decided to do more heavy-duty work on a product line they felt was underleveraged yet potentially very profitable: their video game cabinets. The cabinet is the actual wooden box with a TV screen and control panel that houses the game. Many people don't realize it, but the video game itself is just a computer program. To put the game in an arcade, you've got to put it in a cabinet. And the cabinet's got to be purchased from somebody. Because our client knew why John Smith buys what John Smith buys—like you do for your business—they knew how to build quality products that function well and practically never wear out. While our client knew how to build quality video game cabinets, the owners were not communications experts. They completely took for granted how good their stuff was and never bothered to document their engineering greatness for their prospects and customers to evaluate. That's a very big mistake.

We sat down with the sales, operations and service managers to start the discovery process. The first thing we asked them was about their inside reality. We asked them, "What do you do that makes you so good? What makes you so valuable to the marketplace? Why would somebody want to buy your stuff over the other brands?" They started off slowly with the expected platitudes. "Our cabinets are higher quality." We wanted to know what exactly they meant by "higher quality." So we began a process that we call the "two deep" and "three deep" analysis. This is a methodology our consultants use to dig deeper to get more information.

After some prodding, they finally said, "Well, we reinforce the cabinets more than other companies do." What does that mean? How so? With what? Let's get specific. They went on to explain that most video game cabinet makers use a cleat-and-bracket construction method, which means the wood from each side of the cabinet actually joins together like interlocking fingers. We asked them. "Do you use cleat-and-bracket construction?" They said, "yes." Then they said, almost in passing, "But we also use dowels." "What do you mean, dowels? What's that all about? Why do you do that? What's the benefit? What kind of dowel?" They explained that they drilled 1/2-inch holes in each piece of wood that formed the main pieces of the cabinet, then inserted a 1-inch poplar (hard wood) dowel in each hole and secured each dowel with industrial-strength wood glue *in addition to* the cleats and brackets. We thought that sounded pretty cool. We asked them, "How many dowels are there in each cabinet?" Based on their understated tone, we were thinking maybe 20. They said, "A lot." We asked, "How many? 10, 20?" They said, "No, more ." We said, "Well, how many? They honestly didn't know.

In frustration, we finally said, "Look, who would know? Somebody has to know. You build them here in this factory." We got the production manager on the phone. He didn't know. But he did know the guy who actually drilled the holes, Dan. We asked Dan. Guess what? He didn't know either. He had a machine that drilled them, so he'd never really paid attention. We asked him if it would be possible to count the dowels. He said, "Follow me. I'll show you so you can count for yourself."

Guess how many dowels went into each standard-sized video cabinet? We could not believe it—172 dowels. Then we asked the obvious question. "How many dowels do your competitors use in their cabinets?" They looked at us like we had just asked them what color the sky is on a sunny day in June in Texas. "What do you mean? They don't use *any* dowel rods in theirs." Their tone was, "Duh! Don't you know anything?"

My point is, they were so close to the process and took their construction methods for granted that they couldn't see that what they were doing was anything special. That's because in their paradigm of how the world worked, the only thing that mattered was how much the cabinets cost. They had learned years ago that their customers just wanted the lowest prices, period. They didn't seem to care much about quality. Their menu-board ad slicks had a little bullet point that said, "Hardwood dowel construction." But one little bullet point doesn't tell the story.

Let me ask you this. Do you think that 172 hardwood dowels reinforcing a video game cabinet would make a difference in the durability of the cabinet? Would it last longer? Do you think there would be a benefit to buying it? Of course! But since they had never gotten past platitudes, nobody ever knew how awesome their stuff was.

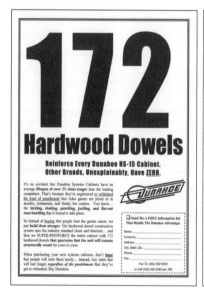

We put together an ad that ran as one of the hopper system faxes. It had a massive, towering headline that took up half of one page that read: "172 Hardwood Dowels Reinforce Every Dunahoe HS-15 Cabinet. Other Brands, Unexplainably, Have ZERO." Do you see what a slam that is on everyone else in the industry? But we didn't just come out and say, "Hey, they suck" and leave it at that. We said, "Hey look, here's how a good systems cabinet *should be* constructed, but for some odd reason we're the only ones that do it." The number "172" in the headline was a gargantuan 3.75 inches tall and 7 inches wide on the page; the words "hardwood dowels" was .75 inch tall under that, and the words "Reinforce Every Dunahoe HS-15 Cabinet. Other Brands, Unexplainably Have ZERO" was just under .25 inch tall under that. This way, the impact is on the number.

Here's a marketing tip for you. If you don't make a big deal out of it, nobody else will either. But if you make a big deal out of it, then others will think it's a big deal.

Under that headline we put copy that educated:

It's no accident that Dunahoe Systems Cabinets have an average *lifespan of over two times longer* than the leading competitor. That's because they're engineered *to withstand the kind of punishment* that video games are prone to get in arcades, restaurants and family fun centers. You know… the *kicking, shaking, punching, jostling and manhandling* that is bound to take place.

So, instead of *hoping* that people treat the games easier, we just *build them stronger*. Our hardwood-dowel construction system uses the industry-standard cleats and brackets and then we SUPER-REINFORCE the entire cabinet with 172 hardwood dowels *that guarantee that the unit will remain structurally sound* for many years to come.

When purchasing your next systems cabinets, don't *hope* that people will treat them nicely. Instead, buy units that will last longer *regardless of the punishment* they've got to withstand. Buy Dunahoe.

And then, according to the *Marketing Equation*, there was an offer for an information kit. As we continued to do our two-deep and three-deep exercises to probe deeper into what defines quality, we also found several undiscovered nuggets. It was like panning for gold in a river and finding softball-sized nuggets that they had somehow mistaken for ordinary river rocks. We found out that other brands of cabinets were held together by just 13 Phillips-head wood screws on each side, for a total of 26 screws. Our client uses 24 screws *per side*, for a total of 48 screws, on top of the cleats and brackets *and* the 172 hardwood dowels.

Moreover, our client only used Allen-head screws, not Phillips-head. What difference could the screw head possibly make? Guess what we discovered? There were dozens of documented cases where vandals had taken an ordinary screwdriver and unscrewed the Phillips-head screws in the cabinet so it actually fell apart. We also found there were *no* documented cases of vandals removing 48 Allen-head screws and destroying the cabinet. We're not talking about big-time vandals here, we're talking about kids playing the games who say, "Hey look, you got a screwdriver? Huh huh."

Another problem with this was thieves. The brains of a video game is called the logic board. It's where the computer is housed and the game is installed. The competitors only protected it with two Allen-head screws and a simple slide bolt that could easily be jimmied open, leaving the $3,000 logic board open to theft. Our client's cabinets housed the logic board in a steel container inside the cabinet that was completely inaccessible without a key.

We created a hopper system piece with this headline: "The Biggest Threat To Your Video Cabinets COULD BE An Allen Wrench And Screwdriver That Some 13-Year Old Kid Took From His Dad's Toolbox"

And then a subheadline that read: "26 Phillips-Head Wood Screws Hold Some Brands of Video Cabinets Together."

Interrupt and engage? I think so. Now to educate; here's how the rest of the ad reads:

Scary thought, but it's true: Some brands of video game cabinets are extremely vulnerable to vandalism. In fact, brands make vandalism tempting to kids who are normally good—because the screws that hold it together are just sitting there, begging to be tampered with. The screw heads are exposed so that any kid with a screwdriver can dismantle it in just a few minutes.

The Good News? Logic Board Thieves Will Make You Forget About Your Vandalism Problems!

The real problems with some of those other brands start when logic board thieves get hold of them. The only thing protecting the logic boards are two Allen-head screws (easily accessible from outside the cabinet) and one measly simple slide bolt which any novice would-be thief can easily jimmy. You are asking for trouble with these brands of cabinets.

Want To Break Into A Dunahoe Cabinet? Better Bring A Crowbar, A Chainsaw and A Pick-Axe.

Dunahoe cabinets are instantly recognized by thieves as OFF LIMITS. It's just not going to get broken into. And, over the course of the cabinet's lifetime, that can mean a savings of thousands of dollars per cabinet to operators. Put your money where it will stay put: Dunahoe.

It goes without saying that there was the standard offer at the end.

The story doesn't end there though. Remember, this whole dialogue about video games cabinets is to show you how it's not only possible, but highly likely, that *you already possess a wealth of information you can easily translate into powerful marketing for your company,* but you just don't know how to get it out of your brain.

As we continued that meeting, we wanted to quantify exactly how durable the cabinets were as a result of this newly discovered, fantastic inside reality. They had some statistics about how long they lasted and how little maintenance they required. But then the funniest thing came up, again in passing. After 20 minutes of discussion, they said, "Remember when we had Mike do the stress test on the HS-27?" And everyone in the room started laughing. We wanted to know what was so funny. They said that when they first developed this particular model, they wanted to test the durability of its engineering and design. They wanted to simulate all of the punishment the cabinet would go through over the course of 10 years in real-life situations.

Then a light bulb went on. Hey, let's get Mike to jump up and down on the control panel and see what happens. The control panel is the part of a video game cabinet that has all the buttons, joy sticks and controls that the player uses to actually play the game. It is the part of a cabinet that is particularly vulnerable to wear and tear because:

1. It protrudes out from the rest of the game to accommodate the player.
2. It's the part of the game that the player has constant contact with. It's the epicenter of pounding and activity.

For these reasons, the control panel has to withstand more punishment than any other part of the cabinet. Why was *Mike* jumping up and down on the control panel? Why not somebody else? Here's why: At 272 pounds Mike was the biggest guy in the company. After Mike jumped up and down, the control panel was visibly weakened in 10 minutes and broke off at 12 minutes.

They viewed that as a failure. So they actually went back to the drawing board, reengineered it with some upgrades they knew would cost more but did it anyway. After a few weeks they had a new prototype, and got Mike up there again to jump up and down. After 15 minutes with no breakage, the model passed the stress test.

Obviously, you can see why everyone was laughing. We were laughing just imagining it. So that gave us an idea. We asked if they could reenact the stress test again for a video. Wouldn't that make a great piece of evidence as a marketing tool? So we set up a test and got Mike up there one more time. Then we created this ad:

We Had the Biggest, Fattest Guy We Could Find Jump Up and Down on Our HS-27 Control Panel for 12 Minutes Just to Make Sure It Could Endure Any Punishment Your Customers Could Dish Out.

Then a subheadline:

Our 272-Pound Punishment Test Failed. So We Re-engineered the Darn Thing.

That's right. The big, fat guy BROKE the control panel clean off after 12

minutes of jumping up and down. Sounds like a story of failure, right? Wrong! That gave us all the information we needed to re-engineer, reinforce and FIX the problem before it got to one of your arcades.

Subheadline:

We Go the Extra Mile to Make Sure That Dunahoe Is the Best Stuff On the Market.

Our "fat guy" test is just one of the things we do to make Dunahoe products the best on the market. We're not interested in selling to operators who are fly-by-nighters looking for the cheapest stuff available. But the other 99 percent know that quality counts and makes you far more profitable in the long run.

Buy The Cabinet That Passed The "Fat Guy" Test. Buy Dunahoe.

Granted, it took us two tries. But it passed for a whopping 15 minutes before we let the fat guy off. No breakage. That's Dynamo quality. Insist on it.

Then there was an offer for the video of the fat guy test. Everybody who responded to that ad joined our hopper system.

Are you starting to see how powerful the *Marketing Equation* is? Do you realize how much impact this could make on your business if you implemented it properly?

After the major pieces of their strategic and tactical marketing plans were in place, we shifted our focus to *Maximizing and Optimizing.* We implemented perpetual selling strategies and upselling strategies that rewarded customers for their loyalty and encouraged them to order more at the time of purchase. We did joint ventures with other non-competing companies to sell our products to their customers and vice versa. We instituted a referral process that increased our customers.

Here's what happened after we put these things in place: First, Top Brass pool went from 5 percent of all pool tables sold to 32 percent. Overall company sales of pool tables went up by 248 percent in eight months. Table hockey went up by 377 percent in the same time span. Soccer only went up by 41 percent, but we didn't really spend a lot of effort there. Video game cabinet sales went up by 202 percent. That's the power of the *Monopolize Your Marketplace* system.

Because of this marketing success, this company went from losing money every month to a net profit of over $7 million. And we achieved this total turnaround in just 10 months! That's right, a $7 million profit in 10 months. One year later, this company bought out its main competitor and consolidated operations to their original facility in Texas. This is the same competitor they had considered selling out to when we first hooked up with them. The sales manager we worked with—the one who instituted our program—was promoted to the vice president of marketing with a big fat increase in salary.

This *Monopolizing Your Market* program is so powerful, the results are so inevitable that you'd be an absolute fool not to take action and implement it on your own behalf. But again, I urge you to discuss your options with one of our consultants. To find out who you should work with in your local area, go to our web site at www.y2marketing.com and click on Find A Consultant To Work With. We have over 1,000 active consultants who implement *Monopolize Your*

Marketplace strategies nationwide. We support them with our employees in our corporate headquarters near Dallas, Texas. For more information on any topic addressed in this book, I invite you to check our web site at www.mymbook.com.

In closing, I again put the case to you: Are you happy with the results you are now getting from your marketing, advertising, and sales initiatives? Are you pleased with your marketing ROI and the growth of your business? If so, I applaud you and wish you continued success. Hopefully I've given you a few ideas to build on. Now, if you are not so fortunate, I challenge you to do something about it. You can turn things around with the MYM system. Put it to the test. You won't regret it. I promise you: You will soon monopolize *your* marketplace.

Index

Why invest $8 to $10 a month in your own leadership development?

You will receive an exponential return on investment.

For the past 20 years, our three monthly magazines have been the best source for the best and brightest insights from all the top consultants, coaches, authors, and speakers on team leadership and personal development.

Now you can subscribe to *Executive Excellence, Sales and Service Excellence* or *Personal Excellence* at a special discounted rate of 25 percent!

Team Leadership ($10/month)
Executive Excellence brings together the best thinking in the world on all the issues that leaders encounter, and offers it all in the most time-effective format.

Sales/Service Leadership ($8/month)
Sales and Service Excellence covers seven dimensions of sales, marketing, and service excellence.

Self-leadership ($8/month)
Personal Excellence focuses on seven dimensions of personal and professional leadership.

There's more! To help you get the most out of your favorite articles and implement new ideas you will also receive FREE:

The *Personal Excellence Plan,* an easy-to-use guide designed to help you create and implement a vision and mission, goals and priorities.

Excellence in Action, found at the end of each article to motivate to implement the insights the author has shared. In addition, we provide you with an *Excellence in Action Guide* to help you put into action those ideas that will bring about desired change.

Executive Excellence Worksheet, the perfect way to bring *Executive Excellence* or *Personal Excellence* into a meeting or team. It's designed to bring focus and vision to your team.

Certificate of Excellence, the best way to recognize and reward people. Use the Executive Excellence Performance System now to bring about desired change!

Executive Excellence
(print or audio)
One-year subscription $119
(4 to 9 subscription are $80 each
10 to 24 are $60 each
25 to 99 are $50 each
100+ are $40 each)
Electronic Subscription: $10 each
Group discounts as low as
$2 per person per year.

Sales & Service Excellence
or Personal Excellence
(print magazine)
One-year subscription $96
(4 to 9 subscription are $55 each
10 to 24 are $45 each
25 to 99 are $40 each
100+ are $35 each)
Electronic Subscription: $8 each
Group discounts as low as
$1 per person per year.

Instant Consultant
CD Archive for just $149

Find a wiser,
better way to
live your life
and lead your
organization.

Invest wisely. Invest in excellence.
To order, call 801-375-4060.

Are You Searching for Solutions

Sustainability • Productivity • Performance • Leadership
Growth • Profitability • Change Management • Team Building

...From All the Right Faces?

Finding solutions is as easy as 1-2-3:

1. Search the *Instant Consultant.*
2. Find Solutions and Applications.
3. Then Put Excellence in Action.

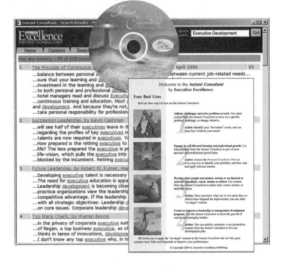

What To Do Next

1. **Talk To A *Y2Marketing* Consultant:** Get an overview "snapshot" of how to implement what you've learned into your business, determine your "Marketing Risk" (how much is at stake when you execute your marketing plan), and chart your best course of action.

2. **Buy the *Monopolize Your Marketplace* Audio CD Program:** The full-length program teaches you how to apply all the *Monopolize Your Marketplace* winning strategies in 11 hours. Each concept is carefully explained and illustrated with several examples.

3. **If your "Marketing Risk" is low to moderate, Join A Marketing Mastermind Group.** Mastermind groups are facilitated by Y2Marketing Principle Consultants on a local level, and are comprised of several businesses that meet regularly to discuss and implement the MYM System. Visit our websites for more information.

4. **If your "Marketing Risk" is moderate to high Engage a Y2Marketing Principle Consultant.** Our Consultants are experienced in working with companies like yours to implement the MYM System step by step into your business. Find a Consultant by going to our website www.mym-book.com, or by calling our Corporate Offices.

Become An MYM Consultant

If you've enjoyed this book, and would be interested in a career working with businesses to implement the MYM concepts, you should consider becoming an MYM Consultant. If you meet the following qualifications, a career in MYM Consulting is for you.

- **Business Experience:** 8 to 10 years minimum; preferably as an entrepreneur or executive.
- **Sales Experience:** An understanding of conceptual selling and Socratic selling.
- **Writing Ability:** A good grasp of grammar and writing skills are essential.
- **Speaking Ability:** Consultants frequently deliver speeches to small and large groups.
- **Time Availability:** Consultants may start part-time; however, full-time is recommended.
- **Financial Ability:** Because of licensing and business start-up fees, a net worth of at least $250,000 is recommended.

We already have over 600 consultants across the United States and Canada, and are actively seeking additional qualified individuals. If this sounds like a possible fit for you, please contact us to request a free audio cd that will give you an overview of the opportunity, the qualifications, and the restrictions.

Order FREE Business Overview Audio CD
Visit www.previewpack.com
Or call (800) 436-4097

These Superior Marketing Strategies Will Make You a Fortune in Your Business.

Learn How to Monopolize Your Marketplace In Just 11 Hours.

Whether you're a business owner, professional, or entrepreneur, *Monopolize Your Marketplace* will teach you how to gain greater control of your marketing RESULTS, distinguish your business from your competitors, and make five, ten or even TWENTY times more money in your business.

SEPARATE YOUR BUSINESS FROM THE COMPETITION. *THEN ELIMINATE THEM.*

What's unique about the *Monopolize Your Marketplace*? **You learn how to market your business so that prospects to see the advantages of doing business with you.** *Monopolize Your Marketplace* shows you how to systematize your marketing so that it produces **very predictable, but extremely profitable results.**

**Any Business. Any Industry. Any Situation.
This Program Will Work For You.**

Regardless of what business you're in, *Monopolize Your Marketplace* will work for you. We've implemented this system into over 10,000 companies in over 350 different industries. The following page provides a quick sampling of some of the small businesses that have benefited.

**_Monopolize Your Marketplace_ CD Program
$299.00
www.MYMbook.com**

What Dramatic Results Will You Get from *Monopolize Your Marketplace?*

- A business-to-business magazine publisher **doubled** the income from his magazine **in just 60 days** by implementing a risk-lowering strategy that allowed his salespeople to get "first-call-closes" 92% of the time. Our system allowed his *worst* salesman to go from $3,200 to $16,800 in sales in just one month.

- A small rubber stamp manufacturer increased his business from about $242,000 a year to about $470,000, adding more revenue in several months than his company had been able to muster in 88 years!

- We helped a high-end flooring store in Dallas' designer district identify a *completely new* profit center that netted the company more than *$250,000 in PURE PROFIT* in one year...with just $746 in extra advertising costs per month.

- MYM helped a plumber increase sales from under $20,000 a month to a record-breaking $147,358 in sales the next January.

- A Texas company that developed property management software credited us with his **3 highest sales months ever**...just from the FREE advice he got from them in a free follow-up consultation after a seminar he attended.

- The owner of a brand new sign company implemented our system and signed *almost $100,000* of orders **before** he even opened his doors.

- A $20 million insurance brokerage firm became the #1 distributor for Philadelphia Life less than 3 months after taking on the product line using the 'Monopolize' strategies.

- An SBA lending bank generated 117 SBA loan leads **in just 2 weeks** the number they had generated themselves in the previous six months... for **17 times less money**

- A property tax reduction company took their direct mail response rate from 4% to 7.1% instantly after implementing a few key components of our system into their marketing plan. Their mailing costs remained constant, but their **profits went up by 250 percent**.

Monopolize Your Marketplace
CD Program
$299.00
www.MYMbook.com